Writing and Doing Action Research

SAGE was founded in 1965 by Sara Miller McCune to support the dissemination of usable knowledge by publishing innovative and high-quality research and teaching content. Today, we publish more than 750 journals, including those of more than 300 learned societies, more than 800 new books per year, and a growing range of library products including archives, data, case studies, reports, conference highlights, and video. SAGE remains majority-owned by our founder, and on her passing will become owned by a charitable trust that secures our continued independence.

Los Angeles | London | Washington DC | New Delhi | Singapore

Jean McNiff

Writing and Doing Action Research

Los Angeles | London | New Delhi
Singapore | Washington DC

Los Angeles | London | New Delhi
Singapore | Washington DC

SAGE Publications Ltd
1 Oliver's Yard
55 City Road
London EC1Y 1SP

SAGE Publications Inc.
2455 Teller Road
Thousand Oaks, California 91320

SAGE Publications India Pvt Ltd
B 1/I 1 Mohan Cooperative Industrial Area
Mathura Road
New Delhi 110 044

SAGE Publications Asia-Pacific Pte Ltd
3 Church Street
#10-04 Samsung Hub
Singapore 049483

Editor: Katie Metzler
Assistant editor: Lily Mehrbod
Production editor: Ian Antcliff
Copyeditor: Kate Harrison
Proofreader: Clare Weaver
Marketing manager: Sally Ransom
Cover design: Shaun Mercier
Typeset by: C&M Digitals (P) Ltd, Chennai, India
Printed in Great Britain by Ashford Colour Press
Ltd, Gosport, Hampshire

Library of Congress Control Number: 2014938626

British Library Cataloguing in Publication data

A catalogue record for this book is available from
the British Library

MIX
Paper from
responsible sources
FSC
www.fsc.org   FSC® C011748

ISBN 978-1-4462-9456-7
ISBN 978-1-4462-9457-4 (pbk)

Table of Contents

List of Tables

List of Figures

Acknowledgements

Many people are involved in the writing of a text, in many different ways. This has been the case for this book, and thanks are owed to the following colleagues:

All who have contributed case study material, and for your very helpful comments on the text, in whole or in part. Your names appear on the following 'Contributors' pages, with thanks for your hard work.

Katie Metzler, my editor at Sage: thank you for your commitment to the project and for making it happen.

Peter McDonnell: thanks for more than I can say, especially the abundance of good Irish stories.

Thank you also to Jaber Al-Asheeri, from the National Institute for Industrial Training, Manama, Kingdom of Bahrain. I explained to him that I always like to include a passage from scripture at the beginning of a book, and was searching the Qur'ân for a passage to communicate the idea that change has to start from within. He drew my attention to the following passage:

For him are angels ranged before him and behind him who guard him by Allah's command. Lo! Allah changeth not the condition of a folk until they first change that which is in their hearts. (Sûra Ar-Ra'd, 13: 11)

Similarly, from the Holy Bible:

And be not conformed to this world: but be ye transformed by the renewing of your mind, that ye may prove what is that good, and acceptable, and perfect, will of God. (Romans, 12: 2)

Thanks also to

Sally Aston	Mark Cordery
Pip Bruce Ferguson	Jane L.Crane
Jenny Carpenter	Odd Edvardsen

John Elliott

Jean Flood

Karen Rut Gísladóttir

Chris Glavey

Steve Gordon

Dot Jackson

Maria James

Anne-Gerd Karlsen

Adrian Klos

Kjartan Kversøy

Lāsma Latsone

Clare Lawrence

Willem Louw

Karen McArdle

Steve Mee

Rita Moustakim

Bente Norbye

Linda Pavitola

Julie Pearson

Tamie Pratt-Fartro

Peter Raymond

Jovita Ross-Gordon

Margaret Riel

Joseph M.Shosh

Alex Sinclair

Anne-Lise Thoresen

Margareta Törnqvist

Jonathan Vincent

About the Author

Jean McNiff is Professor of Educational Research at York St John University, UK. She is also a Visiting Professor at UiT, the Arctic University of Norway; at Oslo and Akershus University College, Norway; and at the Beijing Normal University and Ningxia Teachers' University, People's Republic of China.

Jean took early retirement from her position as deputy head teacher of a large secondary school in Dorset, UK. She went into business for herself, and developed her writing. Her textbooks on action research and professional education are now used internationally on workplace-based professional education courses and on higher degree courses. Jean provides interdisciplinary consultancy work to institutions around the world where she gives lectures and conducts workshops on planning, doing and writing action research.

Jean aims to contribute to personal and social betterment through educational research. She encourages everyone to make their stories public in the form of their personal and collaborative theories of practice; and she firmly believes that each individual is able to contribute to social and planetary well-being by explaining how they hold themselves accountable for what they do. In this way she links education with moral accountability. She tries to bring the university to everyday contexts, and everyday contexts into the university, for it is only by involving everyone, she feels, that the world will become a better place for us all.

Visit Jean at www.jeanmcniff.com, or contact her at jeanmcniff@mac.com

Most recent publications:

McNiff, J. (2013) *Action Research: Principles and Practice* (3rd edition). Abingdon, Routledge.

McNiff, J. (2013) 'Becoming cosmopolitan and other dilemmas of internationalisation: reflections from the Gulf States', *Cambridge Journal of Education*, Vol. 43, No. 4: 501–5015. Available at http://dx/doi.org/10.1080/0305764X.2013.831033

Introduction

This book is about writing action research and doing action research. It is written for practitioner researchers studying for masters and doctoral degrees, lecturers, and early career and more advanced researchers who wish to do action research and write books and journal articles from the experience. It may appeal also to those working in research traditions other than action research who wish to use some of its principles, practices and methods; and for students on, say, qualitative programmes who wish to incorporate action research into a mixed methodologies approach. To meet the needs of these practitioners the book outlines the principles, practices and methods of action research, and explains how to communicate understandings of its nature and uses through texts. The book is not only a 'how to' book; it is also about showing what action research means to different people in different research settings. It shows how you can interweave all aspects of your research and writing practice into a seamless communicative whole where each informs and strengthens the other.

The book has several purposes and related interests. The first is to provide advice for people like those identified above who wish to get their higher degrees and get published. The second is to encourage researchers working in the field to see action research as about openness and criticality rather than about certainty and closure, and combat a current tendency to put action research into a box labelled 'finished business'. A third purpose is to allow me to pursue ideas of life-long interest about how writing can be used for different purposes, and look at the potential significance of these ideas for educational work. The book therefore becomes an account of my own action enquiry into doing, writing and publishing action research, in different contexts and with different people. All the case study material in the book is from colleagues I currently work with, or have worked with across the years, and shows people's capacity to realise their right to research and speak for themselves.

I am interested in ideas about texts and discourses, and the importance of writing. I am interested in language games and how the rules of the game are communicated through texts. I am interested in how writing can be used intellectually as a means of rethinking one's ideas, and politically as a means of self-empowerment. I am especially interested in the politics of writing: how it can be used as a means of thought control, when ideas are communicated through texts and sub-texts that persuade readers not to question what they write and read; and how the publication and therefore legitimation of writing, and the research and researcher it represents, are tightly controlled by those reviewers, editors and examiners who specify what counts as a 'good quality' text, and therefore who counts as a 'good quality' researcher. These ideas inform the writing of this book. I love writing as a practice, and I love its texts, especially books. Therefore, because freedom of thinking is a core value for me, I want to use this book to emphasise the need for openness and criticality in writing, and for the practice of writing itself to be a means of doing this, so that we learn to question and not simply accept what we are told.

The fact that this book is about academic writing gives it a particular slant because, if you are a student, an early career researcher or a lecturer, it is not an option for you not to write for publication, whether as a dissertation, thesis, journal article, or book. You may be committed to doing action research, but you are still in the institutional situation where academics from a more scientific and social scientific orientation still control what counts as research and what should be published. This means appreciating that there is a difference between writing action research and writing action research for publication. In the first case you could write for an audience of, say, a peer practitioner group, but when you write for publication you write for an audience of academic peers who expect the highest standards of academic writing. You can choose the content and form of your text to a certain extent, but you still need to abide by the established rules of writing if you wish to get published.

You can, however, learn to work within the rules through writing imaginatively and creatively. You can learn how to influence the established canon, and so influence the wider politics of the control of knowledge and the production of knowledge and texts. This can be tricky, because action research is still relatively new in universities, and many higher education boardroom occupants tend to be suspicious of it. They are suspicious probably because they doubt the capacity of action research for generating public theory, and because embracing action research would mean accepting as legitimate researchers the 'ordinary practitioners' who do action research.

Yet accepting the legitimacy of action research in higher education and knowing how to write it are now urgent matters for higher education, for several reasons. Mode 2 practice-based forms of knowledge, including action research, are now recognised as of equal validity as Mode 1 disciplines-based knowledge (Gibbons et al., 1994): and they are popular with many practitioners who have registered on higher education courses and lecturers. However, these Mode 2 texts, with their emphasis on processes of personal and social learning, require a different form of communication from Mode 1 texts, with their emphasis on results and outcomes. This can present problems. Writing is still the dominant means of communicating research and therefore establishing the legitimacy of the researcher. So if people don't know how to write, they can't get published; and if they can't get published, they won't be recognised. Their voice will not be heard. The job of supervisors is to help them learn how to write, yet many academic staff themselves express concerns about their capacity in writing, and some actively resist writing, especially when it is stated as a condition of tenure. Also, within the action research community, while there is emphasis on the need to articulate what counts as quality in the study of action research, not so much emphasis is placed on what counts as quality in writing, or on the need to teach people how to write and develop academic literacy.

Various problems follow. Because, for different reasons, many practitioners appear reluctant to write for publication or get their voices heard in the right circles, action research continues to be seen largely as a form of professional development but not as a form of knowledge creation or theory generation. Practitioners continue to be positioned as capable of telling good stories but not of creating knowledge – 'knowledge workers' but not 'competent theorists'. They are encouraged to 'tell their stories' but are not always required to offer explanations and critical analyses of those stories, which, on Foucault's (1979) reading, keeps them in their place within the existing regime. Practitioners frequently collude in the plot. They say, 'Don't tell me about theory. I am happy just telling my story.'

However, although there is a dearth of published outputs by practitioners in the form of articles and books, increasing numbers **are** getting their higher degrees and producing their texts, though not in such numbers as one would wish, and this new body of knowledge is becoming established around the world. While higher education academics are still the main producers of academic texts, new popular bodies of educational activists are appropriating power for themselves. These currently run parallel to established higher education institutions, in the form of Internet and social media networking, open access publishing, self-publishing, and open, especially online review practices. This work is still in its infancy, and procedures are only now beginning to be worked out for establishing what counts as quality in online texts (see Andrews et al., 2012) but the potentials are there for a radical transformation of academic writing and publishing.

All this has implications for you, as a practitioner-researcher, whether studying or supervising. If you wish to influence the status quo, you need to become proficient in debates about knowledge and knowledge creation and dissemination and take an active part in public debates about who has the right to research and write. It is no use leaving it to someone else, because there is no one else. If you are to speak for yourself, you need to know what you are talking about, and how to say it. If you are to claim the right to be a legitimate participant you need to produce texts that will be agreed by the academy as high quality, so you need to know what this involves and how to achieve it. This book will help you do so. It will help you to produce a high quality action research text that will stand, on its own terms, alongside the best in other research traditions, and contribute to a knowledge base where all voices are represented in the wider movement towards social and cultural transformation, where all are entitled to speak for themselves and be heard.

About Writing and Making Public

The book therefore is about writing and getting your work published and thereby legitimised. Doing research and writing it are indivisible, contrary to much public opinion that says you do the action first and then you do the writing. Writing is itself a form of action, and finding ways to improve your capacity for writing is itself a form of action research – you research your practice of writing and making your work public. Doing action research becomes multi-layered: it is about improving the quality of practice in the workplace (including in universities), and also about improving the quality of the practice of writing, at the workplace of your desk, about your action in your other workplaces. It is about improving your practice as an activist writer.

I take the view, with Derrida (1997), that writing is 'the inscription of a communicated idea' (in Deutscher, 2005: 9), a making external in a recordable form that which is internal. Olson (2009) says that writing may be seen as 'the use of visual marks or other artefacts for communication and expression' (p. 6). 'Writing' can take the form of letters and words, film and video, performance, cave paintings, graffiti or thinking. A picture or video may be a text, to be interpreted by a reader. Foucault (1977) raised interesting questions about this, wondering whether, for example, Nietzsche's jottings would constitute his writing: would his laundry list count as a text? A text would always have a sense that it is to be made public, even if the reader is oneself.

The world of writing and publishing has changed significantly in recent years, with a broadened understanding of what counts as literature and accessibility to texts (see Collins' 2010 *Bring on the Books for Everybody*). Hitherto inaccessible scholarly articles are now made available through social media, e-books and open access publishing. When you write you make your physical mark. You also make your political mark – your mark of symbolic power – in that you claim the right to make your mark, a right that is too often claimed only by those sufficiently privileged to know already how to do so and what kind of mark is acceptable in the dominant system of knowledge. You claim distinction (Bourdieu, 1984) in different ways. In your writing, you write your life, as a person who can make a quality contribution to the world.

By doing so, you influence the situation where traditionalist members of the academy control what counts as knowledge and its means of communication. Currently, in higher education contexts, any knowledge that claims validity has to be seen as academic knowledge. This means ensuring that the quality of the content of an action research text and the form of the text itself come up to academic expectations. You need to know the rules of academic writing to get your text accepted as an academic text. This means learning the rules of the game so that you can become a member of the owners' club and begin to change it from within, and you also influence the nature of the club. This is happening now in all kinds of contexts. Legions of what are still known as workplace practitioners are accessing university study and gaining higher degrees for their workplace knowledge. Some in turn join existing staff who are also doing some form of action research; many have worked their way up through the ranks and still feel more at home in their professional traditions than as academics and writers: '... each of us as researchers occupies multiple positions that intersect and may bring us into conflicting allegiances or alliances within our research sites', comment Herr and Anderson (2005: 44). Practitioners need to develop expertise too and extend their practitioner identities to become researchers and writers. Traditions do not stay the same forever. At time of writing, the Royal and Ancient Golf Club in St Andrews, the so-called 'cradle of golf', has agreed to change its 260-year-old men-only policy and allow women to become members. Every tradition can be challenged and transformed.

The aim of this book therefore is to help you to produce a work that will be understood immediately as an academic work, so that the originality, rigour and significance of your practice and its potential impact in the lives of others will be properly appreciated, and you will be recognised as a legitimate participant in the global community of writers. It is about communicating the quality of your work and status through ensuring the quality of the text itself. Medium and message are inseparable, and quality in one reflects quality in the other.

Distinction and Symbolic Power

These issues count towards whether practitioners' research will strengthen their academic reputations, including in the form of securing research funding (Hyland, 2007). Currently, most government money, allocated from exercises such as the Research Excellence Framework in the UK and its equivalent in other countries, goes to top research institutions, often working from a scientific or social scientific perspective and doing research into the disciplines, using traditional forms of scholarship. Practitioner groups often find it difficult to secure strong funding because the funding system leans strongly in the direction of the establishment, not surprisingly since it is created and maintained by the establishment. Derrida (1997) notes that it is difficult to over-turn a hierarchical system when one is forced to abide by the rules of the hierarchy itself. So if you wish to get recognition you have to produce a work that will meet the criteria of the establishment, albeit in its own way. You have to produce a work that will immediately impress your reader in relation to its originality, rigour, significance and potential for 'impact' in the wider world, and its capacity to explicate these issues. Too often practitioner-researchers do not do this or know how to do it. They tend to think that a reader will see immediately what they are getting at, without any meta-text to guide their reading. However, if you do not explain to your reader what you wish them to read, or present yourself as careless through incorrect referencing or a vague use of language, your reader will assume that you are incompetent and reject your work. This is serious. To get accreditation for dissertations and theses and to get your work published, you must present yourself as a person who knows what they are talking about, with confidence, and with the authority of your own experience, scholarship and communicative expertise.

This book goes some way to helping you to do this. It will not replace the sheer hard work of study and learning how to write. You have to work with the ideas themselves in order to write, and you have to practise to understand what writing and getting published involves – and it is a highly competitive business. The book will give you advice about how to do it, but you have to do it yourself to succeed. It is a tough road but well worth the effort. The rewards for yourself are considerable, as are, perhaps, the rewards for others, since perhaps the main criterion for success in action research lies in the fact that you are able to pass on your knowledge of action research. This does not mean simply reciting the principles and practices of action research: it means explaining to others the deepened meaning they can give to their lives through engaging in their personal enquiries. The voice of Douglas Hector, the disreputable teacher in *The History Boys* who insisted that students learn how to challenge orthodoxy and think for themselves, is heard at the end of the play: 'Pass it on, boys. That's the game I wanted you to learn. Pass it on' (Bennett and Hytner, 2006: 107).

Passing on knowledge of action research is a guiding principle for me, too. I judge the quality of my work as in its capacity to influence others to keep their thinking open and fluid, not to be intimidated by power or seduced into an easy life, but to maintain independence of mind and build intellectual resources that help them to do so. This enables them to develop practices and discourses that encourage others to pass on the knowledge, as a way of life. As researchers in action on action for action we test the validity of what we consider the best of our thinking through the stringent critique of peers; we find ways of communicating it to similarly-minded others; and we try to influence those who are not. We make every effort to avoid the convenient slide into fundamentalism through lack of critique. A criterion that has recently entered public discourses about the validity of products is 'ease': one-click consumerism makes for an easy life; one-click assessment leads to ease of legitimation. People deserve more: easy-come easy-go is hardly a means for creating a life of which we can be proud. If we are to claim the right to create our lives, especially through writing, which is a main theme of this book, we need to commit ourselves to the process, and not stint or hold back in any regard.

A Note on Terminology

I need to explain my uses of certain words, specifically the word 'text', and the terms 'academics' and 'practitioners', and 'dissertation' and 'thesis'.

By 'texts' I mean any document that can be read and interpreted. Sometimes a text may be seen as a 'work', a specific artefact such as an article or book. A text is taken in this book to mean a work written for academic purposes – a dissertation or thesis, a journal article or a report. Nietzsche's laundry list would not count.

The terms 'academics' and 'practitioners' are used, where necessary, to denote people who work respectively in official research settings such as universities, and others who work in unofficial research settings such as factories and shops. My view is that all people who do productive intellectual and/or practical work, whether for a living or for pleasure, are practitioners: if they do research, they become practitioner-researchers. People who do research in everyday workplace settings and who are also doing academic work (perhaps studying for a higher degree) become academics by default. I am disputing the use of language that perpetuates the tradition of speaking about 'academics' and 'practitioners' as separate groups of people, with implications of hierarchies and meritocratic order.

Regarding dissertations and theses: in the UK, a masters work is called a dissertation while a doctoral work is a thesis. In the US I believe it is the other way round. In this book I stay with the UK system, though I usually try to hedge my bets by referring to 'your dissertation or thesis' as appropriate.

A Note about the Research Base of the Book

I said on page 1 that this book is an account of my action enquiry into doing, writing and publishing action research. It is a research account, with a database provided by colleagues I currently work with or have worked with across the years. We have produced data about our work together in the form of emails, letters, audio and videotaped conversations, papers, books and other documents. These data are the source of the case study material in the book. I introduce the speakers along the way to give a sense of context. All have read, edited as appropriate, and agreed the text. I have acted as supervisor or co-supervisor for all doctoral studies mentioned, and much of the material appears on my website at www.jeanmcniff.com.

A Note about my Background

It may be helpful for you to know some of my background – that which makes me challenge normative (and hierarchical) attitudes and forms of language. In the 1980s I was a teacher who became a deputy head teacher in a large secondary school. I took early retirement because of a health issue that cleared up over time. At the time, leaving school was traumatic because of the loss of a firm professional identity, but in retrospect it was one of the more fortuitous events of my life, for it made me aware of the need for intellectual freedom and forced me to be free. I went into business, and purchased a small seaside gift shop with a business partner, where we sold buckets and spades and flip-flops. We actually had an unfortunate experience of flip-flop wars with the next-door shop-keeper who wanted to maintain a monopoly on selling flip-flops, so I learned rapidly about the politics of business at grassroots level. Recently I have co-authored *Action Research for Professional Selling* (McDonnell and McNiff, 2014), and am developing a new strand of supporting practitioners' action enquiries in business and business schools.

While running the shop, I continued the doctoral studies I had started while at school. I experienced no contradiction between my identity as a gift-shop proprietor, cleaner, salesperson, negotiator and academic. I also developed my writing and wrote texts at the counter, including two psychology textbooks, a book on action research and my doctoral thesis, while the shop was quiet or during the winter off-season when business was slow. Because the books began to generate interest I began receiving invitations to do consultancy work with higher education institutions, mainly in the form of workshops for academic staff wanting to learn about action research. This practice developed to the extent that I gave up my partnership in the gift shop and focused entirely on writing and consultancy work. In 2005 I was invited by a London-based university college to take up a three-year part-time contract to help develop an institutional research culture, and in 2008 was invited by my present main institution, York St John University, to accept a similar position. I continue to do this work and am happy working with colleagues who wish to engage in their own action enquiries. I have several other similar small institutional roles internationally with the same focus. Hence I see no division between 'practitioners' and 'academics': for me they are words that describe two sides of the same coin. Like Sen (2007), I do not see identity in terms of a fixed set of descriptors: I create my identity with others through the life I live, in all its multiple forms. My current situation means that I can move in and move out of institutions by negotiation. I am fortunate, because I can choose, and I never take advantage of the situation. Recently I have begun, with others, to formalise this work as the HEART project (Higher Education Action Research in Teaching), a collaborative international project that promotes the idea of higher education practitioners studying their practices for specific purposes, and through co-convening the Value and Virtue in Practice-Based Research series of conferences at York St John University (see www.yorksj.ac.uk/value&virtue). If you would like to hear more about these initiatives, please contact me at the email address below.

My epistemological and methodological commitments are to action research, which, for me, is a brilliant way of helping people find ways of improving their learning in order to help themselves and others develop productive and peaceful forms of living. Action research is freely available to all, not only to elites. It is research in action on action for action. This is the focus of the book. But if you wish to participate in public debates and challenge who is allowed into the clubhouse, you need to think like an insider and challenge from within. You need to become expert in the rules of the game and know how to play it to win.

A Note on the Title and Content of this Book

In 2006 I was lead author for a co-authored book titled *Doing and Writing Action Research*. This current *Writing and Doing Action Research* is a re-write of that work; it is not a second edition. The earlier book is now out of date and is no longer in print. All the material in this new book is my original work, with due acknowledgement of sources as appropriate, and represents my current best thinking, developed over a life-time. This thinking will, of course, change through the process of writing this book, and will, I imagine, provide the grounds for new works.

I am hoping to make the point throughout that we should all be confident that we can contribute to human and planetary well-being through dialogue. This is a dialogue of equals, conducted in universities and townships, in zoos and retail outlets, as the case studies show. We are all in this life together.

Please contact me for further information about how to contribute to initiatives or for advice about conducting your action research (or selling flip-flops). I promise that I will respond, perhaps not immediately, but I will.

Thank you for reading this book.

Jean McNiff

Dorset, March 2014

You can contact me at jeanmcniff@mac.com and through www.jeanmcniff.com.

PART I

What is Written in an Action Research Text?

This Part deals with the question 'What is written in an action research text?' It outlines what you need to know and do in order to write an action research text, whether for higher degree accreditation or for publication in journals or as books.

This Part contains Chapters 1, 2, 3 and 4.

Chapter 1 asks, 'What do you need to know about action research in order to write it?' It outlines the differences between doing action research and studying what you do as you do it (which is what many people do in the real world), and studying action research as a topic (which is what many people do in higher institutional contexts). It outlines some of the practical implications for what you write and how you write it.

Chapter 2 asks, 'What do you need to know to write action research? Why do you need to know it?' The chapter outlines the main theoretical issues you need to know in order to do and write action research. It emphasises that you have choices about which issues you wish to engage with and how you choose to use your knowledge, with possible practical and ethical implications.

Chapter 3 asks, 'What do you write in an action research text?' It outlines what subject matter goes into a text, and how to achieve an explanatory level of writing appropriate for an academic text.

Chapter 4 asks, 'What is the form of an action research text?' It discusses what an action research text looks like, and how you can achieve an appropriate standard.

Throughout this Part practical advice is given about what you need to do to produce a high quality academic text. Please note that this Part is more conceptual than the rest of the book. There is a focus on the philosophy of action research, and strong theoretical frameworks are offered to ground ideas and practices. I hope these will help you as you weave together the theoretical and practical aspects of your work.

ONE

What Do You Need to Know About Action Research in Order to Write it?

This chapter outlines what you need to know about action research in order to write it. However, these days this is not quite as straightforward as it used to be, because nowadays it is not possible to say definitively what action research is and what it means, given that there are many different action research traditions, all with varying perspectives. Therefore if you wish to write with authority and understanding you first need to know what the traditions are and what they say.

To help appreciate the different perspectives, first look at what Sowell (1987) has to say about a conflict of visions.

Sowell says that people often have different kinds of social visions: he calls one of them a constrained vision and the other an unconstrained vision. People with a constrained vision tend to see situations as given and closed, so learn how to work effectively within them. An unconstrained vision allows people to see possibilities and opportunities: they exercise personal and collective agency to realise them. A constrained vision errs towards orthodoxy; it is about being, and looks for answers and outcomes. An unconstrained vision is adventurous and on the lookout for new ideas; it is about becoming, at home with openness, optimism and critique.

This chapter looks at how these different visions influence the traditions of action research, and how different people with different visions have at times appropriated and misappropriated action research for their own purposes. The chapter covers the following:

1. The practice of action research as a practice and the study of action research as a topic
2. The misappropriation of action research
3. What does this mean for you as an action research writer?

First, let's consider the differences between the practice of action research as a practice and the study of action research as a topic, and what they mean.

The Practice of Action Research as a Practice and the Study of Action Research as a Topic

Action research is universally acknowledged as about change, collaborative and democratic practices, and a commitment towards humans' and other entities' well-being, including animals and the living planet. Although these days there are multiple traditions in action research, most agree on certain goals. These include:

(a) the generation of new knowledge, (b) the achievement of action-oriented outcomes, (c) the education of both researcher and participants, (d) results that are relevant to the local setting, and (e) a sound and appropriate research methodology. (Herr and Anderson, 2005: 54)

No matter how action research is done, or who does it, these matters are taken as standard. However, there are two key considerations.

First, the fact that action research is about collaborative and democratic practices makes it political. This is nothing unusual; all research is political, with social intent, though the intent may vary from helping others to controlling them. Action research is political because it aims to influence processes of change. This means engaging with different forms of politics, including the politics of research in general, of the social context, of the researcher and of the potential reader. These political contexts form backstories to the main stories of action research. To write and do action research successfully you need to know what the backstories say as well as the main public stories. You also need to think about what influences your own personal backstories as well as the stories you tell publicly.

Second, the rhetoric and practices of action researchers can differ. While many write about the democratic, collaborative, emancipatory and other principles of action research, their frequently territorial practices sometimes deny the rhetoric. This can make life difficult for scholars who take what they read in good faith, and so don't know which story to believe.

To make sense of it all, think about the differences between the practice of action research as a practice and the study of action research as a topic, and how these are communicated.

The practice, study and communication of action research

The practice of action research as a practice and the study of action research as a topic are different and are communicated in different ways. Briefly:

- The practice of action research as a practice refers to what people do, individually and collectively, in particular social situations when they inquire into how they can find ways to improve what they are doing. This is a process of personal and collective inquiry. They communicate these stories through oral and written texts, often emphasising personal and collective struggles and achievements.

- The study of action research as a topic refers to how an observer observes, describes and explains what the people involved in those social situations do. How the observer studies this depends on how they position themselves in relation to the situation, whether as outsider or insider researcher (see below), and what their aims and purposes are. The researcher is usually from higher education and uses a traditional form of academic writing.
- The communication of action research depends on how writers see action research, whether as practices in the life-world or as a topic of study within a particular scholarly tradition. They communicate their understanding of action research through the texts they produce.

Here is a closer analysis.

The practice of action research as a practice

The practice of action research as a practice has been around throughout history, long before people called it action research. At a basic methodological level it can be seen as a general strategy that people and other organisms use when faced with dilemmas, puzzles and problems. It looks like this:

- Identify an issue that needs attention or investigation.
- Be reasonably clear why it needs attention.
- Show to oneself, and probably others, what the issue and its contexts look like.
- Imagine what can be done about it.
- Try out a possible strategy and see what happens.
- Change practice and thinking in light of the evaluation.

This evolutionary process is evident across the living world. When a plant or animal is under attack from a predator it tries to find a way of defending itself. When one person loves another, they try to find ways to get the other to reciprocate. When people get stuck in routines or lose momentum they try to find ways of leveraging themselves into new directions. All living organisms, including people, do this: they find ways of staying alive and well. In the human domain it is especially visible in the social world, and especially in processes of social and technological evolution. Examples of social evolution are judiciary systems, health services and the recognition of human rights. Examples of technological evolution are pitchforks, computers and cars. People have acted to make their lives more productive and fulfilling through whatever means are available. A good example is the military: a General sends out scouts on reconnaissance. They bring back intelligence, which is acted on to inform strategy. The strategy is implemented, and gains and losses evaluated. New strategies are planned, and the cycle begins again.

The practice of action research as a practice may therefore be seen in the process of life itself where everything is in a process of evolution. One event transforms into another in perpetual motion: the oak tree emerges from the acorn where it has lain phylogenetically dormant throughout history. Appreciating these processes means adopting an attitude to the world and, instead of simply taking things for granted and seeing them as objects in one's space, seeing everything as in a process of evolution.

If anyone using this strategy were to articulate it, they would say something like the following:

- What do I wish to investigate? What is my research issue? What is my concern?
- Why do I wish to investigate it? Why is this an issue? Why am I concerned?
- What kind of data can I produce to show the situation as it is?
- What can I do about it? What are my options for action?
- What will I do? How will I do it?
- How will I continue to gather data and generate evidence to show the situation as it develops?
- How will I ensure that any conclusions I come to are reasonable and justifiable?
- How will I modify my practices in light of my evaluation?
- How will I explain the significance of my research in action?

From this perspective, action research can be understood as about people doing everyday actions and studying what they are doing as they try to live productive and meaningful lives. They do this in mundane settings such as doing the shopping, or in more recognised practice settings such as nursing and machine engineering. Practices may be formalised as projects but not necessarily so. Whatever the setting, the case remains that people work imaginatively and collaboratively in an emergent, developmental way. People also use symbolic forms, including language, to make what they are doing explicit: they offer descriptions and explanations for their actions, as well as their reasons and purposes. This process is known as theorising: they explain the significance of their actions for different constituencies, and imagine ways in which they could have done things differently. In this way they can develop cooperative and shared forms of learning that can facilitate the processes of social evolution. Action research may therefore be seen as a form of ethics in action, when ethics is understood as 'a discourse for rethinking our relations to other people' (Todd, 2003: 1). It is always about people thinking, working and creating knowledge together, a commitment towards improvement, that is, a move towards however those people understand 'the good'. It is not knowledge *about* ethics so much as the practice of ethics in action.

These processes are communicated through texts in the form of stories. The Mills and Boon industry, for example, takes it as a standard model: boy meets girl, they fall in love, seemingly insurmountable misunderstandings develop (usually through external circumstances), and one party takes strategic action to resolve the dilemmas. Misunderstandings are clarified, conflicts resolved and lovers reunited. The recipe works, time and again. A book is written and sells widely, helped because the transformational dialectic of its plot is communicated explicitly through the structure of the text.

The study of action research as a topic

The study of action research as a topic also has a long history, extending formally over the last hundred years or so and informally long before that. It adopts a range of forms, from personal accounts of learning and practice to narratives about other people's practices. How it is told depends on the positioning of the storyteller, whether they include themselves in the story or tell it as a story about other people.

In the 1930s the process began to be formalised when it was given the name of action research by Lewin (1946) and Collier (1945) (see Noffke, 1997b; 2009). Action research became a noun, a thing you speak about, not a verb, something you do (in the same way, as above, that the study of ethics is *about* ethics whereas the practice of ethics is what you do in relation with others). This formalisation of action research was a critical turning point, for it meant that while the practice of action research would still be located in the everyday social world, the study of action research would now move into institutions, the main institution being the university. Because the job of academics is to look out for new ideas and trends, they immediately saw the potentials of action research as a possibly fertile topic for development, so they appropriated it.

This appropriation of action research by the academy had specific advantages. Once a topic is identified as a university topic, it is immediately seen as legitimate and worthy of public discussion, especially since the university is still seen as the most powerful body for legitimating what counts as knowledge and who counts as a knower. Moving action research into higher education therefore had positive and negative consequences, depending on how you see things. On the one hand it meant that the development of action research was legitimised across the professions and in a range of fields. On the other, it meant that action research could be misappropriated by academic elites who would adapt it to their own uses, and potentially distort its democratic potentials. And this is what has happened – and what you, as a person doing action research with a view to publishing your work, need to appreciate and engage with.

Staying with the positive outcomes before considering the need for critical perspectives, the take-up of action research by higher education has resulted in a broad action research family with a rich heritage, who write different kinds of texts.

The communication of action research

Most action research texts are written by researchers working usually in higher education settings: the aim is to provide theoretical resources. Most higher education researchers write about action research as a topic of study, a discipline, and often use practitioners' workplace accounts as evidence to show the validity of their theoretical ideas. Most established researchers agree that the practice of action research has a rich heritage; Popplewell and Hayman (2012, online) say:

Action Research has not emerged from a single academic discipline. Rather, Action Research approaches have slowly developed over time within a wide range of disciplines and professions including education, psychology, social policy, community development and international development.

(Note in this extract how 'Action Research' has become a capitalised proper noun, a notional 'it', rather than a set of practices done in real-time and real-space by real people. This is an increasingly common practice in the literatures.)

Focusing on this diversity, here is part of the abstract for a presentation by Steve Gordon and Jovita Ross-Gordon (2014), both from Texas State University, at the 2014 Value and Virtue in Practice-Based Research conference, held at York St John University, where they speak about the history of the different traditions of action research.

Although some scholars and practitioners treat action research as a single concept, there are in fact multiple approaches to practitioner action research, including technical action research, practical action research, participatory action research, self-reflective inquiry, appreciative inquiry, collaborative autobiography and critical action research. These different approaches have varied histories, operating principles, terminologies, phases, and techniques, but what really makes them different from each other are the underlying values that drive them. For an obvious example, critical action research is based directly on critical theory. Esposito and Evans-Winters (2007), proponents of critical action research, believe that 'issues of power, privilege, and difference have to be central to educational research' (p. 222), and 'action research has to take up issues of race, ethnicity, and gender. We cannot conduct research outside of these contexts' (p. 225). Other approaches to action research tend to have multiple theoretical bases. For instance, appreciative inquiry has roots in both social constructivist theory and postmodernism (Bushe, 2011). Also, different versions of the same approach may be based on different values. For example, different versions of participatory action research are grounded in constructivism (Hansen, 2004), critical theory (Torre, 2009), and postmodernism (McCartan, Schubotz and Murphy, 2012).

Virtually all writers in the field acknowledge this diversity of action research. Many locate its historical antecedents in a particular reductionist intellectual tradition espoused by different scientific and social communities. Flood (2001) writes that action research emerged formally during the twentieth century through a critique of this reductionism. He says: 'Reductionism generates knowledge and understanding of phenomena by breaking them down into their constituent parts and then studying these simple elements in terms of their cause and effect' (p. 133), whereas action research is a form of systems thinking.

With systems thinking the belief is that the world is systemic, which means that phenomena are understood to be an emergent property of an interrelated whole. An emergent property of a whole is said to arise where a phenomenon cannot be fully comprehended in terms only of constituent parts. 'The whole is greater than the sum of its parts', is the popularized phrase that explains emergence. (Flood, 2001: 133)

The main categories of texts where you will find studies of action research and some of the most influential voices include handbooks, textbooks and journal articles. Here are some examples.

Handbooks of action research   Handbooks that show the diversity of the contexts and fields of action research include:

Reason and Bradbury (2001, 2008), who say:

We see [action research] as a 'family' of … approaches – a family which sometimes argues and falls out, may at times ignore some of its members, has certain members who wish to dominate, yet a family which sees itself as different from other forms of research, and is certainly willing to pull together in the face of criticism or hostility from supposedly 'objective' ways of doing research. (2001: xxiii)

In their (2008) second edition, they position action research not so much as a methodology as:

An orientation to inquiry that seeks to create participative communities of inquiry in which qualities of engagement, curiosity and question posing are brought to bear on significant practical issues. (2008: 1)

They emphasise it as 'a practice of participation': 'Action research does not start from a desire to changing others "out there", although it may eventually have that result, rather it starts from an orientation of change *with* others' (p. 1: italics in original).

Noffke and Somekh (2009) similarly emphasise the participatory nature of action research, especially regarding issues about the ownership and legitimacy of forms of knowledge:

Action research has been seen as a means of adding to knowledge generated in the academy via traditional methods, but it has also been seen as a distinctive way of knowing. This point is directly related to whether action research is seen as producing knowledge for others to use, or whether it is primarily a means for professional development. (2009: 10)

They emphasise how important it is that:

those using the term action research … are clear in their assumptions about the kind of knowledge(s) they seek to enhance, the traditions they feel are part of their work, the ends towards which their research efforts are aimed, and the social movements with which they articulate. (2009: 20)

Chevalier and Buckles (2013) give a wide-ranging account, explaining how science may be seen in different ways, including an 'orientation to society and the common good on a global scale' (p. 1). They propose 'concrete ways to reconnect knowledge making in the academic world with the diversity of perspectives on reality and ways to co-create meaning' (p. 1). Participatory action research, for them, 'is an expression of science that assumes reflectivity and self-experimentation in history' (p. 4).

Rowell, Bruce, Shosh and Riel (in preparation, 2016) say that their handbook provides 'a portrait of theoretical perspectives and practical action research activity around the world, while attending to the cultural, political, socio-historical and ecological contexts that localize, shape and characterize action research. Cross-national issues of networking, as well as challenges, tensions and issues associated with the transformative power of action research are explored from multiple perspectives' (see https://sites.google.com/site/interhandbookar/home).

One of the editors, Margaret Riel, is Director of the Center for Collaborative Action Research (http://cadres.pepperdine.edu/ccar/), and has taught action research for over a decade at Pepperdine University. She is currently working with a team of dedicated action researchers to develop the Action Research Network of the Americas (http://www.arnaconnect.org). Margaret's passion is to develop resources to help practitioners learn to be action researchers. One of the many superb resources she has produced is a set of action research tutorials (http://ccar.wikispaces.com/ar+tutorial). Each tutorial includes a 10–15 minute video, a set of activities and a set of resources to support the activities. Any instructor or student in an action research programme could use some or all of these activities as part of their study. Additionally teachers could use Action Research Learning Circles (http://onlinelearningcircles.org) to support collaborative inquiry at their schools.

Textbooks about action research Textbooks about action research are everywhere. Whereas in the 1980s there was a handful, today the action research textbook industry is massive. Some of the best are as follows.

Greenwood and Levin (2007) work in industrial, community and higher education settings in Europe and the US. They share a 'strong commitment to the democratisation of knowledge, learning, and self-managed social change' and see their work as about offering, 'as skillfully as possible, the space and tools for democratic social change' (p. 9). For them, action research was initiated by Kurt Lewin in the US and developed in the field of industrial democracy, developed both by the Tavistock Institute in the UK and in the Industrial Democracy Project in Norway. Since then it has had international influence involving 'broad cadres of participants' in dealing with 'pertinent and highly conflictive social problems' (p. 34), as a feature of what has been called Participatory Action Research (PAR). They also espouse Reason's ideas about human inquiry, and Heron's (1996) ideas about cooperative inquiry (see Reason and Rowan's 1981 *Human Inquiry: A Sourcebook of New Paradigm Research,* which is still, for me, one of the best texts in the field).

Burns (2007) in the UK focuses on the idea of systemic action research. Like others who share his vision (including those who draw on complexity theory, including Capra, 1996; Johnson, 2002; and myself, 2000 and 2013a), he speaks about the interrelated nature of social systems, especially in management and organisational development practices, emphasising the need for relational forms of knowing and being.

Coghlan and Brannick (2001) in Ireland focus on understanding organisational life through an action research lens. They see this as when 'a member of an organization undertakes an explicit research role in addition to the normal functional role which that member holds in the organization' (p. xii). I see action research in organisations differently (McNiff, 2000), involving all members of the organisation in researching their practices and negotiating how they can improve themselves, individually and as a collective, for the benefit of all.

The study and theorisation of action research has perhaps been most fully worked out in the fields of education and professional education, and nursing and healthcare. Some of the most influential texts are as follows.

Action research in education **Noffke** (1997b) gives an account of the development of action research in education in 1950s' United States. Like other writers, she identifies John Collier as a founding father of the term 'action research'. She also draws a distinction between the practice of action research in social settings and the study of action research in higher education settings, citing the work of Stephen Corey (1953) who brought critical insights to the potential uses and abuses of action research.

Herr and Anderson (2005) outline the uses of action research for the following fields:

- Organisational and development learning: citing Greenwood and Levin (2007: see above).
- Action science: citing Argyris et al. (1985) and Argyris and Schön (e.g. 1974), about how organisations learn.
- Participatory research: citing Gaventa and Horton (1981) and Freire (1970), who use the term 'Participatory Action Research' to refer to the participation by community in the research field, now further developed by researchers such as Stringer (2007).
- Participatory evaluation: emphasising the need for the involvement of those being evaluated: see also Kushner (2000).

- The work of John Dewey (e.g. 1938) as a major influence, especially his idea of inquiry as a process of identification of problematic areas, which influenced Schön's development of 'reflecting-in-action' (1983) and the need for a new epistemology for a new scholarship (1995).
- The teacher-as-researcher movement in Britain: developed by Stenhouse in the UK (1975), and later by Elliott (1991; 2007) and his colleagues, including Carr and Kemmis (1986) (see also the re-issued *The Action Research Planner*, Kemmis et al., 2014).
- The practitioner research movement in North America, grounded in the original vision of emancipatory and collaborative action research.
- Self-study and auto-ethnography, promoted by authors such as Bullough and Pinnegar (2001; 2004).

Action research in nursing and health care   This is a burgeoning field. Early researchers include the following:

Angie Titchen and Alison Binnie in the UK pioneered action research in nursing (see Titchen, 1993 and Binnie and Titchen, 1998; 1999), grounded in real-life experience. The work of Gary Rolfe (1996; 1998) has also had extensive influence.

Patricia Benner, in the US, working with the Carnegie Foundation for the Advancement of Teaching, has been especially influential in calling for the development of a new knowledge base of nursing through action research (Benner, 1984; Benner et al., 2010).

Action research in nursing is hugely important and widely used (see McDonnell and McNiff, in preparation).

Journal articles   Who to include? Where to begin? So many people, so little space. To cite them all would need a book in itself. Consider some names: Marilyn Cochran-Smith, Bob Dick, John Elliott, Wilfred Carr, Allan Feldman, Stephen Kemmis, Ann Lieberman, Susan Lytle, Bridget Somekh ...

Blogs, websites, YouTube ...   Then there are blogs, websites, fanzines, webcams, YouTube presentations ... and it goes on and on. A wonderful tower, not of Babel because we usually understand one another, but definitely a carnival, a veritable heteroglossia of voices.

In summary, many action research texts are available, and there is no one *Big Book of Action Research*. This can present difficulties for researchers, especially those new to the field, given the many conflicting and contradictory messages about what it is and how it should be done. It means you need to be alert to the hidden messages that seek to persuade you to buy this brand rather than that one. Gone are the 1940s' and 1950s' days when you could have gone into the action research shop to find only one or two bottles of action research on the shelf. Today you can find dozens of different brands, so you need to know what is on offer before you buy one. They also mix and merge with other bottles: sometimes it is difficult to tell what is action research and what is, say, auto-ethnography or narrative inquiry.

However, any text calling itself an action research text agrees common themes, which include the following.

Common themes in action research

- Action research is collaborative and democratic. All voices are included, including the disenfranchised and marginalised.
- It prioritises the well-being of the other (see Buber, 1937; Macmurray, 1957; 1961).
- It is values-oriented: values pluralism is respected and accommodated. (This presents dilemmas about judging quality in practice: would Al Capone be accepted as an action researcher when he claims that he has researched how to bring law and order to the streets of Chicago, without acknowledging the well-being of others?)
- It is self-reflective: see the work of Ghaye (2010) and Winter (1989). Both outline how self-reflection should be a criterion for judging the value of action research.
- It is goal oriented towards social action: see, for example, Bridget Somekh's (2006) ideas about action research for agency in organisational and social change.
- It is open ended, evolutionary and transformational: all things emerge over time as new versions of themselves, adapted to their conditions and contexts (Flood, 2001).
- It is situated and always contextualised: nothing comes out of nothing. Action research links with the literatures of situated learning (Lave and Wenger, 1991) and communities of practice (Wenger, 1998).
- It is critical: this is also taken as a criterion for judging quality in action research: does the researcher show that they have interrogated their own situatedness when reaching conclusions about the quality of their practices and research?

This need for criticality now becomes a major theme because it has special implications for when you write action research.

The need for criticality in writing action research

When you study action research texts and write your own, be aware of the following issues:

- Attitudes towards others in action research.
- Researcher positionality.
- Human interests.
- The need for critical analysis.

Attitudes towards others and different approaches

Be aware that different writers adopt different attitudes towards others in action research, which influences their approaches, and be clear about your own attitudes and approaches. Torbert (2001), Chandler and Torbert (2003) and Reason and Bradbury (2001) speak about first- , second- and third-person research/practice:

- First-person action research is about individual researchers enquiring into their own practices; they produce descriptions and explanations for what they are doing.
- Second-person action research is when a researcher works face-to-face with others in issues of mutual concern.
- Third-person action research extends the research field to wider groupings, such as organisations or international groupings (see Reason and Bradbury, 2001: 6).

Ask yourself: How do you position yourself in relation to others in the research field? Do you study them, or yourself, or you in relation with them? This raises questions about researcher positionality.

Researcher positionality

Are you an insider in the research situation or an outsider who observes the situation, or somewhere between? Herr and Anderson (2005: 32–45) identify the following positionalities:

- Insider, studying their own practices: this involves self-study, autobiography, ethnomethodology.
- Insider, working collaboratively with other insiders.
- Insider, working collaboratively with outsiders.
- Reciprocal collaboration between insider-outsider teams.
- Outsiders working collaboratively with insiders.
- Outsiders study insiders.
- Multiple positionalities.

Decisions about how researchers position themselves are also influenced by whose interests are being served by doing the research.

Human interests

Ask yourself whose interests you serve when you do research in action. Habermas (1976; 1987) sets out three main forms of human interests: technical, practical and emancipatory:

- Technical interests focus on the production of technical rational knowledge with the aim of controlling the natural and social world. Knowledge becomes instrumental activity that emphasises causal explanations.
- Practical interests focus on meaning-making and interpretation, in order to understand the social life-world and its historical and political emergence. The aim is to make practical judgements, usually through hermeneutical methods such as discourse analysis.
- Emancipatory interests help people to understand the influences that lead them to think and act as they do, to liberate their own thinking and resist closure. The aim is to help people take control of their lives by questioning the stories they are told and persuaded to believe (see also Carr and Kemmis's 1986 *Becoming Critical* and their 2005 'Staying critical').

- In my *Action Research: Principles and Practice* (McNiff, 2002 and 2013a), I added a relational interest, about the need for dialogical relationships, where people talk together to improve their learning as the basis of improving their life-worlds.

So, in any discussion about human interests we always have to ask critical questions: Whose interest? Whose theory? Whose voice? Who says? Whose vision? These questions are especially important when you write your text, because it shows how you position yourself and think about the political norms of the action research tradition you have chosen to work in. It also shows how you think about your historical, social and economic situatedness, the form of language you use and the language game you participate in. This is especially important when you claim your knowledge as the truth. Remember what Foucault says:

Truth is a thing of this world: it is produced only by virtue of multiple forms of constraint. And it induces regular effects of power. Each society has its regime of truth, its 'general politics' of truth: that is, the types of discourse which it accepts and makes function as true; the mechanisms and instances which enable one to distinguish true and false statements, the means by which each is sanctioned; the techniques and procedures accorded value in the acquisition of truth; the status of those who are charged with saying what counts as true. (Foucault, 1980: 131)

Where and how do you position yourself in relation to other people in your research, and how do you communicate this? Be aware also that higher education institutions have specific rules about whose voices may be heard, and under what conditions. Often, the messages that texts communicate, or are allowed to communicate, depend on what kinds of discourses are legitimated in universities and how these are communicated through the orthodoxies of writing.

In 2010 I was invited by a group of Norwegian health professionals from the University of Tromsø (hereafter UiT), the Arctic University of Norway, to support their work in learning about and writing action research, with a view to embedding action research in the university. We regarded our work together as an action enquiry, and gathered considerable amounts of data to monitor progress, many in the form of audiotape recordings. Here is part of the transcript of one of the conversations. We are speaking about what counts as theory in academia. Margareta Törnqvist, a member of the group and a teacher in occupational theory, says:

For us in the former Teaching Colleges, unless we adopted traditional theoretical ways, we couldn't get into the academic world. This meant that we lost touch with practices. Professional learning was about applying abstract forms of theory to practice. We became good at discussing theory but not so good at the craft. In my view you have to compare and interlink theory and craft. I believe that action research could be a valuable way of doing this. (McNiff et al., 2013)

Now let's look at some of the more disturbing outcomes of the appropriation of action research, which then amounts to its misappropriation.

The Misappropriation of Action Research

The term 'appropriation' means to make an existing object one's own, such as when singers and storytellers adapt existing works to their own style. In legalistic terms appropriation can become misappropriation when it uses someone else's work, which then becomes theft. In terms of the publication of texts, it becomes plagiarism.

A good example of misappropriation can be seen in the game of football.

Football (soccer in the United States) is considered by many to have been played informally everywhere throughout history, but in its more codified sense had its origins in England. It started life as an open-space activity, frequently played in the streets for entertainment. It is essentially a democratic activity: you can make a ball from any available material, find a space to play, mark out goals and negotiate sides. You play the game by the rules you know or create with the other players.

During the nineteenth century, clubs and associations were formed to develop the game, agree rules and set up associations and leagues. Notwithstanding, football remained open to everybody and most young males would have played football in some way or another. It has been said that you could shout down any coalmine in the north of England and an England centre forward would pop his head up.

Things began to change in recent times. Groups of local business people began to sponsor teams and gradually took ownership of them by becoming directors. The game itself began to be mediated through television. However, with the end of free-to-air television, the means of communication tightened so that distinct groupings came to own the media. They in turn started bidding to have sole access to top-league football matches and gradually took ownership of football. The money they paid soon became the main source of income for the top line football teams. Kick-off times were changed to suit international television coverage.

Consequently a small number of teams commanded a very high income. At the same time the governing bodies of football, such as FIFA, had the power to decide where tournaments would be played; sometimes individuals were found to have influenced their placing. The ownership of football began to be vested in the hands of small elite bodies. They supported and elected each other into the international football associations, formed background deals, and pledged support to each other and to the huge pay-to-view television channels. They bought football clubs as an investment but had no particular interest in developing a long-term relationship with the club: some even borrowed against the assets of the club to purchase it.

Having thus been leveraged, the clubs often found themselves in debt to the owners. Ticket prices for clubs increased, thus pricing professional (now corporatised) football away from the working-class people from whom it had sprung. A new type of supporter emerged, often referred to derisively as members of 'the prawn sandwich' brigade by more traditional supporters. The relationship of many young people with football moved from their personal engagement with the game to watching the match on cable or pay-to-view television. If you walk past open spaces in towns today you will not see many youngsters kicking a football. Football has gone from being a participative activity that involved a large number of people as players and supporters to a spectator sport where people now cheer for multi-million-pound teams, often playing at a far geographical remove from where the supporters live. To maintain continuous and immediate success, many clubs buy in expensive players who are paid huge bonuses, while focusing less on developing footballers from scratch. The demand is for outcomes; processes have largely been forgotten.

You can now get a degree and executive education in the football business and sports industries. Practitioners who attend such courses may actually know just as much about football as the lecturers who teach them, but to have their knowledge legitimated they need to go to university to buy it back in an appropriately packaged form.

Gibson (1993) tells a similar story, how American football has become commodified through the National Football League (NFL). He cites Oriard (1980) as saying:

Perhaps the powers that run the NFL simply do not understand the nature of the game. Perhaps they have become so concerned with packaging and marketing it that they have forgotten it is not merely a product to be pressed on consumers, but a sport that for many Americans has value and meaning unrelated to its investment potential. Perhaps the NFL will slowly but surely kill football because it forgot, or never knew, what football truly means.

(Oriard, 1980, cited in Gibson, 1993: 43)

My concern is that some people in traditionalist universities will kill action research by packaging it in a form acceptable to themselves, while forgetting, or never taking the trouble, to learn through experience what action research means in practice. You can learn action research only by doing it, not simply by learning about it. However, I wish to emphasise here that all is not lost, for members of universities themselves have the power to change the situation, and many are doing so. But to do this systemically would mean an epistemological and professional paradigm shift, a revolution, because it would mean:

- changing the underpinning epistemology of traditionalist universities (Schön, 1995) and their form of logic, from technical rational to relational;
- changing the self-perceptions of academic staff, from authorised knower to unknowing learner, and from external to insider researcher;

- changing the relationship among participants from separatist ('I–them') to inclusional ('we'); and
- changing the form of institutional discourses from didactic ('I tell you') to dialogical ('We learn together, with and from one another').

Achieving this revolution is a hard task, yet it is being done, in many places around the world, as the case studies in this book show. It is a case of how small acts of resistance (Crawshaw and Jackson, 2010) can lead to big acts of transformation. You can be a participant in the revolution, but it carries implications and responsibilities, as spelt out here.

What Does this Mean for You as a Practitioner-Researcher?

Some of the main implications are that you need to develop your knowledge about different aspects of doing and writing action research; this in turn involves engaging with the politics of academic writing as a means of academic legitimation. You need to ensure that you know what you are doing, so that you can communicate the processes involved in doing action research within a literary canon that was originally created by social scientists for reporting work in the sciences and social sciences.

Here are the main things you need to know as a practitioner-researcher, a researcher-scholar, and a writer.

What you need to know

As a practitioner-researcher you need to know:

- What counts as action research.
- Why you have chosen to do action research.
- Debates about action research.
- How you justify your positioning as an action researcher.

As a scholar you need to know:

- What scholarship means (engage critically with texts).
- What critical engagement means.
- What texts do and don't do.
- Different kinds of texts.

As a researcher-scholar you need to know:

- What counts as research.
- What counts as action research.
- Issues of ontology, epistemology, methodology and ways of demonstrating validity.
- Which variants you choose and why – i.e. you need to justify your positionality.

- Critical engagement with the literatures – identifying conceptual and theoretical frameworks.
- What a dissertation or thesis is and does.

As a researcher-writer you need to know:

- How to write for a reader.
- How to produce a text that will keep your reader on your side.
- How to produce a text that will secure accreditation.
- How to get published.

As a dissertation or thesis writer you need to know:

- What your examiner is looking for and how they will judge your thesis.
- How to communicate the authenticity and legitimacy of your positioning in the field.
- How you can defend your thesis and the choices you have made.

Armed with this knowledge, here are some of the things you need to do.

What you need to do

You need to develop strong intellectual resources to help you withstand pressure to conform to orthodox thinking, practices and writing. You can learn a lot from reading and engaging with public discussions about the nature, origins and uses of knowledge of action research, and about democratic and egalitarian movements.

You need to develop your own capacity for thinking and speaking in a dialogical way. This comes naturally for some people; others, including myself, have to work at it. It means always being aware of what effect your words are going to have on the listener or reader, a constant sensitivity to the dynamics of social interchanges and how each positions the other in the discourses.

You need to influence the development of a new epistemology of inquiry, where thinking is seen as emergent, commensurable with the emergent phenomena it encounters and tries to make sense of. Epistemologies (how we think) influence practices (how we act), and practices influence the development of new cultures of practice. By changing your own form of epistemology, you can influence the development of institutional and organisational epistemologies towards learning and the development of unconstrained visions. Research becomes learning; a research-led institution encourages all its participants to learn with and from one another as a life-long strategy.

You need to learn how to write for publication. This means developing the courage to engage with the politics of writing, finding ways to produce texts of such high quality within orthodox structures that you will be able to influence the establishment from within. Further, you will impress others and find that they become your allies who wish to learn with and from you. This happened with *The Muppet Show*. It was originally ridiculed, but when it gained influence and television ratings, anyone who is anyone wanted to be on it. You need to adopt a *Muppet Show* strategy to doing and writing action research, so that your star will shine in its ascendancy, and others will join you for the prestige and the fun of it all.

SUMMARY

This chapter has explored the differences between the practice of action research as a practice and the study of action research as a topic. Benefits from the study of action research as a topic include the production of a range of resources such as handbooks and textbooks, journal articles and online resources. Disadvantages include the misappropriation of action research such that it can lose touch with its roots. You are encouraged to develop your academic and political capacity to engage with contemporary debates and speak from the authority of your own experience.

REFLECTIVE QUESTIONS

Here is a checklist of reflective questions to help you work with the ideas in this chapter.

- Can you explain the differences between doing action research and studying action research? Can you explain how both areas can learn from the other?

- How do you position yourself in the research field? Why do you position yourself like this?

- In what way has the co-option of action research by universities led to its misappropriation? Why do you think this has happened?

- Why do you think some people in higher education are doubtful about the capacity of action researchers to generate academic theory?

- What do you need to do if you wish to establish action research as a legitimate form of theory generation, and demonstrate its validity and legitimacy?

RESEARCH EXERCISE

Write a short text about the following.

Explain how you are doing action research and not social science research. Explain what positionality you adopt in relation to your participants in your practice setting, and to your reader in your text. How do you ensure you communicate these issues through your form of writing?

This now brings us to Chapter 2, which explains what is involved in writing action research, and how you can produce a brilliant action research text.

TWO

What Do You Need to Know to Write Action Research? Why Do You Need to Know it?

This chapter is about what you need to know to write action research, why you need to know it, and what you do with your knowledge. These questions are important because how we use our knowledge makes us who we are, and who you are influences the kind of text you produce.

As a researcher there are certain things you must know in order to do and write research. These include conceptual and philosophical issues, how these help you to understand your practices, and how you use the knowledge in the world for political effect. You can choose whether to know these at a head level only, or whether to commit to them and use them for specific purposes.

The chapter outlines what you need to know, and contains these points.

1. What do you need to know to write action research? Developing conceptual capacity.
2. Why do you need to know it? Developing practical capacity.
3. How do you use your knowledge? Developing political capacity.

When you do and write action research, your knowledge moves from tacit to explicit: your conceptual knowledge (knowledge in the head) informs your social practices (knowledge in practice) for political purposes (knowledge in the world). This is a transformational process:

- Conceptual knowledge (knowledge in the head) transforms into →
- Practical knowledge (knowledge in the practices), which transforms into →
- Political knowledge (knowledge in and for the world).

Ideally, these different kinds of knowledge are integrated coherently within your life. When you write your action research, you demonstrate what MacIntyre (1985) calls its narrative unity; you show how all aspects of your knowledge weave in and out to give deep meaning to your life. However, life and action research are not usually like this: they tend to be chaotic and contradictory (see below for the idea of 'agonistic'). Take care therefore when writing your action research: examiners get suspicious when they read accounts that say everything went perfectly. They look instead for realistic accounts that show how you coped with difficulties and made sense of it all.

So, as a researcher, what do you need to know?

What Do You Need to Know to Write Action Research? Developing Conceptual Capacity

First, consider which conceptual and philosophical issues you need to know to write action research: this means developing conceptual capacity, including knowing how to use an appropriate research language, which enables you to use words to design text. You begin to engage in design thinking and to think like a craftsperson. Consider the idea of craft.

The idea of craft

Thinking like a craftsperson is important because craft is about designing and creating things. You commit yourself to the job in hand and develop appropriate skills and capacities. Sennett cites Shakespeare's Coriolanus as saying, 'I am my own maker' (2009: 9). Creativity is not the prerogative of only a few, as some literatures suggest; it is an inherent quality of being human. We make our lives. Making a life is also a personal, social and cultural activity, because each person is part of and influenced by an existing culture with its own values, discourses and traditions. However, it is possible to influence new directions in the culture, especially through the production of texts that communicate what you have done and how and why you have done it.

To achieve this you need to:

- know the language, including key terminology and concepts; and
- know the main theoretical and conceptual frameworks.

Know the language, including key terminology and concepts

When you do research you use research language. All professionals use a subject-specific language: nurses speak about cannulae; engineers speak about hydraulic systems. Researchers also use a professional language with specific terminology and concepts, including the following:

- Ontology.
- Epistemology.
- Methodology.
- Critique.
- Social intent.

Ontology

This refers to a theory of being, how we see ourselves (different from cosmology, which is to do with one's world-view). Your ontological stance influences how you see other people. Do you see them as an 'It', separate from you, or a 'You', an integral part of your life-world (Buber, 1937)? It also influences how you position yourself in the research field, whether as an insider, an outsider, or somewhere between. Your ontology is linked with your values. This idea can be problematic, especially when people say they believe in values pluralism. What makes Al Capone a villain for many people and Superman a hero? Why?

Epistemology

This refers to a theory of knowledge (what is known), including a theory of knowledge acquisition or creation (how it comes to be known), and a theory of how the validity of knowledge claims can be tested. Questions arise about whether you come to know only through reading books and listening to other people, or whether you can generate your own knowledge. Do people have to be told, or can they think for themselves? Questions also arise about the criteria for judging the validity of knowledge claims. Are they only linguistic criteria, written in documents, or can the criteria be located in the values that inspire the research? If so, which values? Whose values?

Methodology

This refers to a theory of how things are done. Many traditionalist social science researchers see research as the application of a fixed set of methods to the study of a particular situation to achieve a definite solution. Action researchers tend to see it as a creative process of trial and error, working towards a 'best for now' position. The open forms of action research do not aim for an 'end point' (though a formal action research project does); everything is seen as always already, a process of becoming with no beginning or end.

Critique

Critique is the idea of interrogating the normative assumptions of what is said and done and the form of discourse itself ('normative' is understood as what is normal and what should be seen as normal). This can be reasonably straightforward when critiquing other people's ideas but not when it comes to critiquing one's own. It is difficult to keep your own assumptions out of your texts: Said (1991) showed how Kipling's racist prejudices mirrored the mores of the time; my prejudices about the open nature of action research inform this book. It is difficult but necessary to be critical of the ideas you live by. But if so, why?

Social intent

Research is always political, done for specific reasons and purposes in a social context. Why do research? What do you hope to find out? What will you do with what you find out? Action research is even more political, because it means destabilising the way you think, and challenging how other people think, and this has consequences for how you act. How do you act when you have no clear guidelines about how to act?

Know the main theoretical and conceptual frameworks

As well as knowing the language, you also need to know the main theoretical and conceptual frameworks. These are:

- The values and logics of practice.
- Forms of knowledge.
- Forms of theory.

The values and logics of practice

It can be useful to think of practice – what we do – as influenced by, and influencing: (1) a values base (what we value); and (2) a logical form (how we think). Values, logics and practice are mutually influencing: what we believe in and value influences how we think; how we think influences what we believe in; and values and logics influence, and are influenced by our practices. They are in a dynamic transformational cyclical relationship, something like the cyclical form of action research.

However, the situation is not straightforward, and this brings further choices, because different people think differently about values and logics, for example:

- **Values** refers to what we value, what we hold as good. However …
  - o Some people speak about values, such as 'justice' and 'freedom', as abstractions. They say, 'I believe in (this thing called) justice' or 'I believe in (this thing called) freedom'.
  - o Other people see values as embodied in what they do. They don't just talk about what they believe in; they do it. They practise justice and freedom in the way they live. So the abstract values come to life as real-life practices.

- **Logic** refers to how we think. There are different kinds of logic because people think in different ways (contrary to some opinions that say there is only one form of thinking and only one kind of logic).
  - Some people like to think in terms of structures and boxes. They see end points, one 'correct' linear form of thinking. The aim is to achieve closure and final answers. This is a one-track view, stemming from Aristotelian thinking; this informs a technical rational view as the basis of practices such as Taylorism and a cult of efficiency (Callahan, 1962).
  - Some people like to think in terms of 'both–and': you want to be tidy but live in a muddle, or you have great visions but no time to achieve them. This is a dialectical view that contains the idea of contradiction. It stems from the work of the dialectical theorists, including Marxist philosophers such as Ilyenkov (1977).
  - Other people think in terms of unbounded open spaces. They see moving horizons, fluid forms, and different ways of being and doing. This is a dynamic inclusional view that emphasises 'being' rather than 'having' (Fromm, 1978).
- **Values and logics** are not fixed categories:
  - People's values often change; what you choose to do at 16 may change once you get to 40.
  - The way you think also tends to change; you learn to see things in a more mature way over time. A life crisis can change a sense of self-sufficiency into the need for increased social attachment.

  However, if you see values and logics as abstractions, they can become fixed categories. Some people speak about love and justice all their lives, yet seldom achieve a way of living that is loving or just.

These issues are especially important when writing about the practice of action research as a practice, especially when practice is understood as trying to realise one's values, which involves periodically taking stock of what we do. Doing action research is problematic because the underpinning thinking about values and logics is problematic.

Jenny Carpenter was a primary teacher for 11 years before becoming a senior lecturer in initial teacher education at York St John University, where she is also studying for her PhD, focusing on learning and teaching in higher education. In a symposium presented at the 2009 British Educational Research Association annual meeting, she spoke about the frequent contradictions she experienced as a university-based lecturer:

My management and pedagogical aims were to develop my capacity for pedagogical and academic leadership, and to communicate that the programme would operate smoothly partly by reassuring the students that they were in capable hands. These became my guiding leadership and management values. However, I came to wonder whether I was imposing my values system on my

(Continued)

(Continued)

students. Would they feel coerced into agreeing with me against their better judgements, and possibly in areas where their values were contrary to my own? Through engaging with these problematics, and through drawing on the literatures, I have come to understand that values need to be negotiated, and that there are few overarching universal values (Berlin, 1969). Further, I have come to the realisation that I need to problematise the question of values, and perhaps understand values as practices rather than as abstract principles (Raz, 2003) (Carpenter, 2009 online).

Ideas about values, ontology, epistemology, methodology, critique and intent are interlinked, and become a dynamic, self-recreating constellation of forms that are also influenced by context.

As a researcher, you need to show that you are reasonably familiar with these issues and how you use them in your work. You may also identify some of them for your own studies, such as a new epistemology for a new scholarship (Schön, 1995) or standpoint theory (Harding, 2004), to ground your own arguments in your writing.

You also need to know about different forms of knowledge.

Forms of knowledge: The knowledge base of practices

It is widely accepted that there are different kinds of knowledge that you use for different practices. The most common forms are as follows:

'Know that' (also called 'propositional knowledge'). This is knowledge of facts and figures, and involves analytical, often instrumental forms of thinking. You say, 'I know that today is Friday', or 'I know that there are different theories of language'. Verification procedures for propositional knowledge reside in objects such as different kinds of texts ('I know that it is Saturday because I looked at the calendar').

'Know how' (also called 'procedural knowledge'). This is knowledge of procedures and involves skills and competencies. You say, 'I know how to ride a bike'. Verification procedures reside in demonstrations. You show that you know how to ride a bike through riding one.

Ryle's *Concept of Mind* (1949) contains an account of factual and procedural knowledge. These forms tend to be presented in terms of outcomes and results more than processes and experience. Gibson (1993) critiques this view in sport: a focus only on winning the game often means losing your integrity.

'Know', also called 'personal knowledge'. This is tacit, intuitive knowledge that resides in the person but often cannot be articulated (Polanyi, 1967), similar to what MacDara Woods (2000) calls 'knowledge in the blood'. Ask someone how windscreen wipers work without using their hands. Personal knowledge is about wise thinking and action – 'phronesis' in Aristotelian language rather than 'techne'. It is gained through experience and informs practices. Building a bridge involves engineering skill combined with a feel for balance (Levy and Salvadori, 2002): personal knowledge informs empathetic person-centred forms of nursing (Binnie and Titchen, 1999).

Until recently, personal knowledge was not always recognised as academic knowledge but things are changing now: see, for example, the business and management texts of Argyris and Schön (1974) and Hawken (2010). You need to show how you use action research to achieve what Bateson (1979) calls a necessary unity between practical wisdom, rational thinking and procedural capacity. Here again you may encounter difficulties because you are writing action research, with its organic developmental forms, within a traditional academic system that legitimises mainly propositional and abstract forms. This dilemma spills over into forms of theory, which is another area that you need to know about.

Forms of theory: The theoretical base of practices

Broadly speaking, 'theory' means 'an explanation'. When you say, 'I have a theory about something,' you are saying, 'I can explain how and why that thing works as it does'. If you say, 'I have a theory about keys and locks,' you are saying, 'I can explain how keys and locks work' or 'I know why keys and locks work as they do'. To explain something you have to know about it. Knowledge informs the generation of theory: different forms of knowledge inform different forms of theory.

There is no one kind of theory, though some literatures try to persuade you to believe that there is. People have different views about the relationships between knowledge, theory and practice. Here are some of them.

- Some people take a spectator stance and see themselves as separate from everything else. They see knowledge and theory as things 'out there'; this is how they see practice too. They reify them (turn them into things), so theory and practice become separate. Pring, for example, adopts an objectivist view: he says that theory:

refers to a set of propositions which are stated with sufficient generality yet precision that they explain the behaviour of a range of phenomena and predict which would happen in the future. An understanding of these propositions includes an understanding of what would refute them. (Pring, 2000: 124–5)

- Other people see knowledge and theory as 'in here', embodied in the practice. 'Practice' and 'theory' become 'practice-theory', in a dynamic symbiotic relationship. You, the researcher, are also in a dynamic symbiotic relation with other people and your environment. Theory resides in practices and is generated through them to inform new practices, which in turn inform new theory, which informs … ad infinitum.

Important authors who speak about these processes include Dewey, whose (1938) views about experience and inquiry directly influenced the development of action research (see Clandinin and Connelly, 2000; Noffke, 1997a). Dewey was a process philosopher, a tradition that goes back to the ancients such as Heraclitus, and is to be found in the thinking of Spinoza (1996) and later Goethe (Bertoft, 1996). More modern process philosophers such as Bergson (1998) also saw the natural and social world in a state of constant change and development.

In Chapter 3 I introduce the idea of I-forms of knowledge and theory (where 'I' stands for 'Internal' or the personal pronoun 'I') and suggest that practitioners conceptualise their research as the generation of their dynamic I-theories of practice. But if you wish to do this you first need to be clear about how you understand the purposes of research and the need for critical engagement in communication.

The purposes of research

These are widely understood as follows:

- Creating new knowledge, which enables you to make a knowledge claim, that is, explain that doing your research has enabled you to know something now that you did not know before. You test the validity of the knowledge claim in relation to evidence generated from data you have collected.
- Demonstrating critical engagement with your own thinking and with the thinking of others in the literatures.

Achieving these purposes involves:

- Being clear about the relationships in the social settings where the research is conducted and how your language and practices reflect your relationships with others. How do you relate to participants, and how do you position yourself and them?
- Showing the outcomes: in action research this means showing the usefulness of the research for self and others, especially whether you pass on knowledge to others so they also can pass it on and use it to generate their own knowledge.

Why Do You Need to Know it? Developing Practical Capacity

Now think about which of the ideas above you choose to accept, and why you choose them and not others. This informs subsequent decisions including:

- which identity you wish to create and which voice you use; and
- how you think about action and practices.

Which identity you wish to create and which voice you use

Being a researcher and a writer involves adopting researcher and writer identities, and therefore choosing which voice to use. When you work in a workplace, you see yourself as a practitioner and speak with your practitioner voice, probably about your job. When you do research you become a researcher and speak with your researcher voice about knowledge creation and theory generation. When you write you speak with your writer voice about creating texts. Making these kinds of identity shifts is essential because doing research is about learning how to create new knowledge (in action research it is knowledge of practice), and writing it so you can help others to learn.

You also have other identities, including institutional ones, and these sometimes conflict with how you wish to identify yourself. Your institution may wish you to identify yourself in a particular way while you prefer to identify yourself as something else, or you may wish to be both. Sometimes institutions punish you if you don't obey, and the dissonance of trying to live your personal values within an institutional context that has different values can often lead to extreme discomfort. Which identity do you choose to develop? Do you choose to conform? If so, why? If not, why not? Be clear about your reasons and purposes so that you choose wisely and with awareness of potential consequences.

Anne-Lise Thoresen is an assistant professor on the midwifery educational postgraduate programme at UiT, the Arctic University, and a member of the Health Education Research Group mentioned on page 25. She says:

I have become aware that it is possible to have multiple perspectives. I think about my identity as an educator. At the same time I am aware of my identity as a researcher, an educator and a midwife, and these roles are integrated. It's an interesting experience which I want to write about. Maybe as professional educators we can create a new role at the university where we can be health professionals, educators, and researchers. Possibly we can integrate these roles and explain how we manage the process. And we have a responsibility to share our knowledge about how we do this to develop the idea institutionally.

How you think about action and practices

Think about what different writers mean when they say that doing action research is about taking action to improve practices. Ask yourself how you understand 'action' and 'practices', because it is important to be clear about your own meanings.

The idea of taking action is seldom straightforward. Many authors such as Gray (1995; 2002) speak about *agon*, the idea of a contest or struggle. Action is frequently agonistic, and can lead to good or evil, depending on the actor's intentions. Sennett (2009) tells a story about how Hannah Arendt wanted to communicate a vital message to the world: she said that 'people who make things usually don't understand what they are doing' (p. 1). What about when you create your life? What choices do you make? Which values, logics and knowledges inform your choices?

Also, think critically about what it means to take action.

First, remember that 'activity', 'action' and 'practice' are different. Activity is what we do in the moment, whether spontaneous or intentional. We take for granted the automatic activity of breathing; we are focally aware when engaged in a social activity.

Also remember that there are many kinds of action, including:

- everyday action such as watching television or doing the shopping;
- social action, acting with social intent, doing things for other people's benefit as well as your own. According to Weber (reported in Schutz, 1972), social action is action that 'by virtue of the subjective meaning attached to it by the acting individual (or individuals), takes account of the behaviour of others, and is thereby orientated in its course' (Schutz, 1972: 29): individuals act according to how they perceive their relationships with others. Taking social action involves energy, which can transform into collective social energy when people appreciate how their actions really can influence new thinking and action;
- relational action, which goes beyond, but still includes, social action. It is inspired by collective commitment to the well-being of others: see Macmurray's ideas about the self in relation with others (1961), and the self as agent (1957); and
- political action – the section below on page 42 deals with this.

Further, purposeful activities can take the form of practices, more than only action, so be aware of how you choose to represent them. Different people understand 'practice' in different ways. Some see it as ordinary activity: 'anything can in principle be a practice since, in its most literal sense, the term refers simply to the action of doing something' (Lee and Boud, 2009: 12). Others have a more refined understanding: for example, as 'embodied, materially mediated arrays of human activity centrally organised around shared practical understanding' (Schatzki, 2001: 2). Kemmis (2009) and Kemmis and Smith (2007) speak about 'ecologies of practices' that comprise the 'sayings, doings and relatings' of people as they interact with one another in complex social settings.

MacIntyre's ideas about practices are especially helpful. He says:

By a 'practice' I am going to mean any coherent and complex form of socially established cooperative human activity through which goods internal to that form of activity are realized in the course of trying to achieve those standards of excellence which are appropriate to, and partially definitive of, that form of activity, with the result that human powers to achieve excellence, and human conceptions of the ends and goods involved, are systematically extended. Tic-tac-toe is not an example of a practice in this sense, nor is throwing a football with skill; but the game of football is, and so is chess. Bricklaying is not a practice; architecture is. Planting turnips is not a practice; farming is. So are the enquiries of physics, chemistry and biology, and so is the work of the historian, and so are painting and music. (MacIntyre, 1985: 187)

In MacIntyre's sense, doing and writing action research are both practices, involving skills and competences to ensure that the practice has integrity and is a good practice in its own terms. This view chimes with Sennett's (2009) view that being an expert craftsperson calls for connections between skill, commitment and judgement: practice becomes an:

intimate conversation between hand and head. Every good craftsman [*sic*] conducts a dialogue between concrete practices and thinking; this dialogue evolves into sustaining habits, and these habits establish a rhythm between problem solving and problem finding. (Sennett, 2009: 9)

This does not mean, however, that practices may automatically be seen as 'good' in ethical terms. Al Capone made sure his practice was the best it could be: the internal goods he sought were personal power and money. This raises issues about the ethicality of practices, which is essential when writing about what is involved in creating a life.

The ethics of creating and writing a life

The work of philosophers such as Arendt, Dewey, Sennett and Rorty focus on how to develop and nurture praxis, that is, morally committed action. Arendt (1958), for example, differentiates between labour, work and action:

- Labour refers to mundane, repetitive stuff that produces resources to support work.
- Work refers to purposeful activity in the world and the production of artefacts such as books. Work, says Arendt, is superior to labour.
- Action is social and political activity in the world, and depends on labour and work for its effectiveness.

According to Arendt, labour, work and action take place within four possible realms: the private, the social, the public, and the political. She believes that all people are born free; action can therefore become praxis when it is undertaken with social and political intent in the interests of freedom.

Sennett agrees with Arendt's ideas about freedom but disagrees with her hierarchical view of labour, work and action. He says:

This division ... slights the practical man or woman at work. The human animal who is *Animal laborans* is capable of thinking; ... people working together certainly talk to one another about what they are doing. For Arendt, the mind engages once labor is done. Another more balanced view is that thinking and feeling are contained within the process of making. (Sennett, 2009: 7)

I agree with Sennett. Like him, I see everything we do in life as contributing to the good order of the universe. As a child I used to get told off by my teachers when I arrived late at school because I had picked up the worms washed onto the pavement by the rain and put them into friable earth. I still do. Like Orwell, I believe that life is precious: when a creature departs this life, it is 'one life less, one world less' (Orwell, 2004: 98). Kafka is reputed to have said that the meaning of life is that it stops. I disagree. For me, the meaning of life is what we do with it before it stops.

I agree with Sennett that living is a creative practice, and with Tharp (2006) who says that life is a creative work of art. You design and create your life. These ideas are important for action research, for we need to know and explain what we are doing when we engage in creating our lives, and show how we hold ourselves accountable for the gift of life that we did not ask for yet were freely given.

We also need to remember that it is only a tiny proportion of people who are fortunate enough to be able to create their lives as they want. Most people do not have this option. People in sweatshops, victims of abuse and those trapped in unhappy relationships do not have these choices (though we all have options about how we respond to our situations). As a researcher you are one of the privileged few, so it is your responsibility to choose wisely about how you use your knowledge for social benefit, and work for justice and the right of all people to live peaceful and productive lives. You do this through taking action and writing about it and being clear about what motivates you to do it. Knowing this gives you core strength and carries you through the dark hours when you feel like giving up. It is essential that you pursue your research and writing, and here is why.

3. What Do You Use Your Knowledge For? Developing Political Capacity

We said in Chapter 1 that writing is an integral part of doing research. Stenhouse (1983) said that research is 'systematic enquiry made public', to which I add 'with social intent'. The intent, or purpose of doing and writing action research is to exercise one's influence in learning, whether your own learning, the learning of others, or the learning of the social and intellectual formations of which you are part (see McNiff, 2013a; McNiff and Whitehead, 2010; 2011).

Here are some main purposes of writing action research. They draw on Noffke's (2009) influential ideas about the personal, professional and political dimensions of action research, although in my view all writing is political, with different aspects especially relevant for different domains. At this point we focus on the personal; issues of the professional and political dimensions are developed in later chapters.

Think about how writing can help you develop your learning, and what you need to do to let it happen.

Have faith in yourself as a knower

A main story in this book is that all people are born with the capacity for creating an unlimited number of innovative mental and physical acts. While theories such as theories of individual differences explain why only some people can run a 4-minute mile, it remains a tenet of our human condition that we have the capacity to run: no one teaches us. Similarly, we do not need to be taught to be able to think: we cannot *not* think. However, because we are born into a culture (*habitus* for Bourdieu, 1990), we develop dispositions to think in specific ways according to the norms of the culture, including its epistemological system. We do this through listening to the stories that communicate the system. The dominant so-called 'western' (but now virtually global) system of knowledge works from an externalist perspective: knowledge is 'out there', it can be discovered, and, once discovered, will be taken as the Truth. It is assumed that knowledge is unchanging, constituting an objective, self-contained body. This knowledge may be acquired by listening to others who already have it: we can visit the library and read the words of experts. These stories permeate and reinforce the existing culture.

A different story is that you and every other person already have the capacity for knowledge creation inside yourself, as part of your genetic inheritance. You can learn with and from others and they can learn with and from you; but you do not rely on them to know for you, or tell you what to think or believe. This is your responsibility. You have the capacity and the responsibility to think for yourself and to communicate your knowledge to others. You retain power to think and speak for yourself. This means having faith in the power of your personal knowledge.

To write successfully you need to have faith in yourself and what you are doing. This does not mean being arrogant or saying that you know it all. It means holding your knowledge lightly while having a firm conviction of the rightness of your thinking and knowledge.

It is essential to hold your knowledge lightly because you may be mistaken. This is why research is not about pursuing The Truth so much as trying to understand, and about testing the validity of provisional claims to knowledge. Knowledge is never sure; saying that you know something means accepting risk. Having confidence and faith in your capacity for knowing is different from being sure: it is a sense of rightness, while respecting others' points of view. Knowledge contributes to theory, which James B. Macdonald (1995) says is a prayerful act: you demonstrate faith in your capacity to theorise your practice. It is an act of faith. Committing to doing action research, and to writing it, requires courage, because this way of thinking means having confidence in not knowing. Appadurai speaks about the dilemmas involved in doing research, which, he says:

purports to be a systematic means for discovering the not-yet-known. How can you have a systematic means for getting to what you do not know? For example, what you do not know might be so profoundly unsystematic that systematically getting to it is logically impossible. Or it may be that your systematic way is not suited to the most important object that you do not know but ought to be thinking about. So there remains a paradox deep inside the idea of research, and this paradox might explain why it is such a hot-house activity. (Appadurai, 2006: 169)

Exercise your right to research

As a practitioner, you should exercise your right to research. Research is not an elitist activity conducted only by a privileged few but a property of each and every individual. Like Appadurai, I believe that:

full citizenship today requires the capacity to make strategic inquiries—and gain strategic knowledge—on a continuous basis. Knowledge of AIDS, knowledge of riots, knowledge of labor market shifts, knowledge of migration paths, knowledge of prisons, knowledge of law, all these are now critical to the exercise of citizenship or the pursuit of it for those who are not full citizens. (Appadurai, 2006: 168)

Currently, however, only a privileged few are able to conduct research, and within that narrow spectrum, only a tiny minority is seen as qualified and able to do research. A still tinier sector within the already narrow spectrum keep the privilege to themselves by writing in a certain way so as to have their research, and their right to research, acknowledged and legitimised. This forces us 'to take some distance from the normal, professionalised view of research, and derive some benefit from regarding research as a much more universal, elementary and improvable capacity' (Appadurai, 2006: 168). You need to exercise your right to research through communicating its significance: this is a main reason to write and use your knowledge.

Kjartan Kversøy was educated as a chef and a Captain and is now an associate professor at Oslo and Akershus University College in Norway. He supervises masters students and writes mainly about practical ethics. In email correspondence, he explains:

I always try to ensure that participants in action research projects are properly included in saying what is important for them. One aspect is exploring together what a good project would mean for the persons concerned. I have experimented with this and can say that articulating our understanding of quality is empowering for the participants. In the introduction to John Dewey's book *Democracy and Education* (1985 [1916]), Sidney Hook writes that democratic life is impossible unless experts can be evaluated by non-experts. He claims that you do not need to be an expert to evaluate the recommendation of experts. I have tried to show how seriously I take this by asking my participants to tell me, as someone who is positioned as an 'expert researcher' what they think would be good outcomes in our projects. I ask them questions such as, 'What would indicate that this project is good for you?' and 'How do we know whether this has been a good project?' Many of the answers have made me rethink my practices: for example:

- A project is good quality if the documentation is in everyday language.
- The project is good if the results make my work life a little better.
- I hope we are still friends when we finish.

It brings home to me what being a professional educator means and the responsibilities we have to our colleagues. (Personal correspondence)

Realising your natality

Arendt (1958) makes the point that each person, through their birth, brings something new to the world. This means you. You have never existed before and you never will again, at least not in your present form. You are unique throughout all eternity. You occupy your place on earth, and no one can occupy that place for you. It is therefore your responsibility to occupy it well. When you write you explain what you do to deserve the place, and show how you are occupying it to the best of your ability. You realise your natality with responsibility and explain how you are doing so, with other people's well-being in mind.

You also need to speak your truth, as a person speaking with conviction and commitment to your knowledge. This means, in Foucault's (2001) terms, exercising *parrhesia*.

Exercising parrhesia *Parrhesia* means the right and responsibility of each person to speak their truth. This involves choices because speaking one's truth involves risk. In Greek times the carrier of bad tidings was often killed for their trouble; and these days whistleblowers pay the price for honesty and speaking out (Alford, 2001). Speaking one's truth therefore carries specific commitments – these include, says Foucault, commitments to:

- frankness: the speaker believes what they say and communicates the conviction of their commitment to others;
- truth: the speaker knows what truth is and can communicate it to others;
- courage: the speaker accepts the risk of telling the truth.

- criticism: the speaker exercises critique towards self and others; and
- duty: the speaker accepts the responsibility of telling the truth.

In Chapter 10 I link these ideas with those of Habermas's (1987) criteria for communicative competence, with some overlap: these are as follows:

- The speaker speaks comprehensibly.
- The speaker speaks the truth.
- The speaker is authentic.
- The speaker demonstrates appreciation for normative contextualised understandings.

These two sets of criteria are important, for they also come to stand as criteria for judging both the validity of knowledge claims and of your research (Chapter 10).

In summary, then, the issue for you is always about the choices you make. Which values and knowledges do you espouse? Which do you commit to? Why do you do this and how do you then decide to use your knowledge? There are no universal answers to these questions, because each one of us is unique and can think for ourselves. We have free choice, and no one can tell us what to think, although some people try to. It is your good fortune to be able to think for yourself and this brings responsibilities: how do you enable others to do so too? Do you do this, or do you not see it as necessary? If so, why? If not, why not? Being a researcher, and especially being a writer, brings huge responsibilities. If you are to do the job well, you need to know why you are doing it and what you hope to achieve by doing it. Only you can decide.

SUMMARY

This chapter has looked at what you need to know in order to write action research, and the choices this entails about which forms of knowledge, research and theory you will espouse. It emphasises the need to be aware of why you choose specific forms and how you will use your knowledge, and in whose interests. Through doing and studying action research you develop conceptual, practical and political capacity.

REFLECTIVE QUESTIONS

- Do you know the main terminology of educational research? Can you explain what the terms *ontology, epistemology, methodology, critique* and *social intent* mean? Can you use them in sentences?

- Do you know the main theoretical and conceptual frameworks of educational research? Can you explain the different forms of knowledge and theory involved?

- Can you say why it is important to know these things? Can you explain how conceptual capacity transforms into practical capacity, and then into political capacity?

- In what way do your choices influence how you create your researcher and writer identity?

- How do you intend to use your knowledge? In whose interests will you use it?

RESEARCH EXERCISE

Write a short piece about how you engage with the theoretical and practical underpinnings of action research, and how you justify your use of action research. In your text explain why it is important to think about the choices you make when doing research.

In Chapter 3 we consider what goes into an action research text.

THREE

What Do You Write in an Action Research Text?

This chapter outlines what goes into an action research text, and Chapter 4 explains what form the text takes. In many ways it is artificial to separate content and form, because in action research texts the content and form often merge and complement each other, and there are many overlaps. However, separating the ideas into content and form can be useful for analysis.

The chapter addresses these questions.

1. What goes into an action research text? What does your reader/reviewer expect to see?
2. How does your text fulfil these expectations?

Although there are expectations about what an action research text should contain, each person's text is unique, written from their individual perspective and with their critical commentary on the quality of the work. While you need to meet expectations about quality, you should also have confidence that what you write is yours and yours alone.

What Goes Into an Action Research Text? What Does your Reader/Reviewer Expect to See?

Here is a story to set the scene.

As part of my work as a reviewer and supervisor I read proposals and accounts of research in progress. These contain stories of practice and knowledge and under-standing of practice. In early drafts I often read stories told or written at the level of description only. These are 'what next?' stories – they say, 'I did this, I did that'. This describing of activities usually takes the form of 'knowledge-telling' (see below). In the early stages of a text there is often little explanation – 'I did this because ...' or 'I did this in order to …' – or awareness of the need to help the reader to interpret the text appropriately – 'I am saying this because you, the reader, need to appreciate the context …'. It tends to be later in the production process that a work is presented as a well-crafted oral or spoken text that combines levels of description, explanation, analysis, synthesis and explication, and that reads as a scholarly and methodologically rigorous whole.

These kinds of explanatory and critical frames are essential, because it is the ability of practitioners to explain what they are doing and comment on its significance that turns everyday stories into research stories and makes them comprehensible, and it is practitioners' ability to produce quality texts that gets those texts published. Explanations and critique need to run through all texts, whether distinguished by their linguistic print-based form, as most academic texts are, or through texts that include other communicative forms such as dance, music, artwork, performance and multimedia representations, now becoming increasingly recognised as part of higher degree studies. While the presentations may take a non-linguistic form, their significance is still communicated through words, even when the works are presented digitally (see Andrews et al., 2012). To achieve accreditation, the linguistic form of texts needs to be as high quality as the non-linguistic performance, because the work is going to be read by examiners who are in all cases unfamiliar with the research contexts and by many who work in more orthodox print-based traditions.

When we speak about readers' and reviewers' expectations we are speaking about criteria and standards. Criteria refer to what to expect, and standards refer to the value judgements we make about what we encounter. Texts are expected to achieve specified criteria and reach appropriate standards, and these tend to work at increasingly high levels of adequacy.

Here are some common general criteria for all texts, showing levels of progression from general texts, through research texts, to action research texts and advanced level texts.

Criteria for all texts

All texts are judged in terms of basic literary criteria, including:

- The text is interesting.
- It is written authentically.
- It is appropriate for its intended form of publication.
- The writer is confident.

The text is interesting

The subject matter of all texts should be interesting. Horberry quotes Bill Bernbach, 'one of US advertising's most celebrated and influential figures' (p. 19) as saying:

The truth isn't the truth until people believe you, and they can't believe you if they don't know what you're saying, and they can't know what you're saying if they don't listen to you, and they won't listen to you if you're not interesting, and you won't be interesting unless you say things imaginatively, originally, freshly. (Horberry, 2009: 19–20)

You can make any subject matter interesting if you believe in it and tell it with conviction, in your own words.

It is written authentically

This means cultivating the habit of writing as you speak, not as you think academic texts should be written. George Orwell condemned what he called Doublespeak. He said, 'The great enemy of clear language is insincerity. When there is a gap between one's real and one's declared aims, one turns as it were instinctively to long words and exhausted idioms ...' (Orwell, 2004: 216). Raymond Chandler, the American novelist, said: 'I suppose all writers are crazy, but if they are any good, I believe they have a terrible honesty' (cited in MacShane, 1976: 1). You need to let your terrible honesty shine through the academic writing.

It is appropriate for its intended form of publication

An academic text should be written for a specific form of publication, such as a journal, textbook or secondary sourcebook. All forms of publishing offer guidelines. You can find instructions to authors on publishers' websites, and university candidates are given instructions for writing dissertations and theses. You write your text according to the contexts of the form of publication or the instructions.

The writer is confident

You have to believe in yourself and what you are saying. If you are not confident, you cannot expect other people to have confidence in you.

Maria James is a teacher educator at St Mary's University, Twickenham. Her subject specialism is Religious Education and she teaches on masters programmes for postgraduate students. She was awarded her PhD in 2013 (James, 2013). She tells a story of when we started working together in 2005.

My supervisor [Jean] asked me, 'Do you think that your work could have global implications?' I laughed: this would be too grandiose a claim for me ever to make. At the time I was working with a group of academic colleagues who

(Continued)

seemed much more advanced in writing capacity than I was. Jean asked us once to bring along some of our writing for peer review. In a mode of self-preservation I introduced my work as 'a load of piffle'. I had expected a kindly response such as, 'Your work is coming along, continue to work on ...' but Jean sternly remarked, 'How can you expect others to respect your work when you talk about it in such terms!' A lesson was learned. Since then I have never spoken of my work with anything but respect, and I expect others to extend the same courtesy as I seek to respect their work.

Criteria for all research texts

The following are criteria for all research texts.

All research tells stories; different kinds of research tell different stories. All research stories:

- identify a research issue and articulate a research question;
- demonstrate knowledge of their field and subject content;
- say why this is an issue, give relevant contexts and link them with the literatures;
- say what has been achieved (they contain a claim to knowledge);
- describe and explain how it has been achieved;
- provide critical feedback about what they are saying (test the validity of the claim), so that the story may be believed; and
- outline the significance of the research for new forms of thinking and action.

Criteria for all action research texts

In addition, commonly agreed criteria for all action research texts include the following.

The text tells a story of research-based action

This may actually be seen as two interwoven stories:

1. An action story: This is about what you did in your empirical research. You engage with questions and say how you contributed to improving a particular situation.
2. A research story: This is your explanation for why you did what you did, what you learned through the process, and your articulation of its significance for your own and other people's learning and practices. The two stories weave into one (see Figure 3.1).

action
story

research
story

Figure 3.1 Interweaving action and research stories

They do this by explaining the following elements.

1. ***What you know and how you have come to know it***. The story is about your learning as you tried to understand and improve your practice, in order to influence other people's learning. Telling the story involves reflecting on what you have done and producing evidence to support what the story says.
2. ***Your explanations for what you know and how you have come to know it.*** You demonstrate capacity for testing the validity of your story, including the generation of evidence, to show that you have done what you say you have done.
3. ***Your analysis of the significance of your story for your own and other people's learning.*** This involves analysing what you have done, and articulating its significance, especially about whether you are living your values in your practice. It involves testing your ideas against the ideas of others, including key writers.
4. ***Your understanding that there is no meta-story.*** A story is always part of and embedded within a wider story about our histories and cultures (Loy, 2010). Personal stories are told from a particular point in this deeper cultural-historical story: we recognise our situatedness, especially in relation to our forms of thinking and writing. There is never a 'better' story to tell us what to think or write.

Action research texts link values and action

In an action research text you articulate your values, which come to act as the basis of your enquiry. The denial of your values in practice often acts as your starting point, where you experience emotional and cognitive dissonance from the mismatch. Values also come to act as the criteria by which you judge the quality of your practice. If you believe in honesty or freedom, you judge the quality of your practices in relation to whether they demonstrate people being honest and free. The text needs to show the relationship between values and practices.

You conduct your action research ethically

All action research texts should demonstrate how ethical conduct was assured: how access was negotiated, participants were informed and consulted at all stages, ethics documentation was secured and approved by all parties concerned, and permissions sought and granted. In dissertations and theses the documentation needs to be included, probably in the appendices.

Your researcher 'I' is implicit, and explicit if you wish, in your text

Action research may be conducted from different positionalities. Your 'I' is in there somewhere, whether implicitly, or explicitly in the naming of 'I'. However, the research is not about 'me' so much as 'us'. The 'I' accepts the responsibility of taking action in the interests of the other: it is about individuals and collectives acting for one another's benefit.

> Adrian Klos is a Baptist minister serving at Hull and East Yorkshire NHS Trust as their Senior Chaplain. After initially training as a bricklayer he followed his vocation to train as a Baptist minister in Manchester. He writes about his doctoral studies:
>
> I am researching my practice as a Senior Healthcare Chaplain working with a group of eight other chaplains from different denominations, all hospitals-based. My practice of caring for patients involves hearing their voices as they describe and reflect on their experience in hospital. I want to research my practice to develop deeper understandings of it, and to generate my personal theory of practice that may be shared with others, to contribute to their learning. This may present difficulties when working with our community of chaplains. How do I learn to encourage our team to develop transformative research practices? In finding my own voice and combining it with that of my colleagues I hope to be able to make explicit the tacit knowledge that we use on a daily basis. (Klos, 2014)

This has implications for how quality of practice is judged: given the other-oriented nature of action research, it is not enough for a researcher to claim that they have realised their personal values in practice unless they can show how those personal values transformed into actions that benefited others. This means gathering data to show how your personal learning contributed to others' sense of well-being, and explaining this throughout the text.

Criteria for advanced action research texts

Advanced level texts (a dissertation, an article or book) operate by much the same criteria. Additionally, they are expected to abide by the following criteria (here is an amalgamation of instructions I have received from higher education institutions in my role as external examiner and book and journal reviewer).

- Scholarly texts should contain accounts about knowledge creation and should contribute to knowledge of the field.
- They give an account of an enquiry in an appropriately critical, original and balanced way.

- They show improvement in the practice being described, or explain what may have hindered progress.
- They demonstrate critical engagement with the writer's own thinking, with the thinking of other research writings in the field, and, where appropriate, from works of literature.
- They contain material worthy of peer review.
- The story they tell follows a 'golden thread', so it is possible for a reader to see the story woven through the text in a systematic way.
- The work is error-free and technically accurate, with a full bibliography and references.

I also like the advice offered by Sharples about demonstrating the authenticity of a text and the integrity of the writer. Writers should:

- not present unwarranted belief as fact;
- provide justification for ideas, by reference either to the publicly observable world or to an acknowledged authority;
- reference the sources of ideas;
- not selectively ignore facts, but offer all the information that is relevant to an argument;
- acknowledge the limitations of an argument; and
- present the text in a form that is designed to assist, not mislead, the reader. (Sharples, 1999: 165)

The advice emphasises consistently that research is about knowledge and theory. Even though the action of action research may be about finding ways to improve a social situation, the research element is always about creating knowledge and generating theory.

Some of the most important criteria when writing advanced texts, and especially when submitting for a masters or doctoral degree are that the work:

- makes a knowledge claim;
- demonstrates critical engagement;
- demonstrates knowledge of the field and appropriate literatures; and
- contains theoretical matter.

The text makes a knowledge claim

In any research text, you state right at the beginning what your knowledge claim is and its potential contribution to knowledge of the field: that is, you say what you have found out through doing the research that you did not know before, and how this may be useful for others doing the same kind of work. This can be about a substantive issue, such as exploring how a certain procedure will enhance production of an artefact, or it can be an original reworking of other people's ideas. In the book *Steal Like an Artist,* Kleon (2012) says that all art is a form of plagiarism. He cites David Bowie as saying, 'The only art I'll ever study is stuff that I can steal from' (p. 6). While many would not agree with the idea of 'stealing' ideas, it is agreed that you can offer your own configuration of existing ideas. This informs the second expectation of all advanced action research texts: the text demonstrates critical engagement.

The text demonstrates critical engagement

Critical engagement means engaging with your own thinking and with that of others in the literatures. It means you interrogate whatever is said with a view to testing its validity and authenticity. This does not mean automatically disputing things, more that you are ready critically to consider others' ideas, and build original arguments from them, always acknowledging your sources. Not acknowledging sources is plagiarism. 'Critical' also implies engaging critically with your own thinking: as you write you reflect and comment on what you are saying. This becomes a meta-reflection and meta-critique on your work.

The text demonstrates knowledge of the field and appropriate literatures

An orthodox social science text is expected to contain a literature review, which would normally be a commentary on who has written what in the field. It is also expected that the researcher will show how they have applied these theories to their own practices. This is not necessarily the case in an action research text, though you definitely need to show your familiarity with theories in the literatures, and a literature review can help to locate your understanding of an issue. You can also show how you test the validity of your ideas against those of others in the field. This theme runs through your text. You may choose to incorporate others' theories into your thinking, as shown in this book, and you may also show how your work possibly provides an extension of those theories.

The text contains theoretical matter

We said in Chapter 2 that there are different kinds of theory. When you write your stories about generating new ideas from practice, those stories become real-life theories of practice, and the stories themselves become the location of your personal theories: they become your I-theories of practice (see below). They qualify as theories because they contain descriptions and explanations of practice arising from reflection on the practice, and your critical reflection on their significance. Your reader therefore expects that:

- you describe the processes involved (what happened and how it happened);
- you explain to your reader the processes involved (how reflection leads to explanations for practice); and
- you analyse the significance of what you are doing.

Your work is always judged in terms of how well you weave together your descriptions, reflective explanations, critical analyses and meta-analyses, that is, the capacity to analyse the research story and synthesise ideas in relation to the articulated purposes of the research. A main difference between masters and doctoral work is in the progression of depth of understanding and capacity to analyse it in terms of the different levels involved (Chapter 10).

You communicate clearly with your reader

All texts should achieve a high level of communication. The text is judged in terms of whether it is understandable, authentic, truthful, and told in a critically reflective way. This involves demonstrating capacity for self-reflective critique, in-depth scholarship, and the skills of writing for a reader. These criteria also apply to texts that involve performance, multimedia representations and visual narratives. These are not simply descriptive narratives, as seen, for example, on a video of a guide to Paris: they are explanatory narratives, where the actions are explained and analysed.

Tamie Pratt-Fartro holds a PhD in literacy and policy from George Mason University. She is an assistant professor of education at the University of Mary Washington in Fredericksburg, Virginia where she teaches graduate literacy courses to initial teacher licensure candidates and in-service teachers seeking literacy specialist endorsement. In her abstract to the Value and Virtue in Practice-Based Research conference (2014) she writes:

As a literacy coach-educator, I also work as a coach's coach in a high-needs school serving economically-disadvantaged minority students. The purpose of my work is to build capacity in coaches and teachers. Data from coaching logs, which contain specific on-site actions, serve as the foundation for decision-making, yet I had failed to consider them in a holistic manner. Therefore, I wrote numerous narratives to gain a more personal perspective with feelings, frustrations, and wonderings about my effectiveness being explored and questioned. From these data sources, I created a conceptual framework to provide a visual representation of my work at the school to answer the question, 'What is going on here?' (Maxwell, 2013). To further elaborate, I wrote a critical narrative of my interpretations of the framework to position my work within the social and cultural constructs of the school. The results of my inquiry emphasize the ways in which conceptual frameworks can be used openly and critically to evaluate not only how educators work and do research, but to consider how that work is viable and relevant to those we serve. (Pratt-Fartro, 2014)

Here is part of the abstract from Anne-Gerd Karlsen for the same conference, about the need for a masters programme in public health nursing. Anne-Gerd is a Public Health nurse educator at UiT, The Arctic University, and a member of the group introduced in Chapter 1. She writes:

Since 2009, nursing education in Norway has been coordinated through higher degree programmes, many producing clinical specialists including midwives, Public Health and psychiatric nurses. Following decisions by the Norwegian Ministry of Education and Research, and the Bologna process, UiT, the Arctic University of Norway piloted an innovative Masters program in Public Health Nursing in 2011; the first cohort graduates in 2014. However, the shift from post-graduate clinical specialization to masters accreditation has led to questions about which forms of knowledge are appropriate for Public Health Nursing.

The aim of the project was to develop a Master's program enabling students to achieve balanced capacity between professional and academic knowledge. The research question is: How can a masters programme integrate academic and practical knowledge to ensure Public Health Nurses acquire understanding and competence for clinical studies and the profession? ...

These findings are of international interest, highlighting issues about which forms of knowledge are needed in masters programmes. They raise dilemmas about integrating students' practical knowledge and academic competence, and potential contradictions and opportunities in negotiating curricula. ... (Karlsen, 2014)

Now consider how your text can fulfil these expectations.

How Does Your Text Fulfil these Expectations?

Strong conceptual and theoretical frameworks can be helpful. The idea of a conceptual framework refers to the scaffolds, armatures and spaces by which you collect ideas and build arguments. A conceptual framework uses a core concept, such as feminism or creativity, and builds on it to produce an argument that may help the conceptualisation and conduct of the research. A theoretical framework does the same thing in relation to processes of generating theory.

Three frameworks are presented here:

1. The grammar of action research.
2. Framing and re-framing through critical analysis.
3. Academic writing as knowledge explicating and theorising.

The following ideas are grounded in linguistic theory, and are relevant to writing and the production of texts. You do not need an in-depth understanding of linguistics to engage with them, and I hope you find them interesting and useful.

The term 'grammar' tends to refer to the rules that govern the structures and uses of the different components of a language system. By analogy, it may be used to describe the different relationships in all fields of practice. In linguistics, different thinkers propose different kinds of grammar, which are rooted in different ways of thinking and values commitments.

One powerful approach is generative transformational grammar, developed by Noam Chomsky in the mid-1950s as a critique of the then dominant view of structural linguistics as a linear system of interconnected units (Chomsky, 1957). Although Chomsky has radically changed his views since then, the principles of generative approaches remain, and have influenced the development of other fields such as complexity theory (see Chapter 1). The principles of generative approaches are as follows.

We are born with certain capacities, as part of our human condition. In terms of language and language acquisition, it is assumed that the rules of a grammar are already in our make-up, and that language development is part of and emerges through our growth and genetic evolutionary processes. This is a core idea of generative transformational linguistics.

Chomsky refers to the form of language generated by generative grammar as 'I-Language', or 'Internal Language', 'an *internal* property of an *individual*' (Smith, 2000: vii, italics in original), which, he says, should be the proper object of study of linguistics. Internal language refers to the idea that as humans we are born with a genetically inherited understanding of language. He contrasts 'I-language' with 'E-Language' ('External Language'), a body of knowledge about language that may be studied empirically. I-language recognises how tacit innate knowledge transforms into explicit knowledge. These ideas informed my own thesis (McNiff, 1989) and have been developed since.

The main implications of these ideas for action research are as follows:

Practitioners develop their knowledge of practice

All practitioners are able to generate knowledge of practice through studying that practice. This knowledge may be developed and refined in collaboration with others. These collaborative groups form communities of inquiry as they help one another to produce their accounts of knowledge production.

Practitioners develop I-theories of practice

Knowledge of practice may inform the development of practitioners' I-theories of practice. It is not necessary to look outside one's practice situation for a research topic. Because you always work in collaborative relationships, your practice with others becomes your research topic, especially if you study how the nature of the relationships among participants influences how they can influence one another's thinking.

Ecologies of practice: personal and collective

Your practice takes an ecological form at several levels. At a personal level it is possible to see the links between your psycho-biological systems – if you have a cold your thinking may not be as sharp as when you are well. It is important to ensure well-being in all parts of the eco-system to ensure well-being of the whole.

Your personal ecology of practice merges with other individuals' ecologies of practice, thus forming collective ecologies of practice. These in turn are part of wider cultural, socio-economic ecologies. Systems make up other systems and form super-complex systems. These ideas, drawing on complexity theory, link with the idea of the holographic universe (Bohm, 1983) where each part of the system is reflected in the whole and the whole is reflected within each part. They also link with the view (developed much earlier by Spinoza and Goethe – Goethe was influenced by Spinoza) that ecological approaches are always towards dynamic, ever-unbounded forms of thinking and renewable growth. The same processes may be seen at work in the universe and in the human psyche. Further, growth towards open forms of being is in itself ethical, so open-ended and transformational practices may be judged as ethical practices. The ethicality of the practice resides in the process of opening out towards growth and well-being, which requires that researchers pay attention to the other's needs. These ideas may provide useful resources for conceptualising your practices as a researcher and writer.

The second theoretical framework, rooted in the same philosophy, is about framing and re-framing through critical analysis.

Framing and re-framing through critical analysis

The idea of framing is extensively used and reported in the social sciences, and is understood as the perspectives people bring to how they perceive what is happening. People are not always aware that their perspectives have been influenced by their social contexts and experiences, including what they hear or read through the media, or through what influential voices tell them to believe.

Many people use the same mental frames throughout their lives, possibly through not being exposed to other cultures or opinions, or because they are comfortable holding a particular perspective they believe is correct. Staying in the same frame of thinking, which influences practices, can exonerate people from accepting responsibility for what they think and do: a frame becomes a safe place, often to hide.

In *Frame Reflection* (1994), Schön and Rein explore these ideas in relation to the resolution of policy controversies. They say that 'in matters of public policy, disputes are endemic' (p. 3). Disputes are endemic also in ontological debates, about, for example, the right to die when one chooses or whether to regard a person as 'different' according to criterion-referenced assessments (see Gould, 1997). The question we should all ask, say Schön and Rein, is 'different from what?' Nor should this be a matter of cultural relativism. Some practices, including forced marriage or dog fighting should never be condoned. These are not cultural issues so much as about what makes us human.

This idea of systemic dispute is also at the heart of action research, which is about trying to find ways of living with difficulties, explaining to others what you have done, and how you hold yourself accountable for your thinking and actions. Your text shows these struggles, the agonistic base of research in action. This involves a commitment to theory of mind, an understanding that other people will think for themselves and probably see things differently from you. This in itself is impossible for some people because of the emotional and intellectual dissonance incurred.

Schön and Rein ask whether the holders of conflicting frames could ever be persuaded to sit down together to hold a conversation (1994: 45), and cite Kuhn's (1964) idea that scientists might 'see themselves as members of different linguistic communities and become translators' (Schön and Rein, 1994: 47). They also cite Habermas's ideas about an ideal speech situation where 'public decisions are reached by autonomous citizens in a process of unconstrained exchange of opinion' (Habermas, 1984: 102). However, these are imaginary scenarios. My doctoral studies focused on how I could encourage the hostile 12-year-old children I was teaching to engage in the then-new curriculum strand Personal and Social Education. The difficulty was to get them even to engage before we could begin practising social skills.

It is extremely difficult, say Schön and Rein, for people who hold intractably different perspectives to come to see the other's point of view, yet it can be done, as I have experienced while working with different groups who hold conflicting views, but for this to be achieved, we have to be prepared to dislodge our thinking, to think the unthinkable. This is where action research can be helpful, because, if the aim of all research is to create knowledge and generate theory, action research presupposes a form of theory that is of a different kind than traditional propositional theory. Schön and Rein quote Arendt as saying:

From the Greek word for spectators, *theatai*, the later philosophical term 'theory' was derived, and the word 'theoretical' until a few hundred years ago meant 'contemplating', looking upon something from the outside, from a position implying a view that is hidden from those who take part in the spectacle and actualize it ... [As] a spectator you may understand the 'truth' of what the spectacle is about, but the price you have to pay is withdrawal from participating in it. (Arendt, 1971: 93)

As an action researcher, you refuse to withdraw. You actively engage in the action of understanding practice and generating theory from within. Unless you are willing to engage, you will never change anything.

The question now arises, how do you communicate this in your text? This brings us to the third conceptual framework, about knowledge and its communication, and the theorisation of your writing practices.

Academic writing as knowledge explicating and theorising

Several existing models show the mental processes and practical strategies involved in producing a text that you intend to be read by a reader. One influential source is *The Psychology of Written Composition* by Bereiter and Scardamalia (1987): they propose two models involved in composing practices that they call 'knowledge-telling' and 'knowledge-transformation'. 'Knowledge-telling' refers to what the writer already knows about a topic, and texts produced tend to take the form of 'what next?' stories. The writer writes down a concept, then another, and so on until they reach the end of the story: they remain in the content space as they write about the topic. This, say Bereiter and Scardamalia, is the main strategy used by young children, who can evidently handle only one idea at a time. Many adults adopt it too, often when drafting out ideas or writing free-flow text. Initial draft work in the construction of academic texts can often take this form.

However, when the aim is to share knowledge with others (knowledge transfer) it is not enough to stay only in the content space. Now the focus shifts to communicating, so it is necessary to move into a rhetorical space and think about how to use the text itself to try to share meanings with the other. This means thinking about which communicative strategies will best get meanings across. Therefore, when it is a question of knowledge transfer (sharing knowledge with others) the focus shifts to communication: it means adopting 'knowledge transforming' strategies, which represents, according to Sharples, a mental dialogue between content and rhetoric: 'The content space contains the writer's beliefs about the topic, and the rhetorical space holds knowledge about the text, such as its style, structure, purpose and audience' (Sharples, 1999: 23). The writer thinks about choice of content, how to communicate it, and how the reader will understand it. Notionally, it could look as shown in Table 3.1.

Table 3.1   Knowledge-telling and knowledge-transforming

Knowledge-telling	Knowledge-transforming
Here is an account of what I did during the first cycle of my action research.	How do I communicate this point most effectively?
My research focused on how to encourage greater participation by women in management.	Which conceptual frameworks should I draw on that readers will appreciate? Which literatures will I need to consult?
I gathered data from 10 senior women managers, which acted as my baseline data.	How will I represent the data? Which data will I place in the main body of the text and which in the appendices?

Academic texts should be a combination of knowledge-telling and knowledge-transforming, and more: see below. The author writes the story about the research, and communicates its importance to the reader through appropriate communicative strategies.

Knowledge analysis

Writers critically analyse what they have written in light of further reflection and possible reframing, and this provides a further level of knowledge analysis. This often happens through a process of engaging with their own thinking, with other texts and with critical feedback from others. They can do this by reflecting on what they have written, and offering critical commentaries, such as, 'This strategy seemed to work well because …', or 'I have adopted a grounded theory analysis method because …'. This became a main strategy of the masters studies that a group of South African teachers and I developed (2005–2008). Because the UK-accredited programme was delivered in South Africa it meant candidates presented their work to their peers for critical feedback: these presentations were videoed for validation panels at the UK university. This double interrogation of presentations helped presenters to develop communicative and explanatory skills alongside aspects of subject and research knowledge. In the video at http://www.youtube.com/watch?v=eYty6rsiOGA you can see our group speaking about how they have analysed their learning and reconceptualised their identities from practitioners to researchers, and how they have learned to speak for themselves: see also the papers, presented at the American Educational Research Association from Gerrie Adams, at http://www.jeanmcniff.com/items. asp?id=81 and from Tsepo Majake at http://www.jeanmcniff.com/items. asp?id=5, which show the capacity to reflect critically both on the content of their knowledge and on their capacity to communicate it appropriately.

Knowledge synthesis

Galbraith (2009) develops the model by explaining how new forms of knowledge may be produced through the action of linking knowledge-telling with knowledge-transforming into knowledge synthesis. It is the process described earlier, when the action of reflecting on ideas actually generates new knowledge, integrating different kinds of knowledge, namely knowledge about what to write (content), knowledge of how to write it (textual) and knowledge of the need to reflect critically on the form of the text as a communicative device for sharing meanings (communicative).

I now wish to draw on another idea from Chomsky (1965) about levels of adequacy. He says that the potency of a theory can be shown when it moves from observation through description and into explanation, to achieve a high level of explanatory adequacy. In my view, academic texts need to show this capacity for critical reflection. By doing so, the writer may achieve the level of communicative competence, a term introduced by Hymes (1966) in response to what he perceived as Chomsky's too abstract notion of the idea of competence, saying that study of language always needs to be related to its social contexts. I therefore suggest that a new level should be introduced, which is about knowledge theorising.

Knowledge theorising

Theorising refers to the process of explicating ideas, when you as a writer use the process of writing to make clear to your reader what you have come to know and how you have come to know it: in other words, you theorise your writing practices and generate an epistemology of writing practice, which is rooted in the writing process itself and the production of texts. This is the kind of standard that will ensure your work is of a quality that will get it accepted and published. It also indicates an ethical commitment, in that you show how you demonstrate public accountability by accepting responsibility for what you say and write.

I often ask workshop participants to divide a page into three columns, where they write: 'What I did during the workshop', 'What I learned' and 'The significance of my learning'. The task then is to explain the significance of the exercise. This can help them to reflect on, analyse both the importance of what they have done and the importance of reflecting on what they have done, and synthesise it as a communicative whole. Many find that they discover aspects of their work that they had not thought about before.

A main significance of these ideas lies in the fact that they are about emergent and transformational processes. To return to the beginning of the chapter, the process of emergence constitutes a process of theorising and becomes the content: you explain how you have engaged with ideas and practices to try to improve them, how this may be seen as ethical, and how you can explain (theorise) what you have done. Your work is not about arriving at an end point so much as finding new ways of doing things through the doing of them. By the same token, I hope to explore and develop the ideas I am expressing here in future work.

This process goes on in several domains, and engaging with these domains informs your study. Sharples (1999) speaks of writing in the head, writing on the page, and writing in the world; Bolton (2014) writes about writing for yourself, writing for your reader, and writing for posterity. These forms of words are adapted here to communicate how writing action research involves showing the emergence of understandings, capacities and practices towards new ideas, new forms of communication, and new forms of theorising.

Writing in the head: Engaging with your and others' thinking

You show and explain how you have engaged with your thinking and learned to critique it so that it stays open. This involves knowledge-telling and knowledge-transformation. You show the processes of critical reflection where you step outside the story and reflect on, analyse and make sense of what you have said. These parallel processes of offering explanations and reflections lead to the synthesis of the different levels. This enables you to explicate (theorise) how your understandings of your practices make an original contribution to knowledge of your field.

You also show how you engaged with other people's thinking in the literatures. Reading a text is an active process of dialogue with another person who is, as you are, trying to make sense of what they are doing. You note what the writer is saying through writing notes, or keeping a record in a reflective journal. You do not accept everything: you critique and decide for yourself what you will accept.

This enables you to see your text as a reader 'who does not share one's own perspectives' (Sharples, 1999: 104); and it is a reciprocal process. By putting your ideas into the public domain you can invite others also to explore their capacity for thinking and begin a dialogue with you. Production of a text is not the end so much as the catalytic point that opens up a new piece of the enquiry.

Writing on the page: Producing a high quality text

You help your reader understand your story by weaving a golden thread through it. In everyday action research there is no beginning, middle or end of a story: you are always somewhere in the middle. However, when writing the text you need to give it a notional beginning and end, and write a meta-analysis about your thinking and action. You show how words turn into deeds, and how you generate theory out of practice. You tell different stories embedding different levels of explication: your stories of social practice (knowledge-telling), of communicative practice (transforming), of clarifying (analysing), of understanding (synthesing) and explicating for your reader (theorising) form Russian dolls of stories contained within one another.

Writing in the world: Writing for political effect

In your text you explain how you have tried to improve the quality of your practice. Drawing on MacIntyre's definition of a practice (pp. 40–1), you explain how doing your research has enabled you to achieve the internal goods of your practice: as a pharmacist, you have enabled people to receive the medication they need; as a landscape gardener you have enabled people to enjoy life by executing plans for beautiful gardens.

Jane L. Crane is the founder/CEO of 'Adopt A Widow for African Widows' (www. adoptawidow.org). She lives in the USA and travels to Africa on a regular basis. In her presentation to the Value and Virtue in Practice-Based Research conference (2014), Jane describes how she is currently working with widows in Burundi, Africa, a recent post-conflict country (Daley, 2007). The region of Sub-Saharan Africa in general has many widows, including young ones with small children, due to HIV/ AIDS, wars, and the hard life of poverty (Odimmegwa, 2010; Asiimwe and Crankshaw, 2011). Yet a paucity of interventions exists for widows compared to their numbers, so the subject population itself is one in great need of humanitarian attention (Dutt, 2010). Jane writes:

I have devised an Adopt A Widow program, similar to a sponsored-child program, where a sponsor 'adopts' a widow to pay her expenses for a one-year sewing program in which she learns a skill for future self-support in an atmosphere of emotional empowerment specifically for widows. I am testing the model in Burundi through several one-year cycles and interviewing the widows, sponsors, and staff to study the transformation that takes place in all involved, especially the widows. All participants, including the widows, are considered important collaborators in the process of refining and testing the Adopt A Widow humanitarian intervention through multiple action research cycles.

In this presentation, I will tell the stories of some widows currently in the program, in particular how they are important collaborators in the practice-based research. A six-minute video regarding that program is also available for viewing at www.adoptawidow.org. In addition, I have recently completed a book based on interviews with more than 60 widows in seven African countries (Crane, 2014b) and draw on that background in my comments and conclusions. (Crane, 2014a)

Further, you are able to communicate what writing the text has meant for you. You have demonstrated excellence in scholarly practices through your engagement with the literatures, and rhetorical validity through explaining the construction of your text; you keep your thinking open by engaging with others' ideas and incorporating them into your thinking as appropriate. You have shown the internal integrity of your text through these literary devices, and the external validity by showing its usefulness in the world – the 'so what?' of research. You have shown the relationship between practice and theory: theory is seen not as external to practices but located within them. Theory emerges through the study of the practice and is examined through critical reflection and engagement with your own and others' ideas.

These processes of the emergence of theory and the ethicality of open forms need to be made explicit through the content and form of the text. The content needs to explain ideas about the growth of one's own theory of practice, shown through the narrative unity of the text (see Chapter 4).

Yet these aims of showing the dialogical, relational, spontaneous, outward-looking and emergent (and, in my view, ethical) nature of the research can lead to dilemmas, given that the underpinning epistemology of orthodox higher education still errs towards results and outcomes. Action researchers therefore need to find ways of writing their research accounts that honour the integrity of free and emergent forms of research, including the practice of asking questions, within dominant institutional contexts that value the formulation of final answers and conformity to established systems. These matters are dealt with throughout this book.

SUMMARY

This chapter has looked at what goes into an action research text, what criteria are used for judging quality in different kinds of text, and how the criteria will be achieved. Three conceptual frameworks are offered to help you achieve these criteria: (1) The grammar of action research; (2) Framing and re-framing, and (3) Academic writing as knowledge explication. These help you to transfer writing in the head into writing on the page, and politically into writing in the world.

REFLECTIVE QUESTIONS

- Are you clear about what goes into an action research text? Can you articulate your understanding of the need for conceptual and theoretical analyses?

(Continued)

(Continued)

- Do you explain how you generate your personal I-theory of practice from studying the practice? Are you clear about the difference between personal theories and traditional propositional theories?

- Does your action research text demonstrate levels of increasing theoretical complexity? Do you tell the reader what the levels are and how they should be reading the text? Do you communicate the dynamic and organic nature of these aspects?

- Do you appreciate the need to communicate the significance of these matters when producing texts, especially how knowledge in the head can transform into political knowledge in the world?

RESEARCH EXERCISE

Write a short text to explain how you engage with matters of content in action research. Make sure you show how you reflect critically on your practices, and how strong conceptual frameworks can help you to do so. Explain especially how you have generated your personal theory of practice, and the importance of doing so.

We now turn to Chapter 4 and consider how the form of the text communicates the content, and how both content and form need to be commensurable.

FOUR

What is the Form of an Action Research Text?

This chapter discusses the form of a text – how it is written. The content is communicated through the form, so the form becomes the content. The same process happens elsewhere. In a 'staged' wrestling match (Barthes, 2000) the moves are already scripted, so the performance becomes the content. In dance and music, technique communicates the message. In Lewis Carroll's *Alice's Adventures in Wonderland* the poem about the mouse's tale is in the shape of a long tail – a form of visual poetics. The medium communicates the message.

This chapter considers what an action research text looks like, so that the content and form blend as one. This involves appealing to the reader's aesthetic appreciation as much as to their cognitive capacity.

The chapter looks at the following.

1. What is distinctive about the form of an action research text?
2. New genres in action research
3. What form does an action research text take?

What is Distinctive about the Form of an Action Research Text?

This section deals with ideas about:

- readerly and writerly texts; and
- the architecture of texts.

Readerly and writerly texts

When writing any text you can produce a 'readerly' text, a 'writerly' text, or a mix. Barthes (1970) and Sharples (1999) speak about the effects different kinds of text can have on a reader. A readerly text, they say, is written so that a reader sees immediately what the text is getting at. A set of instructions or a manual is a readerly text, and so is a calendar or a bank statement. No great interpretive effort is required for a readerly text: the writer tells the reader how to read it.

A writerly text is written from the writer's perspective, without guidance to the reader about how they should interpret it. The writer aims to show their own personal, often original engagement with ideas, and expects the reader to engage with them too. The text then becomes a living, mediating experience between the writer and reader.

Todorov says that different readers respond differently to different kinds of text. He outlines the stages of a text's itinerary as (1) 'the author's narrative', which leads to (2) an 'imaginary universe evoked by the author', which leads to (3) an 'imaginary universe constructed by the reader', which leads to (4) 'the reader's narrative' (see Todorov, 1990: 42). From an action research perspective, this schema can be understood as an action reflection cycle, when the reader actively engages with a writer's ideas and reframes them as possible new actions and new narratives of action, as in Figure 4.1.

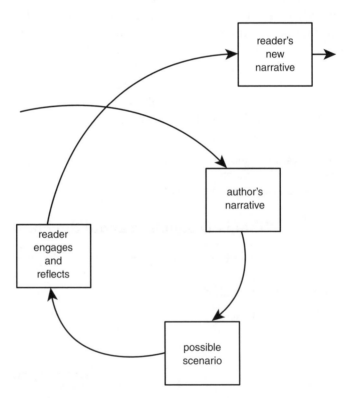

Figure 4.1 Engagement with a text as action and reflection to inform future actions and narratives of action

Most writers initially produce writerly texts, where they explore ideas through writing about them. The challenge then becomes how to think and write like a reader, so that a writerly text turns into a readerly one and the reader can immediately see what the author is saying. I did this when writing this book: I explored ideas through the writing, producing a writerly text, and then revised the text repeatedly so that the form of the text communicated the ideas as a readerly text (I hope!). The movement was from playing with and writing ideas in the head to communicating the ideas through text on the page (see also Bolton, 2014). Achieving this kind of shift comes through focusing on what you want to say, and then finding an appropriate form to say it in.

This point is relevant to Foucault's (1977) idea of the 'death of the author', meaning that the author vanishes once a text leaves their hands and goes into the hands of a reader. It then becomes the reader's responsibility to make sense of the text as they read it. This has implications for the writer, whether they choose to guide the reader through the text or whether they expect the reader to work things out for themselves. It has implications for you, too: your job is to write a readerly text that helps your reader appreciate the importance of your ideas. If you produce a text without giving your reader guidance about how to interpret it, you may find yourself in difficulty.

Learning how to write a readerly text can be greatly assisted by considering the architecture of texts.

The architecture of texts

Sennett (2009) speaks about writing as a form of architecture – a dynamic, engaged practice where hand and head work together in the creation of an artefact. You explore the qualities of your text through working with it. You participate in its creation and construction, which, says Sennett, makes 'thinking like a craftsman … more than a state of mind; it has a sharp social edge' (2009: 44). The social edge is its use value in the world: skilful architecture ensures that buildings do not fall down (Levy and Salvadori, 2002) and that your text communicates what you wish to say.

This architecture is evident in stories: some are linear, a 'what next?' text where the action goes from start to finish, as in a Bauhaus building; and some are dynamically transformational, where different elements emerge at different times, as in Gaudí's cathedral in Barcelona.

This idea of dynamic transformations makes action research texts distinctive. They are different from orthodox social science texts, where the scenes are linear and follow a specific sequence. The rules of action research are about communicating the emergent nature of the research. They are rules of creative design, showing disciplined enquiry through a creative form. The dynamic form of practice improvement, knowledge creation and theory generation are reflected in the dynamic forms of the text, and these dynamic forms have produced new genres of writing.

New Genres through Action Research

Most writing can be classified into genres, such as poetry, narrative, or drama. Each genre has its own traditions and rules about the content and form of the writing (Barry, 2002). A love letter would not usually take the form of a formal essay nor would a philosophical argument be presented as a handbook. Here is an excerpt about what traditional writing in philosophy should look like:

Contemporary philosophical writing is largely impersonal and technical in style. It proposes definitions, makes arguments, criticizes other arguments, corrects previous infidelities and imprecisions in a position, and situates it all in a context of issues current in the discipline. ... The writing of philosophy is now measured by professional standards. Those standards specify that, even where a text is not yet presented in a clear, impersonal and argumentative form, it should, in principle, be translatable into one. (Mathien and Wright, 2006: 1, 3)

Many experimental writers do cross boundaries, but most writers tend to stay within genres that are recognised through an existing body of work (the canon); this communicates the rules, norms and standards of the genre, and the writer picks these up, often by example. You can experiment with form in action research, including your use of multimedia and multimodal forms of representation. Dadds and Hart (2001) speak about 'methodological inventiveness', the need to develop new forms in communicating research, while recognising the problematics of communicating action research within traditionalist forms of writing:

[As supervisors of higher degree studies], we have shared our unease, paradoxically, when practitioner researchers chose to go 'out on a limb', wondering if they would depart too radically from the academic criteria on their Masters' course and fail to achieve the quality standards set by the institution. More importantly, we have also shared a common sense of inspiration when practitioner researchers have reached out for exciting, unorthodox ways of doing and reporting their research and, as a result, taxed the mind of the academy, demanding new thinking about what constitutes legitimate practitioner research at Masters' level. (Dadds and Hart, 2001: 8)

Examples of action research texts that mix genres are: Spiro (2008), who uses poetry and creative writing; James (2013), who uses pictorial metaphors; and

O'Neill (2008), who presents his dissertation in the form of a website, as well as a conventional written text. Other forms include tape-recorded reports for candidates with writing difficulties, and digital dissertations and theses (see Andrews et al., 2012). Butler-Kisber (2010) speaks about sculpture and dance as forms of representation, and poetic, collage, photographic and performative forms of inquiry. She calls for cross-boundary sharing and collaborating, saying, 'Artists and researchers should be working together more often, as should researchers from varying disciplines and who conduct different types of inquiry' (2010: 150). Digital technology is making this kind of research possible through communicating meanings in comprehensible ways.

Narrative form

A main feature of action research writing is its largely narrative form. It is mainly through narratives that humans make sense of and express their understanding of events and experiences (Herr and Anderson, 2005: 64). Action research texts tell a story about how and why the research was undertaken, and what new knowledge was discovered or created. Clandinin and Connelly argue that:

Narrative inquiry is a way of understanding experience. It is collaboration between researcher and participants, over time, in a place or series of places, and in social interactions with milieus. An inquirer enters this matrix in the midst of living and telling, reliving and retelling, the stories of the experiences that make up people's lives, both individual and social. (Clandinin and Connelly, 2000: 20)

Here are some of the distinctive features of narrative writing.

Action research stories often take the form of cycles of action reflection, where the learning from one cycle informs the next over time. These cycles are emergent and transformational, as in Figure 4.2.

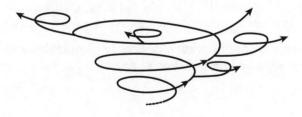

Figure 4.2 Visual to communicate the nature of generative transformational evolutionary processes (see also McNiff, 1984)

To appreciate these issues it may be helpful to consider the form of the underpinning values and logics of the writer, and how these are communicated through the deliberate use of the form of text. Go back to page 13 and Sowell's ideas about constrained and unconstrained visions. A constrained vision draws on a linear epistemology that looks for outcomes and results. An unconstrained vision draws on a transformational epistemology that espouses deconstruction. This means questioning anything that is taken for granted to reveal its hidden foundations. Deconstruction is an accepted part of action research stories, but to show it can be amazingly difficult because we are born into a culture that teaches us to think in certain ways. Deconstruction means interrogating assumptions about thinking while using the same form of thinking that we are interrogating, which involves continually shifting perspectives.

When you write your story of practice, you show how you interrogate the practice itself, how you problematise it. You raise questions about, for example, how people are categorised in terms of race, skin colour, gender, age, capacity and looks, and you question the system of categorisation itself. You question how we learn to categorise ourselves, digging into self-made holes from which we cannot or do not want to escape. We question which specific historical, social, economic and cultural practices have led to our present situations. When you write your text, you question the nature of the text, explaining that it does not simply represent a reality 'out there' but is itself a construction of your own thinking: in other words, you problematise the idea of 'reality' (Norris, 1989). When you write this into your text you show that the text has ironic validity (Lather, 1991), that is, it demonstrates the capacity to reflect on itself. The best action research reports demonstrate this capacity.

These ideas about deconstruction are important for writing your text, because it means that you no longer have specific rules to guide your writing, so you have to create new ones. Lyotard (1984) explains this dilemma for the postmodern writer, which includes action researchers:

A postmodern artist or writer is in the position of a philosopher: the text he [sic] writes, the work he produces are not in principle governed by pre-established rules, and they cannot be judged according to a determining judgement, by applying familiar categories to the text or to the work. Those rules and categories are what the work of art itself is looking for. The artist and writer, then, are working without rules in order to formulate the rules of what will have been done. (Lyotard, 1984: 81)

Further, you can use specific textual devices to communicate your meanings, including voice, style and progression.

Voice

In action research, people speak for themselves. You are the main actor in your story, while working with others who tell their stories. Your story represents a community of storytellers speaking for themselves. The stories are usually first person 'I' stories; action research texts rarely speak about 'the researcher' as a third person. This carries implications, because you have to show that yours is a true story, not your opinion or wishful thinking. This means producing an evidence base, and interrogating how you have deconstructed your thinking so that you are not misled by your own biases.

Karen Rut Gísladóttir (2011), who works at the University of Iceland, is a hearing teacher of deaf children. Her thesis (for which I was external examiner) tells her story of learning how to teach for literacy. She includes the voices of the children as together they try to create and communicate meaning together. One such story tells how Melkorka wrote a draft of an essay in poetic form.

When she showed it to me, I read the entire poem, which I found to be full of meaning and movement.

'What is it that you are trying to say here?' I asked her, pointing to the stanza above. 'I open my eyes,' she explains. 'Everything is moving very slowly but also very fast. I see everything in full speed around me but then … It is like time has stopped for me, but I see how life continues … you know.' She put her hand[s] in front of her face, palms inward, fingers pointing towards each other. Then she slowly pulled them in opposite directions, like she was ripping her face apart. I watched her, not sure of what she was trying to tell me. She saw this in my face.

'See here.' She navigates to YouTube on the Internet. Once there, she searches for a word that, unfortunately, I did not record in my research journal. It brings up a video of a woman with myriad colors moving around her like auras.

'I open my eyes and time stands still for me,' she said, 'but everything is moving so fast.' We discussed this and edited Melkorka's work together to better capture the meaning that she was trying to express in her poem and to transform the written resources already available to her into a more standardized version of written Icelandic. (Gísladóttir, 2011: 26–7; see also Gísladóttir, 2014).

Style

The style of the narrative is personal and speaks about learning processes, unlike traditional social science texts that speak mainly about the subject matter. The style of writing should be user-friendly but not chatty, and positions the reader as a companion who is also involved in deconstruction, especially deconstructing your report to see whether you have engaged seriously with your own processes of reflexive and dialectical critique.

Progression

The progression of the story is transformational. It communicates the underlying connections between the characters in the story, and the connections between the author and reader. Bateson (1979) speaks about the need to develop the capacity to see all things as connected. An action research story makes these hidden connections explicit, between experience and meaning, and between the different aspects of the story.

Lāsma Latsone and Linda Pavitola, both assistant professors at the University of Liepaja University, Latvia, write about the value of researching civic responsibility in the context of Latvia, linking the aspects outlined above. They say:

The research results confirmed the theoretical findings of others as well as pointed to cultural and historical background as profoundly significant for an in-depth understanding of civic responsibility and whether to adopt it as a personal value. As Latvia is still in a transition process from culture nation towards civic nation, cultural tools can be powerful factors both in the process of national identity development, but also in promoting civic responsibility and active citizenship. The research also revealed considerable inconsistency and incoherence between lived values and those defined by society's and individuals' values, and provided evidence of the need to pay more attention to aspects of civic responsibility linked with rights, duties and personal activity that could help to strengthen interactional and transactional links between micro and mezzo systems.

As democratic educators we should aim to deepen students' understanding of the concepts of community and civic responsibility, emphasise systemic thinking, and encourage students to achieve a healthier balance between private and social values; this would possibly contribute towards their greater social involvement and activism for the benefit of wider society. We agree with Gundara (2000) who suggests that we need many more thoughtful, politically educated and active citizens who would seek solutions to conflicts in democratic and intelligent ways, not through violence. (Latsone and Pavitola, 2013: 104)

Transformational and catalytic form

An action research text communicates the generative transformational capacity of the research. Every thing contains its own potentials for new forms: a seedling transforms into a flower, a caterpillar into a butterfly. People have generative capacity for an infinite number of new practices, and each can be an improvement of itself. The enquiry never ends, because each 'satisfactory' ending contains new beginnings.

These ideas have implications for systemic influence because one aspect has the generative transformational capacity to influence new developments. There are implications also for action researchers. Practitioner-researchers can act as catalysts – to influence others to improve what they are doing – but in action research the catalyst itself changes as part of the changing system.

Action research has catalytic validity, therefore, when systemic change happens. This is seen also through the transformational form of the text, where each step acts as a catalyst for, and transforms into the next.

Methodological rigour

Methodology refers to the way you design and do your research and test the validity of your findings. Your text communicates the systematic nature of the research, emerging from seeming chaos. Most researchers experience times of confusion when nothing makes sense. Law (2004) speaks about mess in human enquiry, and Mellor (1998) says that the methodology is in the muddle. Writing a report can also involve periods of intense frustration when the ideas do not come right. However, if you have faith in your own personal knowledge, things do come right, most of the time.

The rigour of your methodology is in its transformational capacity. History is sometimes seen as 'one damn thing after another', a linear sequence leading to closure. A more critical perspective understands how events at one point generate actions at the next. History therefore becomes a transformational process of catalytic moments, where the present holds consequences for the future. This is also the nature of action research. When you ask, 'How do I improve what I am doing?' you are unleashing a set of catalytic possibilities.

These ideas present some of the main features of the form of an action research report. The question now becomes, how do you communicate the process of doing action research in your text?

How do you Write an Action Research Text?

This section is about how to write an action research text. It is possible to structure a text in many different ways, and it is for you to decide which structure best communicates your specific meanings. However, if you are hoping for academic recognition, your text needs to fulfil agreed academic criteria, as set out in Chapters 9 and 10. At this point I would like to outline what I see as a useful and realistic armature, or scaffold, around which to write your text. This is not the only way, but it works for me, probably because it reflects the same common-sense set of questions people ask when faced with dilemmas in everyday situations, as outlined on page 16. I hope it works for you, too.

We begin with a basic action plan that shows the main steps in doing action research. The plan can also provide a framework for writing your action research story, perhaps as a dissertation or thesis. When you write your dissertation proposal (Chapter 8), you explain how you are planning to conduct your research, so you write in the future tense: 'This is what I hope to do and this is how and why I aim to do it.' When you write up your research (Chapter 9), you tell the story in the past tense: 'This is what I did and this is how and why I did it.'

Different frameworks for dissertations are proposed in Chapter 9, but a general framework for an action research text looks like this.

- Introduction to the research story.
- The research story:
  o What did I want to investigate? What was my research issue? What was my practical concern?
  o Why did I want to investigate this? Why was it an issue? Why was I concerned?
  o How can I show what the situation was like initially? How did I gather baseline data to show the situation as it was?
  o What could I do? What actions could I take?
  o What did I do?
  o How did I gather data to show ongoing developments and generate evidence?
  o What did I find out?
  o How could I show that any conclusions I came to were reasonably fair and accurate? How did I test the validity of my provisional conclusions?
  o How could I articulate the significance of my action research?
  o How did I modify my ideas and practices in light of my evaluation?
- Conclusion.

The questions of the action plan may become chapter and section headings, as follows.

Introduction

The following points go into your introduction:

- Tell the reader what the research is about. State your claim to knowledge, and give a brief overview of how you will test its validity. Say why you have chosen an action research methodology.
- Say that the report is about yourself and your learning, so it is written in the first person. Your 'I' is the focus of the enquiry, but it is not 'all about me' so much as how I can contribute to other people's flourishing.
- Introduce yourself to the reader. Say who you are, where you work, and anything special about your circumstances that led you to do the research.
- Say briefly what the main findings of the research are, and what their potential significance could be.
- Give a brief overview of the chapters ahead.

Now tell your reader that you are going to write your research story.

Your research story

The contents of your story are as follows (to note: you may also use the headings below as chapter headings).

What issue did I want to investigate? What was my concern?

This section says what the research was about, and contains the following points.

- Say what you wanted to investigate. This is your research issue: perhaps the nature of relationships in your organisation, or creating online learning environments. It could have been a problem, or something you were interested in, or an evaluation of your present situation.
- Say you were studying your practice in the contexts where these issues were happening, in order to find ways of understanding and possibly improving the situation.
- Explain that you were concerned because you were not living in the direction of your values. Perhaps organisational structures, or established ways of working were preventing you from realising your values; perhaps you were denying them yourself, acting in ways that were contrary to what you believed in. Say that you undertook your research to find ways of realising your values more fully.
- Now articulate your research question.

Your research question You formulated a research question in relation to the identified concern. Your question took the form: 'How do I improve ...?' You can use different words, but the underpinning idea is that you were trying to find a way to improve something. For example:

- How do I help to improve the relationships in my organisation?
- How do I encourage people to use this new technology?
- How do I create better online learning environments?

A special point: The problematics of 'I' and 'we' Sometimes you may be involved in a collaborative project, where your 'I' turns into 'we'. Take care when writing up this kind of project. If the project was genuinely collaborative and the voices of all participants are heard, then you can probably use 'we'. If it is your voice only, and you are speaking on behalf of others, clarify whose ideas are whose, and make sure that you are representing others appropriately. In most reports, 'we' refers to the action in the workplace, while 'I' am the one who reports what I am learning through the action 'we' took in the workplace. 'My' learning is grounded in my interactions with other 'Is'.

Why was this an important issue? Why was I concerned?

This section deals with the reasons for your concern, and why it was a concern. It discusses issues of values and contexts.

Values As noted in Chapter 2, values are the things you value, such as friendship and kindness. In traditional reports, values tend to be spoken about as abstractions. Raz's (2003) *The Practice of Value* speaks about values in an abstract way. In action research, values become manifested as how we do what we do. If we act with kindness, we live the value of kindness. If we involve everyone in public debates, we act democratically. Your job as researcher and writer is to show how you lived your values so that they became practices and did not remain at the level of words.

Your values inspire and provide the reasons for your research, as well as its purposes. They also act as the basis for your conceptual frameworks. The ideas you espouse, such as justice and freedom, and the literatures you read about these ideas (see Arendt, 1958 about justice; or Berlin, 1969 about freedom) stem from your values.

Contexts Set out what your research contexts are. These can be as follows.

Personal contexts Say who you are, where you work, what your working conditions are like. Say anything special about yourself. Were you made redundant at the age of 40? Did you have difficulties in school because you are dyslexic? What does your reader need to know about you? Do not write your life story, just enough to let the reader see the relevance of your personal contexts.

Locational contexts Say where your research took place: in a hospital or union building. Describe anything special about the place. Perhaps it was geographically remote, or in an area of outstanding natural beauty. Give any special details that will help your reader understand the context: perhaps insufficient resources or a history of institutional bullying?

Research contexts Outline what the literatures say about your field of enquiry. Show how you incorporate other people's ideas into your own thinking, as well as critique them. You cannot agree or disagree with them unless you explain why the ideas are relevant. This means showing that you have read them. Do not simply drop names. Bassey (1999: 6) cautions against what he calls 'genuflection', 'sandbagging' and 'kingmaking' – practices designed to look good, pad out the writing, or shore up an author's weak scholarship.

Policy contexts Say what the current policy is in your area. What is the policy around rescue services, or emergency waiting times, or urban planning? Must you meet targets or produce outcomes? These may be important contextualising features.

Any other especially relevant contexts Do you work with offenders or young people at risk, or in a botanical gardens or zoo? Are you deaf, or especially gifted in a particular field? If so, say so. Help your reader understand why information about your contexts is central to the research.

Combining values and contexts Now combine these ideas about values and contexts. They provide the background to your research and give reasons for why you took action. Say what you hoped to achieve, and whether you were in a position to do so. This means talking about your research goals. It may not be appropriate to say, 'I wanted to change the situation,' because the only things we can ever change in a sustainable way are our own thinking or behaviours. It is more realistic to speak about influencing others' thinking and practices, encouraging and helping them to change themselves.

Writing and Doing Action Research

How do I show what the situation was like initially? How did I gather data?

Explain what the situation was like when you began your research, and produce data to show it. This data can be in the form of reports and other documents, such as statements and participants' communications. It can also be photographs and videos. You can produce quantitative and qualitative analyses. You can use any and all data to show the situation as it initially was. You can tell stories from your own history, as well as stories from archives, or vignettes from personal experience. Let the reader see what was going on, so that they can empathise with you when you say you felt you needed to take action.

Speaking about data involves considering the people you asked to get involved in your research. These were your participants, critical friends and observers. It also involves speaking about ethics.

Participants Say who you invited to take part as research participants. These fall into at least three groups:

> **Research participants** You invite participants to be directly involved in the research, as the people whose learning you are trying to influence. They can be your colleagues, students, patients, or customers. Remember the focus is on you, not them; you are investigating your practices in relation with them, not theirs in relation with you. Remember also that they are your equals and they should be treated as such.
>
> **Critical friends and validation groups** You ask these people to work with you and give you ongoing critical feedback on your research. Your validation groups are a formal gathering, including critical friends by negotiation, to give you feedback on the potential validity of your evidence and research claims.
>
> **Observers** These are the colleagues and interested parties you invite to observe you in action, or otherwise as appropriate.

Ethics Involving people in research means you must get their permission. Say how you did this, and include a blank copy of the letter requesting permission as an appendix in your report. Also put the letters granting permission into your appendices. Blank out real names and addresses, or anything that could identify participants. If they wish to be identified, put a note from them to that effect in the appendices, otherwise readers may ask questions about authenticity and your sense of responsibility. Say also, as appropriate, that you have sought and gained the approval of institutional ethics committees to pursue your research.

Generating evidence It may be appropriate at this point to speak about how you generated evidence from the data. Depending on how you organise your ideas, you may do this now, or you may prefer to leave it until you speak about gathering data on an ongoing basis (see below).

What could I do? What did I do? What actions did I decide to take?

You now had choices about what to do. You could act or walk away. Having considered all angles, you decided on one. Talk about the risks involved, and the dilemmas about whether to accept them. Then say what you decided to do, with real intent.

How did I continue to gather data to show the situation as it developed?

Talk about how you gathered the data, stored it, analysed it, and made sense of it, so that you could turn it into evidence.

Monitoring the action and gathering the data Explain how you monitored your action and gathered data about it. Say which data-gathering techniques you used, and whether you used the same ones throughout or used different techniques at different points for different purposes. You gathered data about your actions and your learning, and also about what your research participants were doing and thinking. Say how you negotiated this with them, perhaps to include extracts from their diaries in your report, or from tape-recorded conversations. You must show how you negotiated the use of the data to reassure your readers and reviewers that you were acting ethically. You also need to produce any disconfirming data, which showed that your research was not going as planned, so you took this as a steer for new action. Unless you explain that you considered all angles, your readers will ask questions about whether everything was as neat as you say it was.

Storing the data Say where you stored your data archive, as computer files, or in file boxes, and explain how you categorised it. Say that you were aware of the importance of systematic storage so that you could access the data easily when it came to interpreting and analysing it. Also explain how you ensured the data was secure, such as storing it on a password-protected computer.

Interpreting and analysing the data Explain that you knew you would not use all the data, and would select only key pieces to use as evidence. Be clear about your criteria for the selection of data, that is, only those data that are specifically relevant to your research question and ultimately your research claim. The question and the claim are aspects of the same thing. Your question asks, 'How do I improve what I am doing?' and your claim states, 'I have improved what I am doing'. Your data acts as a bridge between the two, along which you walk as you implement your action plan. The criteria you identify for the selection of data into evidence are therefore the criteria you identify to show the validity of the claim. Say what these criteria are. Say also how you coded and sorted the data, possibly by using a grounded theory data analysis approach (see, for example, Cresswell, 2007).

Criteria, standards of practice and standards of judgement Criteria and standards are involved in making judgements. Criteria refer to what you expect to be the case, and are set in advance. When you go to a hotel, you would have certain criteria in mind – cleanliness, comfort and service. Standards refer to the quality with which criteria are achieved. In all cases, criteria, standards of practice and standards of judgement are linked and informed by our values. In the case of professional practices, we judge quality in terms of the extent to which we realise our values, such as warm relationships. Our criteria, standards of practice, and standards of judgement are manifestations of our values. You would be expected to engage with these ideas throughout your text.

How could I show that any conclusions I came to were reasonably fair and accurate?

Say that you know the importance of testing your claims to knowledge. You are not simply expecting people to accept your claims. You have gone through rigorous validation processes to test their validity. These have involved the following.

- You have tested the validity of claims that you have improved the quality of your practice against your values. You are reasonably sure that they are justified. You have drawn on your personal knowledge (Polanyi, 1958) as the grounds for the validity of the claim. These values are always oriented towards the other's flourishing and sustainable growth.
- You have tested their validity against your capacity for self-critique and deconstruction. You have demonstrated your capacity to stand outside your action research and comment critically on your emergent understanding.
- You have checked their validity against theories in the literature. You have shown that your knowledge claims have theoretical validity.
- You have checked them against the critical feedback of others, in the form of critical friends and validation groups. You have shown these colleagues your confirming and disconfirming data, and have acted on their advice. You have placed the transcripts of conversations with critical friends in your appendices, and minutes of validation meetings. You have asked validation groups to consider your criteria and standards of judgement when testing this validity, and whether you are presenting your claims to have acted truthfully, sincerely, comprehensibly and appropriately (see Habermas, 1976).
- You are now testing the validity of your claims by submitting your text to the critical evaluation of your readers and reviewers. If they approve it they will grant it validity and legitimacy.

How could I articulate the significance of my action research?

Show that you appreciate the meaning of your research, in terms of its potential significance and possible implications for yourself and others. The people who would benefit from engaging in it would be:

- Yourself. You can inform your further learning and practices through what you have learned, including your capacity for reflexive and dialectical critique. You can become more conscious of the dynamic nature of your values, criteria and standards of judgement.
- Your colleagues, students, parents, and other parties who would benefit personally from reading your work. They may be able to adopt or adapt your ideas to their practices.
- Social and cultural formations. These are the existing social and professional groupings that claim social and cultural capital and make statements about the way things should be. If you can influence their thinking, they will in turn influence the social and cultural order in which they have a strong voice.

How did I modify my ideas and practices in light of my evaluation?

Say how you intend to continue the action in your workplace, and also through doing research. There is no getting off this process now you are on it. One cycle leads to the next; issues that emerged now become new beginnings. Say what you have learned from the experience, and whether you would consider doing things differently. You have refined your insights, and are better equipped intellectually to engage in further action reflection cycles. You have developed a critical mind, and there is no going back; once you have made your eyes different (Polanyi, 1958: 137), you see things in a different way, and you cannot unlearn this.

SUMMARY

This chapter has looked at the form of an action research report. It has discussed some key formal features, and how these can be incorporated into an action plan. The action plan, engaging with questions such as 'How do I improve my practice?' can be used as a starting point for writing. The form of the text is judged in relation to specified academic criteria, as well as the demonstration of critical engagement with your own thinking and with the literature.

REFLECTIVE QUESTIONS

Here is a checklist to remind you of the key formal features of your report:

- Have you produced a readerly-writerly text? Do you speak directly with your reader? Do you anticipate that your reader will bring their own interpretations to the text? Do you explain how you wish the text to be interpreted?

- Does your report manifest its underlying logics and values through its form? Do you position your reader as a thoughtful, creative person? Do you write in a way that communicates open and transformational thinking? Do you show how your research adopted a cyclical form?

- Does your text adopt a narrative form? Do you tell a research story?

- Does your text show processes of deconstruction? Do you show how you have deconstructed your thinking, and have problematised issues rather than taking them for granted? Do you communicate how the research is located within social, economic, historical and political contexts? Do you explain the possible influence of your research on those contexts?

- Is your text transformational and catalytic? Do you explain its potential for educational influence? Does it show methodological rigour?

RESEARCH EXERCISE

Write a short text to explain how you engage with issues of form in writing. Explain how you justify what you write and how you write it. Explain how this amounts to metacognitive reflexivity.

We now move to Chapter 5, which discusses some of the most practical issues involved in becoming a writer.

PART II

Becoming a Writer: Researching Writing Practices

This Part explores what it means to become a writer, and some of the practicalities involved.

It contains Chapters 5, 6 and 7.

Chapter 5, 'Becoming a writer' is about having faith in yourself and your tacit knowledge and your capacity for learning; your writing begins here.

Chapter 6, 'Writing a good quality text' outlines what it takes to turn your tacit knowledge into the explicit form of a text that readers will wish to read.

Chapter 7, 'Planning for the production of texts' enters the world of the political where texts may be used to influence other people's thinking.

Practical advice and robust theoretical resources are offered throughout.

The chapters are organised to reflect what Noffke (2009) communicates as 'the personal, professional and political', and Sharples (1999) expresses as 'Writing in the head', 'Writing on the page', and 'Writing in the world'. These transformational and cumulative processes show how personal values and ontological commitments may transform into texts that have potential for influencing the creation of a more peaceful and productive world for all.

FIVE
Becoming a Writer

This chapter offers ideas about what is involved in becoming a writer, much of which involves getting to know yourself and how you write, and learning to develop your capacity. Technical issues of how quality is judged in texts is in Chapter 6, and how to achieve it is in Chapter 7.

This chapter focuses on what becoming a writer involves, what it means, and what you need to do as a result. It discusses the following issues:

1. Developing a writer identity
2. What do you need to know about being a writer?
3. What do you need to do to develop yourself as a writer?

Developing a writer identity

Earlier we discussed the need to develop an extended sense of identity, from practitioner to researcher to writer. This is not a linear process where you leave behind one identity to take on another, but a cumulative one, where you hold all your identities together as an expanding vista of transformational practices. It is a generative enterprise where you shape and design your life towards more open and creative forms, and develop cognitive spaces and structures to help communicate the processes involved. You can show, as Hofstadter (1979) does, how formal systems can interlink and, in shifting their own patterns, come to form new eco-systems as described in Chapter 4.

Becoming a writer involves different capacities, the main ones being: (1) a sense of faith in yourself and your own knowledge; and (2) faith in the work of words.

Faith in yourself and your own knowledge is the foundation of being a writer: a sense of 'having control over how you write and trust in your ability to make progress' (Sharples, 1999: 128). This can present dilemmas for action researchers writing in traditionalist higher education contexts, where texts are usually supposed to report results rather than show processes. It is not easy to have faith in yourself and your original ideas in a context where you are expected to have the answers beforehand as in traditionalist settings. The difficulty is exacerbated when you do action research, which, because it is about charting and initiating processes of change, means you do not know where you are going until you get there. The difficulty is even more exacerbated when it comes to writing the project up because many writers do not know what they are going to write until they write it: the ideas emerge through the process of writing. This is where it is important to have strong faith and commitment to what you are doing.

As noted in Chapter 2 Macdonald speaks about theory as a prayerful act, an expression of belief (Macdonald, 1995: 181). He saw theory as 'the development of frameworks from which designs can be generated rather than theory as the testing of designs' (Macdonald, 1967: 166, quoted in Pinar, 1995: 4), the same view communicated by saying that practitioners generate their theories of practice from studying the practice from within the practice. The research that leads to the generation of theory is grounded in an 'individual style of life that is self-aware, self-critical, and self-enhancing' (Allport, 1955; cited in Macdonald, 1995: 17).

Macdonald drew on the work of different process philosophers, including Polanyi, who refers to faith in one's tacit knowledge as a 'fiduciary component'. Polanyi says that we know more than we can tell: we have a massive fund of tacit knowledge, and we need to have faith in its power, in spite of the uncertainties:

Personal knowledge is an intellectual commitment, and as such inherently hazardous … into every act of knowing there enters a passionate contribution of the person knowing what is being known, and this coefficient is no mere imperfection but a vital component of the knowledge. (Polanyi, 1958: viii, 312)

Further, once we commit, we can never go back:

My eyes have become different; I have made myself into a person seeing and thinking differently. I have crossed a gap, a heuristic gap, which lies between problem and discovery. (Polanyi, 1958: 143)

This same process of transforming tacit knowledge into explicit knowledge works at the level of practice where values transform into living practices, and at the level of writing where ideas transform into words on the page. It works primarily through having faith in one's work. This can be difficult when your supervisor requires you to produce the first draft chapter of your dissertation while you are still playing with ideas, yet this is what you need to do to move your ideas along. Most experienced supervisors appreciate the tensions involved yet also know that you work your ideas out through writing them, so do not jib at the idea of producing a draft chapter without quite knowing what it will contain. The process of writing can help you work it out.

Bente Norbye is a research group leader at UiT, the Arctic University. She speaks of her experiences of facilitating the research group introduced in Chapter 1:

Part of my responsibility as group leader is to support the academic writing of colleagues. This is why we have arranged a writing retreat. It is important for colleagues to work out ideas together, to meet the institutional expectations of publications. We write collaboratively and work out our ideas through dialogue and through the process of writing. (Transcript of research group tape-recorded conversation, McNiff et al., 2013)

Having faith in the works of words

The idea of having faith in the works of words is taken from Doxtader (2009) who documents some of the processes from 1985–1995 that led to the Truth and Reconciliation Commission in South Africa. 'In the name of a beginning, reconciliation begins with a belief that there are words which hold the potential for all things to become new' (Doxtader, 2009: ix). In the context of apartheid, he says, to turn sworn enemies into engaged opponents 'reconciliation's fragile words come to constitute the potential for politics and a politics of potential' (p. ix). His question becomes: 'How do words of reconciliation transform human relationships?' (p. x). This could be a main research question for all action researchers.

The job of writers is to work with words. This means having faith in their words and their capacity for using words. Nor is it simply about single words, but about turning words into text to communicate the meanings of practices to influence social and political domains. Turning words into text can be problematic. When you struggle to communicate an idea, you may find that words stay as separate entities, little stickers that you stick down onto the page, one at a time, yet when the ideas begin to emerge and take over your mental space they transform into sentences and carry you along; you develop a heightened sense of awareness of yourself as you create text; you get caught up in what Csikszentmihalyi (1990) calls 'flow', in this case, the flow of creative writing.

Here are some ideas about how to do this and what you need to know about being a writer.

What Do You Need to Know About Being a Writer?

When you write you are always in relationships. You are never a stand-alone writer; you are part of a culture with its own history and ways of making meaning. In part, this influences how you make meaning. You are in multiple relationships, including:

- you and your relationship with yourself and others;
- you and your relationship with your text;
- you and your relationship with your reader; and
- you and your relationship with the world of which you are a part.

Edward Said communicates these relationships in *The World, the Text and the Critic* (1991). He says that, as a writer, you bring a critical perspective to bear on your relationships. This is essential in academic writing too, especially when writing through and about action research, which means deliberately taking action in the world in order to influence others' epistemological and personal-social practices. Writing action research becomes a new form of social and political action.

You and your relationship with yourself and others

Aim to be confident about how you understand yourself. This raises questions about how you understand the concept of identity, which influences whether you believe you can turn yourself into a writer. Do you see identity as a once-and-for-all given, or is it a moving process? Is your identity fully created at birth, or are you able to recreate yourself throughout life? For many, identity is conferred by being born into a specific culture. There is the joke about the man who wants to work in Northern Ireland. When people ask him his religion, he says, 'I'm a Jew', and they ask, 'Are you a Catholic Jew or a Protestant Jew?' Some people create their identities in terms of other people: Katherine Mansfield's (1922) story 'The Daughters of the Late Colonel' tells of the two daughters of a domineering father who needed to ask him what to do when he lay already dead in the parlour. 'We must ask Father', they say. Identity becomes a prison; for some it becomes a safe place to hide. 'It is our culture,' says the bomber; 'we safeguard our culture because it makes us who we are.' In Sen's (2007) view, seeing identity in terms of a fixed set of characteristics reinforces an attitude that everything is fixed and unchanging. This means you can give yourself over to the context you are in and not try to do anything about it.

> ... violence is promoted by the cultivation of a sense of inevitability about some allegedly unique – often belligerent – identity that we are supposed to have and which apparently makes extensive demands on us (sometimes of a most disagreeable kind). (Sen, 2007: xiii)

Doing and writing action research means being critical about how you identify yourself in relation with others. Do you see others as in your space, satellites orbiting your central planet? Ngũgĩ (1993) challenges the so-called western epistemological tradition where European culture is the centre, the norm against which everything else is assessed. He speaks about the need to shift the centre elsewhere, but here misses a critical point, because challenging the idea of a reified centre means committing to the process of removing the centre altogether. We are all centres and therefore none of us is. When we recognise that we are in relationships with others, we focus on the relationships more than on the objects that form the nodes in the relationships (see Figure 5.1).

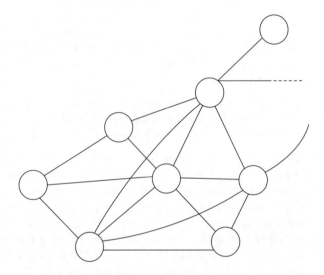

Figure 5.1   Connectivity among nodes in relationships

I like Lodge's (2003) ideas about writing and consciousness: he says we can learn more about consciousness through reading works of literature than through scientific methods. Similarly, Kohn (2000) says that consciousness may be understood as 'the basis of theory of mind, the ability to think what another individual might be thinking' (p. 4). This is what we do when we write: we communicate ideas about how we come to understand others and ourselves through our texts.

Clare Lawrence is a published writer and has chosen here not to use her real name. She writes in an email to me:

Our son was diagnosed with autism when he was three. I am a teacher, and I understood how difficult it is for the education system to meet the complex

(Continued)

needs of a child with autism. What do you do with a child who can read but seldom speaks? Learning how to work with our son became the topic of my action research.

Our answer has been to share his education between home and school. The schools have been wonderful, and we have learned so much! Our son is now choosing his 'A' levels, is independent and self-assured. He is at home with his autism, which he sees more as a strength than a disability.

Throughout I have shared what we have learned through writing. I have written six books, articles for teaching journals and parenting magazines, newspapers and blogs. I have had feedback from mums and dads, grandparents and teachers. So why not convert all this into action research? I know what we have done and what has worked. I have theories about why it has worked and could work again. I want to influence other people's thinking.

Academic writing, though, is not quite the same. You can't 'just say it'. Everything has to be backed up with explanation and evidence. My assertions that 'I know this works!' just don't cut it. How do I know it works? What do I mean by know?

I have focused so far on my son's quest to learn: about what he experiences (often in unusual ways) about other people and what they mean to him and he to them. Now it is time to focus on my learning. Is my understanding of research methods so very different a challenge from my son's grappling with his place in this world or what process to use to decide if a boy in the playground is friend or foe? If I have helped him to develop the technique of using data to make decisions with composure then perhaps I too can learn to meet the demands of my own investigations. (Lawrence, personal correspondence, 2013)

Now look at some of your relationships with your text.

You in relationship with your text

As a writer you need to feel comfortable with your text and its production. This means getting to understand your own process of creating it, becoming conscious of the seven-eighths of a text that lies hidden beneath the surface, what Hemingway evidently called the 'iceberg principle'. Hemingway said that readers intuit the history and meanings of stories and is reputed to have written the following 'six word novel':

For sale: Baby shoes, never worn.

Fershleiser and Smith (2008) developed the idea further, recording six-word stories by famous people: for example:

I asked. They answered. I wrote. (from Sebastian Junger)

Stole wife. Lost friends. Now happy. (from Po Bronson)

Try writing your dissertation or article in six words to find its real focus (incidentally, Horberry, 2009, assuaged the potential tragedy from Hemingway's story by saying that the shoes were probably the wrong colour).

To feel comfortable with your text, aim to understand among other aspects:

- Your writing style.
- The process of drafting, composing and editing.
- The need to think like a designer.
- Linking your content space and rhetorical space.

Your writing style

Writers work in different ways and develop different styles, using different strategies and frequently combining them. Sharples (1999) cites the poet Stephen Spender as being the first to identify two different types of writer:

those who write as a way of finding out what they want to say (which he called Beethovians) and those who write to record or communicate what they have already prepared (which he called Mozartians). Recently, researchers have given these types of writer the more helpful name of Discoverers and Planners. (Sharples, 1999: 112)

Discoverers use the process of writing to work out ideas: they discover what they want to say and make their tacit knowledge explicit. Planners think carefully about what they are going to write before doing so. Most people probably use a mixture of both. Here is some of my writing from 1990 about combining the processes. Drawing on Chomsky's (1986) ideas of competence (what we know at a tacit level) and performance (what we do in practice), I wrote:

In writing I tap my tacit knowledge (Holly, 1989). I externalise my thought-at-competence through my action-at-performance. My writing becomes both the symbolic expression of thought (this is what I mean) and the critical reflection on that thought (do I really mean this?). My writing is both reflection-on-action (what I have written) and reflection-in-action (what I am writing). The very act of making external, through the process of writing, what is internal, in the process of thinking, allows me to formulate explicit theories about the practices I engage in intuitively. (McNiff, 1990: 56)

Discovering and planning are essential to successful composing. Often it can be helpful simply to produce a first working draft to see what ideas you have, and not stop to sort or arrange the ideas into a specific form; this comes later when you can see what is there and begin to make sense of it, rather like emptying the contents of a box onto a table to see what you have and wish to keep.

The processes of planning, composing and editing and revising

Planning, composing and editing and revising are all elements of writing a text. Planning means thinking about what you wish to write and how to write it; composing is the act of writing; and editing and revising is the process of making changes to your text in light of your critical evaluation of your reading of it. This process itself is a form of self-reflective enquiry in action, where reflecting on and evaluating the quality of the writing you have composed leads to a revision of the original and to further cycles of re-writing where you re-plan and re-compose.

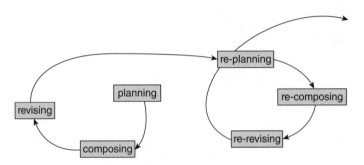

Figure 5.2 Ongoing cycles of re-writing

General advice would be to aim to write a rough first draft to get an overall shape of the text. You can do light editing as you go; this can include moving pieces of text around and paying attention to the sound patterns of the words, sentences and paragraphs. There is no one way of doing this: each person finds their own way. This reinforces the need to have faith in your own process of becoming a writer.

Willem Louw is a clinical psychologist living and working in New Zealand, where he works with a specialist Māori mental health team as well as in private practice. I was external examiner for his PhD thesis (Louw, 2011). In response to my questions about the issues in this book, he wrote:

The first draft of my thesis was a 50-page personal narrative where I wrote about events and insights that were emotionally meaningful for me. It read like a short story and contained no quotations, no academic language at all. It was writing from the heart only. I needed to do this first, as I had terrible doubts about my ability to write academically and hit writers' block usually after the second sentence. This was my own solution to just making a start and keeping at it. (Louw, 2013: personal correspondence)

Think like a designer

Deliberately learn to think like a designer. This can be difficult for those prac-titioner-researcher-writers who prefer to stick with their professional identity as an engineer or plumber. It can take intellectual energy to make the mental switch to thinking of oneself as a writer and then a designer. Yet writing is about creating text and involves design thinking. This often takes the form of an action enquiry that can use visual methods such as symbols and flow dia-grams, as in, for example, Figure 5.2. It reinforces the idea that the words 'action research' refer to a creative way of thinking and designing in action domains, as when taking action in the social world and in the literary world.

Now think about Sharples' (1999) ideas about content spaces and rhetorical spaces.

Content spaces and rhetorical spaces

In Chapter 3 we said that when you write you create different kinds of conceptual spaces and link them where possible: this is when you think about ideas. Now think about rhetorical space (how you write) to reflect on your content space (what you write): this is when you think about how best to communicate your ideas to others. This can lead to what Schön and Rein (1994) refer to as a process of refram-ing: you begin with an idea but reframe it in light of a more fully developed idea.

John Elliott is Emeritus Professor of Education at the University of East Anglia. In a 2013 text, he speaks of a project by Hogan (2010) that revealed the need to provide teachers with 'diagnostic and action-hypotheses' to reframe:

... to examine, test, refine and further develop in relation to their own pedagogi-cal practices. Hence, it was hoped that other teachers might avoid constantly 'reinventing the wheel', while having space for exercising personal judgments in an on-going process of collaborative professional knowledge construction.

Speaking of action research as 'work of the spirit', Elliott says:

This kind of knowledge base may seem terribly mundane and ordinary to repre-sent it as the work of the spirit, but this under-estimates the 'heartwork' involved in over-coming prejudices and pre-dispositions to achieve the levels of self-understanding it represents. Such an achievement depended on a shared com-mitment to an educational aim and a willingness to acknowledge that many of the prejudices and pre-dispositions that hinder its realisation in practice are held in common. The work of the spirit in teaching depends on the formation of com-munities of practice. Its major enemy is the culture of individualism that still shapes teaching and learning in many school systems and in doing so distorts the development of 'educational practice'. (Elliott, 2013: 15)

The 'other' is a key figure in doing and writing action research and requires specific commitments from you as researcher-writer. In practice contexts such as clinical or industrial settings we judge the quality of what we are doing in relation to whether we can show the realisation of personal values for the benefit of the other: for example, as a nurse you judge the quality of your practice in relation to whether you feel you are contributing to patients' flourishing.

Jonathan Vincent, who is studying for his PhD, has worked in a range of educational settings, including special needs and mainstream secondary, and now works as a lecturer in education studies at York St John University. In his abstract for the 2014 Value and Virtue in Practice-Based Research conference at York St John University, Jonathan speaks about his commitments to university students with autism. He writes:

The medical definition of autism describes it as a spectrum of 'impairments' (Wing, 1996) and characterises it broadly as a social and communication disorder. Rather than physical or cognitive, the challenges that university students on the autistic spectrum tend to face are those of a social and emotional nature and for this reason autism has been termed an 'invisible' disability (Rose, 2005). Historically, Higher Education students with disabilities and particularly those on the autistic spectrum have been under-represented in terms of student voice (Hendrickx and Martin, 2011), compared with their neurotypical peers.

I am involved in the Stratus Writing Project, a participatory project that seeks to serve as a platform for autistic students to tell their valuable insider stories about student experience at university and beyond. My paper details the participatory process that has taken place over the course of the last 18 months and outlines some of the key findings from the project, as analysed by the students themselves. In an effort to be true to the principles of emancipatory research, it is envisaged that one or more undergraduate students will participate in the delivery of the paper as co-researchers. (Vincent, 2014: 1)

Through encouraging students to write for publication, Jonathan shows how he enables them to realise their capacity for independent living and thinking by writing their own narratives.

Similarly, Odd Edvardsen from UiT, the Arctic University writes about how he helps others to help themselves, specifically while working as a member of the Trauma Foundation Care team, a Norwegian-funded NGO working in post-conflict countries, including Iraq, Lebanon, Laos, Cambodia and Vietnam (see http://traumacare.no: see also Edvardsen, 2006). In an account in McNiff (2013a: 197–9) he explains how he and colleagues help citizens in landmine-infested areas to learn how to deal with injuries without the assistance of often-unavailable expert medical expertise.

You have a strong responsibility to your reader as follows.

Demonstrating authorial responsibility

As an author you have responsibility towards your reader. Your reader knows only what they read on the page and what you choose to tell them. This has specific implications for what and how you write.

Maria James, introduced on page 51, writes in response to questions about the need to write for a reader:

Through writing my doctoral thesis, it emerged that I sometimes fail to write for my audience. While I am considered an articulate oral communicator, apparently I do not always communicate on paper with the same clarity. I expect others to be on my wavelength and I find it hard 'to stand away' from the text. Often, the page has served as an inhibitor to expression and yet at the same time I work out much of my thinking as I write. Perhaps it is when I use writing in this cathartic way that the problem becomes exacerbated, for I am not always certain what may emerge. (Personal correspondence, 2014)

Demonstrating linguistic responsibility

Your use of language reveals how you position yourself in relation with your reader. You can easily communicate a sense of the rightness of your opinion through the fact that you write in a particular authorial voice, through, for example, the subtle introduction of values-laden terminology. Clark and Ivanič (1997) show how the manipulation of simple lexical items can prejudice a reader's perceptions: commenting on extracts from a newspaper, they compare the terminology of specific items, such as 'our boys' are 'dare-devils, brave and loyal' whereas 'their boys' are 'cannon-fodder, fanatical and blindly obedient' (p. 30).

Experienced examiners and reviewers are seldom taken in by these strategies. They look for a critical perspective from authors, and the author's own capacity to reflect on their writing style and possible prejudicial use of language (see also pages 137–8).

Demonstrating communicative responsibility

It is your responsibility to explain things to your reader and not expect them to work things out for themselves. If you use a specialised word that your reader may not know, explain it. Provide signposts in the form of section headings; write clearly; design the layout of your text so there is a lot of white space that enables your reader to read easily and fluently. These matters are all under your control, and show you as a responsible writer and a successful communicator.

Demonstrating epistemic responsibility

Code (1987) speaks about the need for epistemic responsibility. It is the responsibility of all, especially those who are publicly positioned as intellectuals, to use their knowledge wisely and in the services of the truth; unlike Heidegger, who used his intellectual powers in the services of the Nazi regime (Lilla, 2001). This has special implications for you and your relationship with the world: when you become critical you do not give in to persuasive subtleties. Chomsky comments:

Journalists generally have professional integrity. Typically they are honest, serious professionals who want to do their job properly. None of that changes the fact that most of them reflexively perceive the world through a particular prism that happens to be supportive of concentrated power. (Chomsky, 2005: 150)

Learn to see the prism: learn to think for yourself.

You in relationship with the world

The responsibility of writers hinges around this capacity to interrogate whatever is supportive of concentrated power. In Chapter 3 we spoke about the need for critical reflection on the stories we tell and are told, as do Foucault, Orwell, Said, Zinn and others. They make the point that it is not only about challenging what is written in texts and the production of texts, but what systems of power are in place to control what counts as a text, who says, and how the system continues to remain in power.

This has special relevance to people like you who write academic texts because you are positioned, rightly so, as an intellectual, someone who can think for themselves. Dragons lurk here, because, as Orwell points out:

If you had the kind of brain that could understand the poems of T.S. Eliot or the theories of Karl Marx, the higher-ups would see to it that you were kept out of any important job. (Orwell, 2004: 39)

For Said, this moves to the heart of the matter: 'In effect I am asking the basic question for the intellectual: how does one speak the truth? What truth? For whom and where?' (Said, 1994: 65).

This book is about how you can exercise your educational influence in the thinking of those who are also subject to the power of institutionalised systems that refuse you entry to the club. There are dangers also if you are admitted to the club, because, instead of beating the system so that you are admitted to the club, you may find that the system beats you. Clark and Ivanič (1997) explain how schools 'co-opt children into dominant values and contribute towards their socialization into the dominant ideology' (p. 50). They cite the work of Kress who comments on how children are taught to write in specific writing styles:

The learning of the genres involves an increasing loss of creativity on the child's part, and a subordination of the child's creative abilities to the demands of the norms of the genre. The child learns to control the genre, but in the process the genre comes to control the child. Given the cognitive and social implications of these generic forms, the consequences for the child are immense. (Kress, 1982: 11)

The task of the intellectual therefore demands that they write in such a way that they communicate what is important in human living and show how this is commensurable with their own values of personal and intellectual freedom and social integrity. 'The intellectual does not represent a statue-like icon', says Said, 'but an individual vocation, an energy, a stubborn force engaging as a committed and recognizable voice in language and in society with a whole slew of issues, all of them having to do in the end with a combination of enlightenment and emancipation or freedom' (1994: 55). He goes on to point out that:

The particular threat to the intellectual today ... is not the academy, nor the suburbs, nor the appalling commercialism of journalism and publishing houses, but rather an attitude that I will call professionalism. By professionalism I mean thinking of your work as an intellectual as something you do for a living, between the hours of nine to five with one eye on the clock, and another cocked at what is considered to be proper, professional behavior – not rocking the boat, not straying outside the accepted paradigms or limits, making yourself marketable and above all presentable, hence uncontroversial and unpolitical and 'objective'. (Said, 1994: 55)

Nor, in my view, does this mean presenting yourself as 'a radical' or 'alternative' or 'cool' by wearing a certain hairstyle or speaking in a certain way, but of writing from the heart, with sincerity. You do this from the narrow political perspective of getting the PhD, getting your work recognised and accepted by elite journals on its own merits, within a broader perspective of the Political, to influence processes of change such that you enable others to see what is being done to them, or they are doing to themselves, in the name of freedom. You encourage them to challenge dishonesty, to exercise their 'terrible honesty' (see page 51).

Learning to become a writer means having faith in the works of words: 'What is above all needed is to let the meaning choose the word, and not the other way about', says Orwell (2004: 118). It means having faith in yourself so that you use your words to produce texts that will challenge existing systems of power that aim to confuse and subdue, and exercise your best efforts so you will be able to speak for yourself in spite of constraints, and not be silenced.

What, then, do you need to do to develop yourself as a writer?

What Do You Need to Do to Develop Yourself as a Writer?

Here are some of the most important aspects to consider before you commit to the challenge of speaking your truth in a corporatised higher education world that largely does not want to listen. You need to:

- research your practice as a writer;
- learn your craft: work at it;
- learn through reading;
- become cosmopolitan;
- be self-critical and aware of your own positioning; and
- have faith in yourself and find opportunities to engage.

Research your practice as a writer

The New Testament verse says: 'Be ready always to give an answer to every man who asketh you a reason for the hope that is in you, with meekness and fear' (Holy Bible, 1 Peter 3: 15). Similar sentiments may be found in other Holy Books, all calling for acceptance of responsibility for hope.

Responsibility for hope comes from researching your practices and offering an account of what you are doing and why you are doing it. You ask, 'How do I improve what I am doing?' and give reasons why you wish to improve it. You gather data and generate evidence to show that you have improved it, and you test the validity of your conclusions against the critique of others.

Learn your craft: work at it

You cannot hurry the business of learning to write. You can write at speed but you cannot rush it, so learn to have confidence in the wait. Supervisors need to be aware as well as candidates: it sometimes takes a long time for ideas to emerge. Sometimes mimesis helps: we copy others' works, not in the sense that we steal their work but that we study their techniques, their use of language, and adapt it to our own. This means first becoming an apprentice and learning from others: Sennett (2009) says that an apprentice would become a 'journeyman', travelling often for years to learn their craft in the workshops of others. Writers do this: your entire life as a writer becomes one of learning from others and your own experience, and putting what you have learned into practice:

The most important advice I or anyone can give you about how to write is to start writing. Writing itself is its own best teacher. You can never learn to write by thinking about writing; you have to *write*. (Page, 1998: 32, italics in original)

Learn through reading and talking

Meet people in books and seminars and lecture halls. Go to conferences: many researchers go to conferences simply to present papers, not to confer. It is important to talk with people, see how they see things and learn from their experiences. Books and journals are not static entities: they contain other people's work with words. Go to museums and galleries where sculptures and artefacts represent other thinkers' ideas, and think with them as you look at their work. Look at this lovely description of a library, by al-Takriti:

Instead of seeing the usual information-packed inanimate objects lying on shelves, I suddenly envisioned a cacophony of passionate debates, insults, romances, genocide defenses, patriarchy justifications, and all the other phenomena one might find in a vessel filled with millions of texts in hundreds of languages. ... the books ... harangued me in shelving blocs – fiery Albanian nationalists here, pious Hanafi jurisprudents two rows across, followed by stern Ottoman apologists and whispering Sufi sensualists. I pondered what the complete absence of such books would mean. At least the cacophony would end, I figured – but what then? (al-Takriti, 2010: 93)

al-Takriti goes on to say that this musing helped him to appreciate what written texts meant to humankind. 'Without such texts,' he says, 'there are no recorded debates' (p. 94). With texts, libraries act as repositories of ideas and librarians become curators of knowledge.

Become cosmopolitan

Don't stay at home: travel and take your notebook with you. Record ideas as you walk around cities; read the *Rough Guide* or *Lonely Planet* guides. Read Theroux's (2012) *The Tao of Travel*: he says that when we travel we discover ourselves as much as others. Walking a city becomes a case of putting yourself in the shoes of others as they live in it. We encounter the other on their own terms; we become cosmopolitan. Hannerz (1990) defines cosmopolitanism as 'a stance towards diversity itself, towards a co-existence of cultures in the individual experience', which is 'related to considerations of the self as well. Cosmopolitanism often has a narcissistic streak: the self is constructed in the space where cultures mirror one another' (pp. 239–40).' I like this idea: in a 2013 article I wrote:

It is this idea of 'consideration and construction of the self' that is the main theme of this paper, because developing a cosmopolitan mindset involves not simply learning to get on with the locals at a surface level (observing national days, particular forms of greeting and eating together), though this is an obvious starting point, but actually committing to a deep level respect for the traditions and values of others and internalising the insights. This means not simply taking the insights out of the suitcase when one is a guest in the other's place but actually carrying the insights into one's life, regardless of time and place. It means becoming a different person in the world, becoming comfortable with trying to see things through other people's eyes, while maintaining one's own sense of judgement around what it means to be a person who shares the world with others. It means bearing in mind the comment made by John Hume, when he was leader of the SDLP at the beginning of the peace process in Northern Ireland, that decommissioning begins in the mind, not in the laying down of arms. In the practical philosophical terms of thinkers such as Bohm (1996), Buber (2002) and Macmurray (1961), it means developing a dialogical attitude, that is, an openness to the other and a willingness to listen and learn, and use the learning to inform one's own judgement about what is right and wrong. (McNiff, 2013b: 502)

Your text becomes a travel guide as you construct your invisible city (Calvino, 1974) and take others on a walking tour of it. It becomes an interactive map.

Be self-critical and aware of your own positioning

I learned to challenge my own learned racism through choosing to work in South Africa. It was horribly uncomfortable at times, but the learning lasted for life. I deliberately made myself different. We need to put ourselves in places where we would rather not go, which can be disorienting. A colleague commented once of his experience of our group work: 'This is like escaping to where I can't find the place to escape to.' You deliberately disorient yourself: you become a stranger to yourself. Levinas (1998) says that in trying to understand others we strip away our reservations towards the other: 'saying' becomes 'wholly sign, signifying itself' (Levinas, 1998, cited in Todd, 2003: 108). We actively create our identities in relation to the other: 'Responsibility for the other is the very structure of subjectivity', says Todd, 2003: 109). We look in the mirror and see a different person from the one who looked back yesterday. But you don't live in yesterday: today is today, and there is a lot of learning to do. Have faith in yourself, trust in the process and do it.

SUMMARY

This chapter has offered ideas about what it takes to become a writer. Developing a writer identity is about having faith in your different relationships: with yourself, your text, your reader and the world. It emphasises that writing is a craft that needs to be learnt and practised using different strategies. It also emphasises the need to be critically aware of your reasons and purposes for wishing to develop your writing practices.

REFLECTIVE QUESTIONS

- How do you see yourself as a writer? Do you see the importance of writing as a reader for a reader?

- Do you remain aware of your different responsibilities as a writer? Do you demonstrate these responsibilities through your text, and explain to your reader that you are doing so?

- Do you see the need to research your writing practices, the same as you research your social practices? Do you see how you can adopt an action research approach to writing as a practice?

- Why is it important to read and talk with others, to become cosmopolitan in thought and deed, and to be self-critical and aware of your own positioning?

RESEARCH EXERCISE

Write a short piece to explain how you are researching your practice as a writer using an action research methodology. Explain how this may help you improve your writing knowledge and skills. Be vigilant with ideas about the need for self-critique and awareness of your positioning as a researcher in practical and writing contexts.

Chapter 6 explores these issues in more detail.

SIX

Writing a Good Quality Text

This chapter sets out what is involved in writing a good quality text. The research focus shifts from ***doing*** to ***writing*** action research, from talking about the signified to the signifier, from what is being written to the process of writing itself. The question still takes the form, 'How do I improve what I am doing?' but now asks, 'How do I write a text that readers will want to read? How will readers appreciate its quality? How do I communicate the originality, rigour, significance and potential influence of my research?' Achieving this means knowing how to produce a good quality text and then evaluating and ensuring its quality in relation to appropriate standards of judgement.

The chapter addresses these issues:

1. What are the criteria/features of good quality action research writing?
2. How do you produce a good quality text in order to achieve the criteria?
3. How is the quality of the text judged?

These issues are especially significant in light of the fact that you are writing and submitting an action research text for legitimation in a higher degree setting and thus placing it in the public domain: your text fulfils Stenhouse's (1983) idea that 'research is a systematic process of enquiry made public' and, from an action research perspective, the extended idea that it is about improving practice with social intent (McNiff, 2002). This can be a tricky business because, as noted throughout, traditional academic writing operates a strict gatekeeping practice to ensure that its traditions are protected. Also, your text will belong to your readers more than to you, and they will make judgements about its quality in terms of their own criteria and standards of judgement. You therefore need to know what readers are looking for, and give it to them while maintaining the integrity of your own ideas, scholarship and research. You need to produce an action research text that will qualify both as a good quality text as well as a text for academic legitimation.

What are the Criteria and Features of a Good Quality Action Research Text?

Here are some criteria that readers look for in any text.

General criteria

- Is the work readable?
- Is it well structured?
- Does it speak to my experience?
- Is it fiction or fact? How can I tell?
- Is it interesting?
- Does it hold my attention?
- Is the form of language appropriate?
- Do I feel inspired after reading it?

Academic readers are looking for the same things, and more. They are hoping to see that the work fulfils the following academic criteria.

Academic criteria

The work:

- contains a claim to knowledge and makes a contribution to knowledge of the field;
- demonstrates critical, original and balanced engagement;
- demonstrates and explains the impact of the research;
- shows understanding of the research context;
- shows improvement in the practice described, and if not, explains why not;
- is written in an appropriate form;
- contains material of peer-reviewed publishable merit; and
- is error-free and technically accurate with a full bibliography and references.

These are matters of competence in knowledge of content, process and communicability. The criteria of comprehensibility, authenticity, truthfulness and appropriateness, developed by Habermas (1976) for judging communicability, are especially helpful and look like this:

a. **Comprehensibility**: is there clarity in expression, structure of the text, and use of language?
b. **Authenticity:** does the author tell a story that shows over time and through interaction how they have established their authenticity in showing a commitment to live the values they explicitly espouse?
c. **Truthfulness**: are the research claims justified, to show that this is a true story and not a work of fiction?

d. **Appropriateness**: does the author show awareness of the values base and biases of the normative background, especially how cultural and historical forces have contributed to the present context?

Look at what is involved.

a. Comprehensibility

Making something comprehensible involves several practices, most importantly remembering that you are writing for a specific market. This means using a form of language that will appeal to that market and structuring the text so the meanings are clear. Clark and Ivanič (1997) emphasise that texts are always produced within a social culture, which is made up of people who are themselves constituted by their historical, political and other social traditions. A text is never context-free. It is a story within other stories, and, as Loy (2010) notes, there is no meta-text, no big story that contains other stories. You therefore need to make sure you know who your reader is, and write for them.

 This means being aware of your own writing habits and how you construct your text. As noted in Chapter 5, in your first drafts, perhaps you write more for yourself as you work out ideas (you write a writerly text), but ultimately you have to write for a reader (a readerly text). Readers will confer validity on your claims and legitimacy on the text, so get them on your side by writing in a way that respects their own knowledge and form of language. Readers in general look for writing they can enjoy and that speaks to their experience. Therefore the form of expression, use of language, structure of the report, and presentation of the text all need to be clear. This involves developing a writer's identity and practising the skill of writing and committing to sustained work (Chapter 7).

 Here are some key aspects involved in achieving clarity of expression, clear structure, and fluent presentation of the text.

Clarity of expression Be aware of the language you are using, and speak directly to the reader's experience. Many people think that an academic report needs to be written in 'Sunday best' language, which is not necessarily the case. Everyday language is fine for an academic text. This does not mean triviliasing the language or the ideas; it means speaking directly, with minimal fuss, aware that you are speaking to an educated reader who knows the field and who wants to hear what you have learned. They want to hear you speaking about your particular contribution and explaining the significance of it for different constituencies. It is your responsibility to tell them, clearly and to the point.

 Writing an academic text means using a form of language appropriate for an academic reader. They would expect to see your use of professional terminology, and engagement with scholarly debates. This can have implications for some researchers who need to switch language codes for different places, such as changing a workplace dialect for an academic dialect. You leave your language of primary schooling or direct selling in the school or sales workplace and engage more in theoretical debates about the nature of pedagogies (Pollard and Tann, 2013) or direct selling (McDonnell and McNiff, 2014). It is your responsibility to learn the received dialect; in a university context, this is an academic dialect.

Minimalist form Speaking directly involves a minimalist form of language, which means writing in a plain, uncluttered way. Avoid using words such as 'highly' or 'extremely', unless you are using them to make a point, and take out every 'very'. Avoid hyperbole, the kind of exaggeration that invites exclamation marks. Do not write 'It was fantastic!!!' or 'This was the best thing ever!'.

Do not use two words when one will do. In 'This was a very beautiful and pleasant house,' take out 'very' and choose between 'beautiful' and 'pleasant'. 'This was a beautiful house' says what you mean in a way that does not overburden the reader. Your reader has limited concentration span and patience, so do not smother them with words (in the sentence you have just read I took out the initial 'Bear in mind that ...'). Be ruthless in editing. If a word does not earn its keep, it has to go.

Avoid expressions that say you know it all. Avoid 'surely' and 'obviously'. What is obvious to you may not be obvious to anyone else. Avoid self-congratulatory comments: 'I believe I am demonstrating something that no one else has thought of before ...' Yes, perhaps so, but your reader will not warm to you. Avoid rhetorical questions: 'So how is this to be demonstrated?' They tend to frustrate even the most patient reader, who wants to hear your ideas, not answer empty questions.

In brief, avoid preciousness, which can be distracting and irritating. Go for a plain, simple style, written with authority and discipline.

Orwell drew up a list of dos and don'ts:

- Never use a metaphor, simile or other figure of speech which you are used to seeing in print.
- Never use a long word where a short one will do.
- If it is possible to cut a word out, always cut it out.
- Never use the passive where you can use the active.
- Never use a foreign phrase, a scientific word or a jargon word if you can think of an everyday English equivalent.
- Break any of these rules sooner than say anything outright barbarous (Orwell, 2004: 119).

Clarity of structure Derrida spoke of a text as a 'heterogeneous, differential and open field of forces' (Derrida, 1986; cited in Deutscher, 2005: 33). Achieving clarity of structure means organising your material so that your reader can easily find their way through this open field of forces. You can achieve clear organisation by structuring your text through pedagogical and textual devices, such as the following.

Signposts Signposts usually take the form of headings and sub-headings. Editors talk about 'A', 'B' and 'C' headings to denote sections and sub-sections of the text. These are usually given different weights and fonts, and use devices such as capitals, bold and italics, like this:

THIS IS AN 'A' HEADING

This is a 'B' heading

This is a 'C' heading

If you use a software programme such as Word, your headings may already be built into the programme. It is up to you to choose a headings system, but once you have chosen it, stick with it so as not to confuse your reader.

You can use other devices such as boxes or shading, margin notes and visuals. Keep it simple. Signposts provide a means of navigating the text, so avoid using a system that is so complex that the reader needs a codebook to work out what the signposts mean. Learn that you use a table when communicating data in a verbal form, and a figure to communicate in a more pictorial form; and learn how to label tables and figures according to the chapter they are in – Chapter 3 would have 'Figure 3.1' and Chapter 8 would have 'Table 8.2'. Learn also that 'Table' goes above the box and 'Figure' goes below it.

Advance organisers These are devices that orient the reader by giving an advance summary of the text, its key features and significance, and anything special to watch out for: these are rhetorical and pedagogical devices. Advance organisers are often matched by end-of-text summaries. The reader should be able to read the advance and post summaries, and see immediately what the text is about. Using these devices means: 'Tell them what you are going to do, do it, and then tell them what you have done'. Remember that you are writing a pedagogical text, so it is your responsibility to walk with your reader through the text, not expect them to walk with you, and not let them get lost.

Correct grammar

Correct grammar involves correct spelling, punctuation, sentence construction, paragraphing, and use of words. Many books are available to help. You should invest in a good dictionary and thesaurus. You can find a lot of information on the Internet, such as the difference between 'each other' (two people), and 'one another' (more than two people). Develop an ear for the sound of sentences to get a sense of sound patterns and rhythms; you can do this by listening to someone reading aloud, or reading aloud yourself.

Study the literature to see which publications use single or double inverted commas. Watch how writers use sentences to communicate one idea at a time, and build these sentences into separate paragraphs to communicate sets of ideas. See how they develop an argument through the skilful use of text. If you find it difficult to use correct grammar, do your homework and find ways of improving (see the academic criterion about error-free and technically accurate presentation). If you lack confidence around these issues, perhaps because you are dyslexic or if English is not your first language, find expert help through a professional copyeditor or first language speaker. Remember that it is not the responsibility of your supervisor to correct your language. You have chosen to do this programme of study, so it is your responsibility to find expert help where necessary. Experts usually charge for their services, so it is a matter of what you are prepared to do to achieve your degree. (But watch out for plagiarism, or getting someone else to do your work for you – see Chapter 7 for advice.)

Avoid repetition

Often in a text, less is more: under-statement can be better than over-statement, especially in academic texts. Say what you have to say once, and leave it at that. Avoid repeating favourite quotations. Keep a list of quotations in your notebook and tick them off once you have used them. It is easy to forget which ones you have used in a lengthy text, so be systematic. Also, avoid repeating favourite individual or strings of words, such as 'it would appear that ...' or 'this is arguably the best ...'

These are a few techniques from a vast repertoire of writing skills that make a text comprehensible to the reader. Repeat: the best way is to practise the skill of writing. This involves reading the work of successful people in the field for rhetorical skill and technique as well as content, noting what they do (and do not do), and following their lead while developing your own style (but do not copy their words or work).

Here is a second criterion for effective communication.

b. Authenticity

This criterion refers to your capacity to tell a story that shows over time and through interaction how you are genuinely committed to living as fully as you can the values you claim to believe in. Authenticity refers to the idea of commitment, that your judgement is sound and consistent and that you maintain the integrity of your values towards the other's well-being, in this case, your reader. Through what you write and how you write it, you can show that you are genuine – someone who does what they say they are going to do. This can be difficult, because the only thing your reader knows about you is what they read about you, so you need to reassure them that they can believe what you say through your form of writing and presentation. Specifically, people need to know that you can be trusted in your actions, research and scholarship, as follows.

Can your actions be trusted? Explain how you can be trusted in terms of your actions, how you did what you did with good intent and with the motivation of contributing to other people's flourishing. This means you would spell out your values near the beginning of your story, and show how, over time, you did your best to live them in practice. You talk about your commitments, and you also show them in action.

Julie Pearson, a senior lecturer in Physical Education at St Mary's University, Twickenham, writes about the turn in her understanding of the focus of her research, from self to other. She writes:

My research story explains how I have moved from looking inwards to my self while trying to realise my professional values about education, teaching and learning and Physical Education, to interrogating those professional values so that I began to look outwards and think in terms of the social good rather than the personal good. (Pearson, 2014)

Can your research be trusted? Show that you can be trusted in terms of your research and capacity for methodological rigour. This involves giving explanations for your actions, and producing a strong evidence base to back up your claims. It involves showing how you gathered data, tested it rigorously, linked it with your research question and aims, and analysed it in a disciplined way. You need especially to engage with disconfirming data, which told you things you did not want to know, and explain how you took action accordingly. Explain how you searched your data for key pieces that you could turn into evidence. When you make your claim to knowledge, you need to justify it and not expect people simply to believe that it happened as you say it did.

Can your scholarship be trusted? Show that you can be trusted in your scholarship. Honour all academic conventions, and put your references in good order. When you cite a person's name, make sure it is relevant to its context, and is not simply decorative. Also show that you have read the work in question. Remember Michael Bassey's (1999) point about avoiding 'kingmaking', 'genuflecting' and 'sandbagging'. It is easy to pretend that you have read widely by picking up names and giving summaries you have read elsewhere. Some readers may be fooled some of the time, but over the length of a work, an experienced reader will pick up whether or not the researcher has actually read those works. If you refer to Foucault, remember that your examiner may be an expert on Foucault's work, and may wish to have a detailed discussion with you about a specific aspect.

Aim to show your authenticity through your writing. Do you write with passion and conviction, with the authority of your own experience? Do your words ring true? Do you show that you are confident in your ideas, or do you cover up by waffling? It is of course possible to mislead people through skilful technique. Groucho Marx (some say it was George Burns, others Sam Goldwyn) was famous for saying that once you can fake sincerity you've got it made. Remember that your reader is experienced and has developed an ear for a text, in the same way as a wine taster develops a nose, so they will raise questions about any writing they do not consider authentic.

Now think about how you show that you are telling the truth.

c. Truthfulness

Claims to knowledge are also called 'truth claims', so your report needs to show that you are telling the truth about what happened. This is especially relevant to data gathering and analysis, and the production of evidence to test your claims to knowledge.

The processes of establishing the validity of a truth claim are as follows:

- The claim is grounded in a question identified at the beginning of the research. This is usually about how you can live your values more fully in practice, such as 'How do I help unemployed people to get a job? By so doing, how do I realise my values of freedom on behalf of the other?'
- You explain why the question is important.
- You monitor the action and gather data to show the research context, especially about how freedom is or is not being practised. You keep your data in your data archive.
- You try out new freedom-oriented practices, and gather more data to show yourself and others in action. You help long-term unemployed people to develop their technology skills so they can find new employment.
- You ask critical friends and validation groups to scrutinise your data in relation to your research question. All offer critical feedback. You try to get triangulation, comments from at least three different points of view.
- You check the relevance of the data against your original values. They enable you to select pieces of data that show how the research question is being addressed.
- You identify those data that can now stand as evidence. Again you subject this evidence to the scrutiny of critical friends and validation groups. If they agree that the evidence is relevant and meaningful, you can use the evidence base to test the validity of the emerging claims. So validation meetings comprise several processes, including: (a) listening to the research account; (b) scrutinising methodological issues including gathering and analysis of the data; and (c) agreeing (or not) the validity of the knowledge claim.
- You explain the significance of your research for educational influences in learning.

Processes such as these demonstrate the methodological rigour of the research. It is a question of establishing the validity of the claim to knowledge through establishing the validity of the evidence base.

These processes apply to multimedia representations, the same as linguistic ones. A visual narrative would have to demonstrate validation procedures. Examples are available to show good quality writing that includes video-data. Most multimedia work uses video-data to create an evidence base (for example, Yee, 2012), and new work is emerging where a complete thesis can take multimedia form (O'Neill 2008, accessible at www.ictaspoliticalaction.com).

Joseph M. Shosh chairs the Education Department at Moravian College in Bethlehem, Pennsylvania, where he teachers literacy education and teacher action research. He is an initiator of the Action Research Network of the Americas. He writes:

> Moravian College's action-research graduate program for practicing teachers requires degree candidates to engage in writing to learn opportunities about their professional practice. Teachers develop an ontological and epistemological stance from which they engage in multiple cycles of inquiry, documented within a Google Docs field log, including participant observation journal entries, syntheses of interview and survey data, and critiques of student work. Reflective, analytic, and methodological memos penned throughout the research process undergird the coding of data and development of theme statements. The master's theses written by the program's 175 graduates are available for review and download at http://home.moravian.edu/public/educ/eddept/mEd/thesis.htm (Shosh, 2014).

Establishing the truthfulness of a claim within an academic context involves testing it against the literature. Key writers come to act as virtual critical friends (real if you contact them). Engaging with the literatures lends credibility and authority to the report, and strengthens your credentials as a researcher.

d. Appropriateness

Appropriateness refers to your awareness that you and your situation are influenced by values, including those that contextualise current economic, political and social situations.

It is essential to talk about your values, which ground and drive your research. Sometimes people are not aware of their values, or even that they have values. Some people think that values refer only to socially acceptable ones, but cruelty is as strong a value as kindness, and the desire for power can be stronger than a love of peace. Try writing down the values that inspire your life, or talk with a critical friend about why you do the work you do, and what is rewarding about it.

> Pip Bruce Ferguson has worked as a staff developer for many years. She has a particular interest in action research and collaborative writing. A New Zealander, she is currently working in staff development at Dublin City University. She outlines some of the dilemmas of introducing new assessment procedures (the Performance-Based Research Fund: PBRF) that require participants to make their achievements public into an institutional culture that disapproves of the practice. She writes:
>
> *(Continued)*

(Continued)

The Wānanga (a Māori tertiary learning institution) had been established as a pan-tribal, multicultural institution, but one that was based on sound Māori values and processes. Our staff and student cohorts were welcoming to all who wished to join in the work, so my appointment as Research Manager, given that I am not Māori, attracted little negative comment. ...

The PBRF raised issues that needed careful consideration. There is a Māori proverb that translates, 'The kumara [a sweet potato] does not speak of its own sweetness', and this is deemed to mean that one does not praise one's own work. But to achieve the highest scores in the PBRF, researchers had to engage in a blatant self-promotion process, claiming ownership of work at the highest level possible in order to maximise personal grades, and hence payment of research funds to the institution. We knew that this would make many feel extremely uncomfortable. There is also a sense for many Māori that knowledge is not the possession of an individual, but is developed through group processes, and often is the result of work by those who have gone before, such as ancestors or elders.

Writing of the dilemmas involved, she says:

So, here's the problem. I was subsequently taken to task by my then line-manager, not the person with whom I had, in consultation with senior staff, introduced and promoted the PBRF. This manager accused me of introducing 'viruses without vaccines', in other words that I had done similar destructive work to that of British soldiers who had evidently given American Indian tribes pox-ridden blankets, resulting in the deaths of thousands. ... my 'virtuous' action in seeking to ensure that TWoA got its fair share of the research 'cake' had had negative consequences beyond what I had envisaged. (Bruce Ferguson, 2013)

Most of us experience cognitive and emotional dissonance when our values are denied in our practices (Festinger, 1957). We can use our research as a means of over-coming the contradiction. This is often the starting point of an action enquiry. You ask, 'How do I improve this situation here?', understanding that the way to improve a social situation is first to improve your own thinking and learning.

It is important to appreciate that your espoused values can also be the outcomes of persuasion, often through the media. Marlin (2002) explains how propaganda can become an art form to persuade people to believe things they actually don't believe in. The experiments of Milgram (1973) show this in practice. People tortured others, against their better judgement, because they were persuaded that they were doing the right thing. You are also subject to these forms of persuasion, through the messages you receive from the culture. You therefore need to show that you have developed your capacity for critical thinking.

This involves deconstructing what you say. What do you communicate when you refer to patients as 'them', or say, 'It's either them or us'. How do others feel when you say 'No' to their ideas; and what do you communicate when you say about people with physical impairment or learning difficulties, 'It's not their fault'. Your report will communicate, through your use of language, whether or not you live your espoused values.

These are some of the criteria that your reader is expecting from the form of language of your report. The issue now is, how do you write this kind of language?

Here are some ideas about how you can do so.

How do you Produce a Good Quality Text?

Here are some ideas about how to produce a good quality text. These include logistical issues, such as finding time and space to write, as well as editorial issues such as drafting and proofreading. Some of the most important strategies are as follows.

1. Planning, composing and revising.
2. Inviting critique.
3. Proofreading.
4. Academic conventions.
5. Engaging with the literatures.

Planning, composing and revising

It is commonly assumed that writing a text involves three phases: planning, composing and revising. Here are some ideas about what they involve.

Planning

Writing a successful text means being passionate about your topic. Organise your ideas by thinking about the issues that grip your attention. This takes discipline: it is generally easier to daydream than think constructively. If you are struggling to get the ideas right, think about them last thing at night and let your mind do the rest. In the morning the ideas will usually have sorted themselves out. Organising your ideas may take several days or weeks, but they will eventually come right if you have faith in your own capacity to make sense of your experience.

Composing

Many people mistakenly believe that their first draft is the final version. Sorry, it does not work like this. You will probably need multiple drafts before you have a final document. Even the most experienced writers need to produce multiple drafts as they are writing.

The first draft is where you work out the ideas. This will probably be a lengthy text because you may not stop to edit until later and reduce the word length. Your later drafts refine the ideas, eliminate superfluous words and get to the point. The first draft of the book you are reading was far different from its final form, and a lot of paper and ink cartridges have been recycled. Your drafts will become more focused and relevant as you engage with the advice of critical friends and with the ideas.

Revising

Revising is where you read your text with a dispassionate critical eye to see if it makes sense and reads well. If anything in your text does not make sense to you it is not going to make sense to a reader either. Make sure every sentence relates to the others, that the ideas are coherent and the argument is clearly expressed, and that words are used to their best advantage. This means you have to read it to yourself many times, and each time make sure that every word counts. Read the text out loud and listen to your voice. If anything does not ring true it is not right and you need to change it. Edit with a critical eye. This can be hard for writers who are often reluctant to throw out ideas (see Stephen King's 2012 comment that you have to 'kill your darlings'), yet it is part of the discipline of becoming a writer whose work readers will want to read. Take out all repetition, frilly words, pretentiousness, and other redundancies. Keep focused, to the point, and speak in a language that your reader will understand. You can of course experiment with different genres or style. Researchers sometimes use poetry or drama in their works, but they also make clear to the reader how these different genres should be engaged with and understood, and why they are using them.

Inviting critique

Critique is essential to sorting out your ideas. Other people's responses to your thinking and writing will help you move forward, as well as reveal flaws in your arguments or errors in your writing. Talk with your critical friends, and listen to what they have to say. If they suggest that your ideas are mistaken, don't get defensive: listen and rethink. If they point out a flaw – perhaps you have not properly tested the validity of a claim – look again and rewrite. It is better to rewrite before submitting your document when an examiner may possibly reject the work. Share your text with colleagues at intervals and ask for critical feedback, but don't expect them to respond immediately. Respect their time and commitments, as they respect yours.

Proofread to make sure that your manuscript is error-free and technically accurate. Read critically to see any errors in grammar, including spelling, punctuation and syntax, and ensure that you obey the conventions of academic scholarship. Check that your references in the text match those in the bibliography. Make sure the dates match and that you have all the names of the authors in the bibliography. Citations such as 'Brown et al.' may appear in the text, but all authors' names must be written out in full in the bibliography. Check your references against your text multiple times. This is serious. In a doctorate, the regulations of most institutions maintain that a thesis may be passed with minor modifications, but too many errors may mean that the thesis be recommended for revision. It is in your own interests to proofread thoroughly. If you cannot proofread yourself, engage the services of a professional proofreader to do it for you. Remember that their job is to work with your text as a text, not in terms of the concepts or ideas, and ensure that all the technicalities of presentation are correct, so do not expect them to comment on the quality of what you have written (though some do if you ask them).

How is the Quality of the Text Judged?

Your reader judges your text in relation to the general and academic criteria on pages 54–7, demonstrated by your communication of ideas through the use of language. If you show that you can do this, you can claim several kinds of validity for your text, including:

1. Content validity
2. Rhetorical validity
3. Ironic validity
4. Catalytic validity
5. Educational validity
6. Academic validity

Content validity

This refers to whether or not a study actually achieves what it says it will do. In the case of your text, it becomes whether the text achieves all the criteria of a good text in terms of the different issues listed below.

Rhetorical validity

The word 'rhetoric' is used in different ways, in the literatures and in this book. In Chapter 5 it referred to the devices you employ to guide your reader through the text. Here it is used in a slightly different though related sense of helping a reader to make sense of what they are reading. All texts aim to communicate messages, and they use writing techniques to do so. You do this too. You are hoping to persuade your reader that they should validate your claim to knowledge and give you your award. You are presenting your work as your best understanding, though you acknowledge that you still have much to learn.

The art of rhetoric can be both overt and subtle. It can be used in educational ways, when people are persuaded to think for themselves; and in colonising ways, when they are persuaded to do things against their better judgement. Your text aims both to persuade (it demonstrates rhetorical validity) and also to educate (it demonstrates educational validity), so you need to use language in such a way that you help others to make independent and valid judgements about their own work.

You therefore need to make explicit what you are trying to communicate, first in relation to your practice (your standards for judging the quality of your practice), for example:

- My work shows how I have enabled marginalised children to speak for themselves (Cahill, 2007).
- I have become a more reflective practitioner (Pearson, 2014).
- We have developed a community of researchers and writers (Karlsen, 2014).

You also need to set out how you have done this (your standards for judging the rhetorical validity of your text):

- I show, through the use of language, that my account is comprehensible, authentic, truthful and appropriate to its context.
- My writing demonstrates, through the use of language, my capacity to exercise my educational influence.
- I use textual devices to clarify any ambiguities in my account.

Ironic validity

This idea, made popular by Lather (1991), has been a feature of textual analysis at least since the 'linguistic turn' of the mid-twentieth century (Norris, 1989), when philosophers such as Derrida (1997) began to make clear that language was socially constructed, and used to achieve specific human interests. Foucault (1994) especially asked how it was possible for the subject [person] to tell the truth about themselves. The question arises, how is it possible to reflect on the use of language while using that form of language? Critical analysts such as Said (1991) explain how literature can communicate the norms and values of a culture so that what is said becomes taken for granted; and Wittgenstein (1953) explains how people use different 'language games', with unspoken norms. He says that most people play language games for specific purposes; Chomsky (1991) says we often do so for our own ends.

To overcome colonising practices, says Derrida (1997), it is necessary to make the familiar strange, to see things through critical eyes. This means putting yourself in the other's shoes, and recognising yourself potentially as Other to the other (Buber, 2002; Ricoeur, 1992). In terms of your text, it means putting yourself in the shoes of your reader. Your reader is looking for your awareness of how you may be communicating normative assumptions, your capacity to deconstruct your own thinking, and your explanations for how you are doing it.

You therefore need to explain how you have done this (your standards for judging the ironic validity of your text), for example:

- At this point in my narrative I step back and comment on how I have spoken about my practice.
- When I speak about my management practices, I clarify my understanding of management as involving collaborative working practices.
- While I am maintaining that my claim to have improved my practice is justified, I am aware of the need to produce authenticated evidence to test the validity of my claim, and to show how I have subjected it to rigorous critique, on the assumption that I may be mistaken.

This also is an example of your capacity for demonstrating rhetorical validity.

Catalytic validity

Catalytic validity (Lather, 1991) is about how you can re-orient and refocus your research so that you can understand reality in order to transform it, a process Freire (1970) termed conscientization. Catalytic validity involves both a recognition of the reality-changing influence of the research process, as well as consciously channelling this influence so that participants gain self-understanding and self-determination through their involvement.

Educational validity

'Educational' in this book means a practice that aims to encourage others to think for themselves, and make wise choices about how they should act. This means using language in a transparent way and setting out explicitly what you think is the significance of your work, and the significance of your capacity to communicate it. Doing this is not arrogance, but a sign of how you hold yourself accountable for judging your capacity for educational validity.

Explain how you have done this (your standards for judging the educational validity of your text), for example:

- I have used a form of language that encourages people to be critical.
- I have shown through my text how I have communicated my capacity for critical deconstruction.
- I have used a self-reflective form of language in my report.

These issues emphasise key themes: the tentative nature of knowledge claims; the need to test them to establish their validity; the need for reflexive and dialectical critique (Winter, 1989), which informs the ironic validity of your text. Your reader is hoping throughout to read a mature, self-reflexive account that demonstrates your capacity to engage thoughtfully and energetically with your own thinking, and show how this has enabled you to become more critical and considerate in your practice.

SUMMARY

This chapter has considered some of the technicalities of writing as a means of communication. It has looked at how the generalist and academic criteria of good quality writing can be achieved to ensure the comprehensibility, authenticity, truthfulness and appropriateness of a text. Attending to these kinds of practical issues can contribute to ensuring the quality of a text in terms of its originality, significance, rigour and effect on other people's thinking and practices.

REFLECTIVE QUESTIONS

Here are some reminders of the main ways in which you can make your text accessible to your reader.

- Is your text comprehensible? Do you take care in clarity of expression and use a minimalist form? Is the structure clear? Do you provide signposts and navigational devices? Do you use correct grammar and avoid repetition?

- Do you come across as authentic? Do you show that you can be trusted as a researcher and scholar? Do you communicate the values base of your research and show how you are trying to live them in practice? Does your text demonstrate originality, while observing traditional academic criteria?

- Are you truthful? Can people believe you? Do you explain how and why your knowledge claims may be believed? Do you include appendices as part of your evidence base? Do you include all research documentation including ethics statements to show your responsibility as a researcher and writer?

- Is your text appropriate for your social and academic context? Do you explain how your values may be different from those of your institution or community? Do you demonstrate how you are interrogating your own and others' normative assumptions, and have learned the importance of speaking for yourself?

- Is your text of a high technical merit? Have you produced a well-structured, well-argued text? Have you checked for errors, and ensured that your bibliography is accurate? Have you produced a clean text that is visually appealing and that your reader will want to read?

- Do you claim, implicitly or explicitly, different kinds of validity for your text: for example, rhetorical, ironic, catalytic and educational validity? Do you select from different kinds of validity the ones that are right for you?

RESEARCH EXERCISE

Write up your action enquiry into your writing practice so far. Explain how your writing practice has improved, or not, and say why this may be the case. Explain what is important about researching writing as practice, and how this is at the heart of research practices.

If you have done all these things, you have probably produced a text that is a pleasure to read.

In Chapter 7 ideas are explored about how to use the knowledge and skills gained so far for the production of texts that will go into the public domain.

SEVEN

Planning for the Production of Texts

This chapter is about planning to write and produce texts. This is perhaps easier said than done because, while everyone can write, not everyone finds it easy to be a writer; and being a writer is not simply a matter of developing capacities, as outlined in Chapter 6, but also of getting yourself organised to write and dealing with the day-to-day practicalities of producing a text.

This chapter outlines some of the issues to think about. These include:

1. Golden rules.
2. Planning and getting organised.
3. Drawing up action plans for writing.
4. Meeting deadlines.
5. Coping with difficulties.
6. Understanding legal issues.
7. Watching your language.

Golden Rules

The production of texts involves two main golden rules:

- Practice, habits and routines.
- Selling ideas.

Practice, habits and routines

There is no substitute for practice ('practice' as a noun and 'practise' as a verb in British spelling). It takes a long time to produce a text. Like everything, it can take years to develop the capacity for good writing, which operates at multiple levels, including skills, and factual, procedural and personal forms of knowledge. Learning to write also develops with maturity. My early texts were all passion and little discipline, and an urgent desire to speak my mind. I hope the passion is still there, and I still speak my mind, but now, I hope, tempered with discipline and greater respect for others' points of view.

Practice means hard work. Twyla Tharp, world-famous choreographer and dancer, speaks about the importance of practice and building up habits and routines for developing creativity:

I will keep stressing the point about creativity being augmented by routine and habit. Get used to it. In these pages [you find] a perennial debate, born in the Romantic era, between the beliefs that all creative acts are born of (a) some trans-cendent, inexplicable Dionysan act of inspiration, a kiss from God on your brow that allows you to give the world *The Magic Flute*, or (b) hard work.

If it isn't obvious already, I come down on the side of hard work. (Tharp, 2006: 7)

I agree. There is simply no substitute for practice and work. The aim is to make it all look easy. 'Ginger Rogers supposedly once asked [Fred Astaire] why he worked so hard; he replied, "To make it look easy"' (Tharp, 2006: 175). Perhaps Stephen Pressfield has the best advice: 'Do the work!' (Pressfield, 2011), or Richard Branson's (2006) 'Screw it, let's do it!' (and it earned him a knighthood). Just get on and do it and accept the consequences.

Aim to develop the habit of practising. Do some writing every day, even if only three lines. When working on a text, maintain regular contact with it. If you leave it for only one day you will forget what you have written and waste time getting back in touch with it. Keep the text in your head and see it as some-thing that gives you a buzz, not an arduous job to be done. Make it a joy – only you can do this, but it means adopting an attitude that sees life as something to be enjoyed, not for struggling through.

Selling ideas

Drawing on an idea from John E. Kennedy of the 1890s Royal Canadian Mounted Police, Horberry (2009: xii) comments that writing is 'salesmanship in print': when you write you move into the business of selling. You aim to help your customer (reader) purchase a product or service (idea) that they need; your aim is to turn the need into a desire. Before writing this book I co-authored another one titled *Action Research for Professional Selling* (McDonnell and McNiff, 2014), and learned a good deal about sales. A key principle of selling is that the sales process is informed by the idea of AIDA (Attention, Interest, Desire and Action). The aim is to attract the customer's attention, capture their interest, arouse their desire for the product and inspire them to take action (buy it). You do the same when you sell an idea: you aim to influence others to engage with and consider accepting your idea. In the *Selling* book we also pointed out that universities are nowadays in the business of selling, both ideas and also services such as courses: as Pink (2012) says, we are all in sales now. Further, the world of selling has moved away from earlier stereotypes of the hard selling, predatory salesman. Selling is now seen as a dialogical encounter where each party enables the other to achieve what they wish. This is your job as a writer too: you sell ideas to your reader that will enrich the quality of their, your and others' lives. Your text represents a dialogical encounter between you that helps you both achieve what you would like, often in terms of a realisation of your values.

A key question in the selling-purchasing relationship that customers ask is, 'What's in it for me?' Your reader asks this too. They look at your text and ask, 'What's in it for me? What will I get out of reading this text? Am I prepared to spend my time and energy on it?' Keeping this question in mind can help you write in a way that aims to capture your customer's attention and maintain their level of interest so they will buy the idea or book you produce. Always keep your customer in mind, and deliver to them what you believe they want.

Planning and Getting Organised: Logistical Issues

Planning to write involves understanding and developing your writing practices and thinking about logistical issues, including time, space and resources, and what the final product will look like. This means thinking about how, when and where you are going to write.

How are you going to write?

Think about your preferred way of writing, including the following.

Your preferred mode and medium

Writers work in different modes, where 'mode' means a 'resource for making meaning' such as 'image, writing, layout, speech, moving image, and gesture ... all used in texts' (Kress and Bezemer, 2009: 169); and with different media, where 'medium' means:

the substance in and through which meaning is realized and through which meaning becomes available to others (cf. 'oil on canvas'). From that perspective, print (as paper-and-print) is medium; by extension, the book is medium, if differently; the screen another; and the 'speaker-as-body-and-voice' yet another. (Kress and Bezemer, 2009: 170)

Aim to experiment with different modes and media, including longhand and mind maps, and with computers, pencil and paper and virtual messaging. There is no 'right' way; each person finds their own best way. Experiment with different ways and decide what is best for you. Also be prepared to adapt to changing scenarios and shifts in mood.

Digital technology has significantly changed practices in writing and the means of production and dissemination. Many writers comment on this. bell hooks (2003) says:

I've handwritten all my books. I like to handwrite because I find that I think differently when I do. Computers are seductive in that you feel that you don't have to edit and rework as much because the printed text can look so good, and if you have a good printer it looks even better. So for me the stages tend to be that I work something through in my head, and then I start writing it. (hooks, interview transcript in Olson and Worsham, 2003: 119)

Chomsky (2003) says that the computer has revolutionised his writing:

Once I was able to use the computer, I discovered that there were a lot of things that I could do that I'd never done before. For example, I've never done much editing, simply because it was too much trouble; I didn't want to retype everything. And I never did much in the way of inserting and rearranging and so on. Now I do a fair amount of that because it's so easy. Whether that shows up differently for the reader, I don't know. But I know I'm writing quite differently. (Chomsky, interview transcript in Olson and Worsham, 2003: 54–5)

In my own writing area I have paper, pens and pencil, draft printed writing in a ring binder, and a computer. I also have a notebook where I jot down ideas as they appear, keep a record of changes I make to a work in process, and note sources. I do a lot of longhand writing to work out ideas and create the text, type it onto the screen, print it off and edit the hard copy, and then re-type. The process takes a cyclical action research form, where I think, try out, evaluate, rethink and revise, and try it out again.

Sometimes I type direct and edit the text on the screen. Perhaps it depends on my mood, the type of writing and the job in hand, or whether it is a piece of text outlining practical issues or one that deals with complex ideas with multiple linkages: in this case I often take days or weeks to work out ideas, often when off-task in the garden or doing the shopping. A computer screen helps me focus on a piece of text for close analysis, but I need to see the overview in hard copy to work with it and refine it. This is my way of working, but not everyone does it like this. You need to become confident with your own way. Take care of your eyes, too, because computers can dry them out, so have a small bowl of water on your desk for humidity and drink lots of water.

Be aware of your writing patterns and rhythms. Do you prefer writing at a specific time of day, perhaps in the morning or evening? Is there a special time of day when you are most creative? One of my best times is early in the morning when my mind is uncluttered, but the very best time is in the middle of the night when I wake with ideas swimming around and have to write them down lest they disappear with the dawn. At these times I am in a kind of hypnagogic state, neither asleep nor awake, when the ideas simply flow of their own accord (I am told that people experience this also during periods of focused meditation). Evidently it is a quite common experience, recorded by Mavromatis (1991) who tells how many famous people, including Dickens and Edison, deliberately or accidentally used it to encourage their creative spirit, as in, for example, the story of Kekulé:

I was sitting, writing at my text-book; but the work did not progress; my thoughts were elsewhere. I turned my chair to the fire and dozed. Again the atoms were gamboling before my eyes. ... But look! What was that? One of the snakes had seized hold of its own tail, and the form whirled mockingly before my eyes. As if by a flash of lightning I awoke; and this time also I spent the rest of the night working out the consequences of the hypothesis. (quoted in Japp, 1989, cited in Mavromatis, 1991: 193)

For me, it is an experience, mainly visual but where all the senses work together, a combination of various sensory metaphors. I don't try to analyse it and am grateful that it happens. I also do not recommend that you encourage this state: a good night's sleep is probably the best basis for creative and productive writing.

Be aware of the way you write and your expectations. I used to believe I needed acres of space in front of me before I could write. Perhaps this was because those acres of space were available, but today they are not. Because of the nature of my work it is difficult to find stretches of time, so I have learned to write in the cracks, using half-hour slots to write three sentences, or, when the mood is right, to jot down ideas and sentences when standing in a queue. Rowena Murray (2002) also advises using strategies like this to maximise time and reduce wastage. I occasionally use a voice recorder (inexpensive devices, now available on smart phones) to record notes, which I type up later. If you are serious about being a writer, and the writing begins to write you, you will find time and space, no matter what.

Some people need their own space to write. This is not practical for some, because most people share living areas with others, so your writing space needs to be negotiated. You could try asking people to clear a space for you at certain times. J.K. Rowling tells how she wrote much of her early *Harry Potter* books in cafés because she had nowhere else to go. Alan Titchmarsh, the famous TV gardener turned author, is reputed to write his books in a garden shed. I used to do a lot of writing on planes and trains and while waiting in airports, but my writing habits seem to have changed and I now use travel time to read, because being a writer means also being a committed reader. The main thing is to find a space where you can write, and just do it. Do not use lack of space as an excuse not to write.

Remember to shift your location while writing, take frequent short breaks, and avoid staying in one position too long. Hemingway used to stand, typing on a chest-high typewriter. I also stand a lot to avoid sitting too long in one position. Take regular exercise – bend and stretch and move about frequently. You will also find that exercise helps you think. Horberry (2009) recounts how a colleague recommends yoga exercises because, she says, standing on your head lets ideas fall into it.

Drawing up Action Plans for Writing

Certain tried and trusted strategies for planning and achieving your writing schedule are as follows.

Identify targets and plan how to achieve them

Know where you are going and plan the steps for getting there. Be specific about what you wish to achieve, be realistic about your targets and keep them achievable. Table 7.1 shows a broad action plan for writing a doctoral thesis in four years.

Table 7.1 Action plan for writing your doctoral thesis, 2015–2019

Year 1	Desk research to investigate current thinking about topic. Identification of research issue and question, engagement with issues of values, imagination of solution. Round 1 of data gathering. Interviews and focus groups with all participants to establish base line data. Maintenance of reflective journal. Reading about substantive and methodological issues. Regular meetings with supervisor and critical friends. Progress report 1. Informal validation meeting. Draft writing Chapter 1.
Year 2	Continue desk research. Round 2 of data gathering. Implement proposed solutions. Focus on transforming data into evidence. Articulation of standards of judgement. Continuation of reflective journal, encourage participants to maintain reflective journals. Regular meetings with supervisor. Progress report 2. First formal validation meeting. Continued reading. Draft writing Chapters 2, 3 and 4.
Year 3	Evaluation of implemented solution. Generation of evidence from all data. Maintenance of reflective journal. Progress report 3, and plan for thesis. Regular meetings with supervisor. Second formal validation meeting. Continued reading. Draft writing Chapter 5, 6 and 7.
Year 4	Writing up of thesis. Regular meetings with supervisor. Third formal validation meeting. Submission of thesis and viva.

Make a list of things to do, such as a literature search or first round of data collection. Draw up a chart and put it on your wall or desk. Keep it as a regular feature of the writing task and visit it frequently. Tick off jobs as you do them, as in Table 7.2.

Table 7.2 Identifying tasks and checking them off

Job to do	When?	Done?
Identify critical friends and invite their participation	January 2015	✓
Distribute ethics statements	February 2015	✓
Interview participants and gather first round of data	April 2015	Not yet
Decide on categories for analysing data	May 2015	Not yet
Begin to sort the data	May 2015	Not yet

Break the job up into manageable chunks

Break large tasks into smaller more manageable chunks. Focus on the first step, then the next. Have a start and finish date for each step. This will help give you a stronger sense of jobs accomplished. Don't over-commit, and be prepared to negotiate second deadlines. Put timelines on everything, and create a visual representation so you can see where you are, as in the tables above. Seeing that you are making progress is encouraging and gives a sense of achievement that buoys you up. Be prepared to negotiate your timetable with yourself, and allow extra time for contingency plans. For example:

Table 7.3 Progress chart

Job to do	Task 1	When?	Done?	If not, when?
Literature search about methodological issues	Look for different methodological approaches.		✓ ✓	
	• March 2015: Phenomenology		Not yet	July 2015
	• June 2015: Qualitative Inquiry		Not yet	September 2015
	• August 2015: Narrative Inquiry			
Interview participants in Setting 1	Gather data about their initial research question	March 2015	Not yet	April 2015
Negotiate access to participants in Setting 2	Gather data about their initial research question	April 2015	Not yet	April 2015

Keep a writing diary

Keep a daily writing diary. Write down what you have written, what you feel about it, and resources used. Note quotations used and tick them off in the 'quotations' file you maintain from your reading. Be conscientious about this. It can give you a sense of achievement. Note the texts you have read and tick those off from your reading list. Keep on top of your writing and don't let words run away with you: keep them under control too.

Keep a record of your accomplishments

Keep a record of your accomplishments. Work at your plan and don't stop until it's complete. Change the date if you must but never give up on the goal. You can get an app for drawing up and maintaining schedules, and there are plenty of ideas and visual representations on the Internet. Keep your action plan available at all times. Put it on your computer or in your file, and consult it every day.

Meeting Deadlines

If you are systematic about keeping to your anticipated timetable, you will achieve deadlines. Being punctual is part of your professional practice. Your supervisor or editor expects you to deliver on time and will not tolerate excessive overspill. At worst, you can negotiate an extended time but do not take this for granted. Supervisors and editors are busy and have their own schedules and lists of other texts demanding attention, and if you miss a delivery date you may well find yourself put back in the queue. You may even miss the deadline for submission altogether. The message is, get yourself organised, do the work and deliver on time. Also, do not over-commit: know your limitations and work within them.

Jenny Carpenter, introduced on page 35, writes about her writing practices:

When I start to write, I need to have read a lot first. I set myself a title and a word limit then split the word limit into smaller chunks. For each chunk of words, I identify a sub-heading. For example, if I was writing the introduction for my PhD proposal, I would plan for 500 words and the sub-headings 'who, what, why, context'. These would sit in a diagram similar to a concept map or brainstorm. I would then add brief notes under each sub-heading in a different coloured pen, and, after this, use a third colour to reference my reading and literature for each sub-heading. This would be my first draft, a visual spider diagram with key words and references. Then I would write, using complete sentences and paragraphs. Because I have my framework for the content, the writing seems to flow. I find that my first draft has to be written physically in a notebook rather than word-processed. I need to inter-nalise what it is I am writing by physically using colours and diagrams. I then feel confident to write a structured piece of work. (personal communication)

When does the writing start?

This is a major aspect of producing a successful text, especially an assignment such as a dissertation. Many people believe you can leave the writing until all the data have been gathered in, but this is not the case. Data gathering and analysis are only a part of the research; writing is an equally important part. You should begin the writing right from the start of the research project, for example by keeping a reflective journal, and doing pieces of practice writing about issues. Get into the habit of producing progress reports. These and other writings can act as data about your own learning and actions, and may find their way into the final report.

Often people ask where to start writing a text. If you think there is an answer you will never start. Start anywhere, and write what you feel like writing. All texts start in the middle of other texts, and you will change what you write in any case, so start and the writing will take care of itself.

Stay in touch with your supervisor or editor

Supervisors and editors can offer support and sometimes negotiate schedules. They are experienced in juggling multiple projects, so stay in touch and ask for help when you need it. Institutions also offer counselling services as well as practical help with technology or contact with support groups. Do not suffer in silence. Your happiness is important.

Coping with Difficulties

Difficulties come with the job so anticipate them and learn to cope with them. It is not all going to be problem-free. Sometimes people get tired of writing, or lose faith in what they are doing, or unexpected delays crop up. This is understandable because producing a text, especially a lengthy one, takes time and sustained effort. So you need to develop ways to deal with whatever situation presents. Two of the most common are looking for ideas and getting unstuck when you are stuck.

Looking for ideas

Plenty of strategies are available when you are looking for ideas. One of the best books on the topic, for me, is Twyla Tharp's (2006) *The Creative Habit*. Tharp says that a secret of encouraging your creativity to come alive lies in preparing to be creative. She speaks about developing rituals and routines to get yourself into a receptive state of mind. First, this means getting rid of the demons that remind you of your biggest fears, such as:

1. People will laugh at me.
2. Someone has done it before.
3. I have nothing to say.
4. I will upset someone I love.
5. Once executed, the idea will never be as good as it is in my mind.

(Tharp, 2006: 22)

Tharp's advice is to face up to your anxieties and deal with them. The people you respect will not laugh at you; everything has been done before in some way so nothing is really original; and we all have something to say. Even if you don't know how people will respond, you need to remind yourself that you're a good person with good intentions who is trying to create unity, not discord; even if the ideas are not perfect or hugely original they are good enough to get a degree or get published. Her advice is to see the thesis in your mind's eye; see the book with your name on it and feel it in your hands; see your loved ones' faces at graduation; hear the applause.

Similarly Page (1998) suggests strategies for evoking your creative spirit. She recommends seeing everything you do as an experiment and quotes Kierkegaard as saying, 'To dare is to lose one's footing temporarily; to not dare is to lose one's life' (p. 186). Work persistently: 'Out of the process of working will come the brilliant ideas that will give your writing its signature quality' (p. 186). Find supportive allies who will give you positive though critical feedback on your working ideas.

Maintain a reflective diary

Keep a reflective diary where you write down events and your learning from the events. This helps you keep a record of your learning, and how it influences your practices. As noted earlier, learning, reflection and action form a self-reflective spiral. Your diary can be a goldmine when you are searching for ideas: what you recorded then as half-formed ideas emerge over time into fully-fledged important insights. You can develop a diary as a print-based document, on your computer as a regular document, as a video diary (think of explorers who maintain a video diary) or as part of a social network, where you develop a blog on a website. This helps you to keep a record of your developing ideas and others' responses to them. You can develop them all as a multimedia diary, mixing text, visual and auditory messages to keep you on track.

Getting unstuck when you are stuck

When you run out of ideas or get lost trying to sort them out, stop writing and do something else. Horberry (2009: 28) recommends that you:

- change location (try a meeting room or the kitchen table instead of your desk);
- change tools (computer for pencil and vice-versa);
- try automatic writing (write non-stop about your subject for several minutes); or
- stare into space (this really does work)!

Have confidence in your tacit understanding that you know what you want to say, and let your mind do the rest. This can take time, sometimes days. Do not try *not* to relax. Even the most experienced writers acknowledge that they have to stop from time to time to let things settle in their mind. Many postmodern writers say that you don't write the text so much as let the text write itself. However, don't pretend that you are stuck when in fact you don't want to work. Good writing stems from a small amount of talent and a large amount of hard work.

The experience of not knowing what to say next is often called 'writer's block'. If this is your experience, get to know what fires you up to the extent that you want to say something. You can:

- read an article;
- view a picture;
- listen to someone speaking; or
- any other stimulus;

all of which makes you want to say something because you are:

- angry;
- enthusiastic;
- sympathetic; or
- any other emotion that makes you want to speak.

Then, as soon as you feel that you want to get back to writing, sit at the desk or the computer and work at it. Bring all your discipline to the task, and just stick with it until it comes right, as it will. This is the sheer hard slog and determination involved in being a writer.

Develop face-to-face and virtual support networks

Support networks are important for finding and lending moral and emotional support to colleagues. You can offer critical feedback by acting as critical friends who comment on one another's draft writing, and companionship and an understanding voice when the going gets rough or when there is something to celebrate. Your supervisor may organise a support group, but if not, do so yourself.

Support groups can meet face-to-face or through digital technology. I took part in an international online group who met using Second Life technology. It was an interesting experience psychologically and technologically and great for bringing people together to discuss ideas and share their research. Many such programmes exist today, as well as online conferencing facilities such as Skype, and many are free to download. Most universities provide conferencing facilities for postgraduate candidates as well as technological support in how to operate them. There are mixed advantages, but a main one is that people can come together from anywhere in the world through virtual as well as face-to-face contacts. At time of writing I am developing a Higher Education Action Research in Teaching (HEART) network that aims to bring together people internationally in higher education institutions (HEIs) who are studying their practices as HEI-based practitioner-researchers. The aim is to develop ideas and make them public. The annual conference on Value and Virtue in Practice-Based Research, at York St John University, aims to do the same, parallel to the HEART project.

If you have access to the Internet, your opportunities are boundless. You can develop blogs, websites and chat rooms to find support from others, and provide it in return. The Internet offers space for a new public sphere (Chapter 14), where people may come together, on an equal footing, to discuss matters that are important to them, and that may be developed as their individual and collective action enquiries.

Understanding Legal Issues

Writing often takes the form of work in the public domain, and if you put it there, you are responsible for what you write. This can present serious problems for scholars in terms of how they communicate their meanings and commitments through the language they use. Two of the most serious these days are plagiarism and the need to watch your language so as not to communicate potentially prejudicial stances.

Plagiarism

When you put your text in the public domain, it becomes part of the social order, which is run according to certain laws. One of these laws deals with intellectual property. A person's ideas are their property, as much as their car or house, and original ideas must not be used without permission or acknowledgement. Using someone's ideas without acknowledging the source is plagiarism, and plagiarism carries serious penalties.

It is sometimes difficult to know where one person's thinking leaves off and another's begins. Sometimes collaborative colleagues work with an idea rapidly, which develops through their interactions. This joint production needs to be acknowledged. In official exercises such as the UK Research Excellence Framework it must be stated how much time each party spent on the work, and due recognition recorded.

When you use someone's idea from the literatures or from everyday conversation, you must acknowledge your intellectual debt. If citing ideas from the literatures, write their names into your text and give the source such as a journal article or a website blog, and the page reference. Learn how to cite references properly – there are plenty of books on this topic, computers have built-in programs, and your institution or publishing house will give you specific guidelines. Always check that every reference in the body of your text is also in your list of references. If you miss out a reference you will jeopardise the quality of the text and could be penalised.

Do not use any part of a text that has already been published without giving its source. Doing so amounts to cheating. This applies to material from the Internet. Sophisticated programs are available to help readers detect whether the material exists elsewhere, but for your own integrity, you should never cheat. This applies also to re-using your own work. Sometimes people use material from a previous assignment in a current one. This is unethical and dangerous. If an examiner chose to go through the entire record, as sometimes happens for quality assurance purposes, and they find that a candidate has used the same material in different assignments the candidate could be disqualified. Plagiarism of any kind can carry severe penalties, so be aware.

At the end of the day, it has to be accepted that some candidates do cheat and get away with it. Most people, however, produce original work whose ownership and quality they can stand over. We should all be proud of what we do.

Watching your Language

Take care with your language, and ensure that it is free of racist, sexist, ageist or other discriminatory nuances. This is a serious legal issue, because anti-discrimination legislation is in place to prevent this kind of language. It operates at different levels of subtlety.

At an overt level, you must not use language that makes defamatory, inflammatory, or false statements about others. You must be prepared to take public responsibility for your language: if you don't, you may find that your article will not be published or your thesis not accepted. Similarly, you must not quote other people's work in ways that distort their original meanings by, for example, taking their words out of context or slipping in an extra word to change the meaning into one that you wish to communicate. Your examiners and editors have read the same material as you have and are experts in their field, which is why they are examiners and editors.

At a more subtle level, you must take care not to communicate ideas about others that your reader may find offensive. This was often the case in literary works (and often remains so), before matters of discrimination became high profile. This is not simply a matter of political correctness but of recognising our shared humanity and the dignity of difference (Sacks, 2003). For example, Said (1991) challenges Jane Austen's perpetuation of Empire by casting her characters in stereotypical roles; Biko (1987) challenges racist stereotyping, the idea that 'we are faced with a black problem' (p. 23), that people of one colour are different from people of another: 'Being black is not a matter of pigmentation – being black is a reflection of a mental attitude' (p. 48). He also notes hierarchical and patriarchal relationships: 'I am against the superior-inferior white-black stratification that makes the white a perpetual teacher and the black a perpetual pupil (and a poor one at that)' (p. 24). Similarly, in *Custer Died for Your Sins*, Deloria (1988) observes how Indians are portrayed: Indians always have 'a plight'; many white people claim an Indian Princess as an ancestor; Indians will benefit from the administrations of religious (usually Christian) organisations. To achieve these benefits:

Indian children were kidnapped and forced into boarding schools thousands of miles from their homes to learn the white man's ways. Reservations were turned over to different Christian denominations for governing. Reservations were for a long time church operated. Everything possible was done to ensure that Indians were forced into American life. (Deloria, 1988: 8)

However, note in this text the generic use of 'he' and 'him', a common irritation in texts and just as bad when replaced by a generic 'she' and 'her'. 'Mankind' is supposed to refer to all humanity, and 'You guys' is everywhere. Hotel desks are manned, not staffed. Sojourner Truth's 1951 cry, 'Ain't I a woman?' challenges the supremacy of black women scholars as speaking on behalf of all black women without allowing 'ordinary' women to speak for themselves. The form of words 'people of colour' ignores the fact that white is a colour too, and normalises whiteness. Corcoran and Lalor (2012) assume that university lecturers can offer critique and do not even think of 'practitioners', let alone include them.

Steve Mee is a senior lecturer in lifelong and interprofessional learning at the University of Cumbria. He writes about his work with people with autism:

In my role as an academic I support people living with autism. As part of this support I try to help these colleagues speak for themselves in the public domain to give them a sense of pride in their work, and to influence many non-autistic people's stereotypical views of autistic people. Recently, therefore, I collected some of their first-hand accounts, written in their own words, and submitted the collection to a publisher who had expressed interest, and who then sent the manuscript out to review. Two of the three reviews were positive and one was negative. In response to whether the text should be accepted for publication, the first reviewer stated:

'No. Not in its current format. The book begins and ends really well, but the individual contributions are disjointed and sometimes read as a bit of a 'rant'. I understand that the author wants the individuals to take ownership for their work.'

The second reviewer stated:

'Yes. The author has presented a collection of personal reflections on living with autism. This has been achieved sensitively and with real understanding of autism and the ways in which people who have autism perceive themselves in the world. It enables the reader to stand alongside the writer and see life through their eyes and emotions.'

The third reviewer stated:

'Yes. The author's style is easy to read and well structured, the language used is appropriate and accessible and you feel that you really get to know the people that have contributed to the narratives.'

Some of the authors in this book are very angry about the first reviewer's response to their autism: two, for example, have suffered post-traumatic stress disorder as a consequence of their experiences at school. Expressing this might be seen as a 'rant' or, on the other hand, 'standing alongside their emotions'. One says:

'The diagnosis I received throughout my time with the mental health teams was constantly 'Depression'. Bloody right I was depressed, suicidal for most of the time. If I'd been seen by a clinician with autism for my diagnosis, things might have been different. Why would this have been the case? Simple: only an autistic person can immediately spot another autistic person.'

Interestingly the first (negative) reviewer described the book as ending and starting well, referring to chapters written by me, the neurotypical author. They also suggest 'a large amount of editing and condensing' to make it accessible for the trainee professional.

So what kind of decisions have to be made to enable the voice of the marginalised person to be heard by those in the mainstream? How do we resolve the dilemmas? (Mee, 2014)

It is this kind of essentialist thinking that Butler (1999) challenges when she speaks about the need to trouble our thinking, to challenge the very underpinning epistemology we use when we think. Essentialism as a tradition has a long history, dating back to Plato and Aristotle, whose ideas about ideal forms and categories informed generations of people who thought, 'This is who we are and this is how we should be'. It is the kind of thinking challenged by Coetzee in his *White Writing* (1988) and others who say that one person knows what is good for another, not in the sense of, say, saving a child from burning themselves, but in terms of what is good for other people's life trajectories, a form of cultural imperialism, a licence to 'do good'. This kind of thinking is evident also in many action research texts, where it is assumed that one party knows what is good for another, and undertakes an 'intervention' to improve the quality of the other's life. Even the grammar of 'improve the quality of the other's life' is an imperialist form, betraying a sense that it is in one person's capacity to improve something for another. In Marx's terms, in the *Eighteenth Brumaire of Louis Bonaparte,* quoted in Said (1995: xiii), there is an assumption that 'They cannot represent themselves; they must be represented'.

In summary, watch your language. Be aware of your own assumptions and where they come from, and take care not to let them creep into your text. This is difficult, especially if you are brought up racist, as so many people are, and all the more reason why you need to plan carefully when producing a text as one you can be proud of.

SUMMARY

This chapter has focused on how to plan for the production of texts. It has offered advice about building up momentum for writing, drawing up action plans, ensuring that you can produce and deliver a text to specified conditions, anticipating and coping with difficulties and finding ways to avoid them.

REFLECTIVE QUESTIONS

- Are you confident that you can develop understanding of your writing practices, including your writing patterns and rhythms, and what is involved? Have you developed awareness of your writing preferences, including mode and medium?

- Can you draw up action plans to ensure you will deliver a text that meets readers' and reviewers' expectations?

- Are you confident about how to deal with unforeseen difficulties? Have you ideas about how to get unstuck, if and when necessary? Will you put in place appropriate supports and contingency plans? Are you aware of legal issues, especially about matters of plagiarism? Will you watch your language in terms of how you position yourself and others?

Identify a text you wish to produce and draw up an action plan for doing so. Show the detailed steps involved, and how you intend to achieve your anticipated output. Write your plan on a wall or desk chart and use it to guide your daily activities.

We now move to Part III, which considers writing for academic accreditation. It begins with Chapter 8, which sets out how to write proposals.

PART III

Writing an Action Research Text

This Part is about writing an action research text for masters and doctoral degrees. It outlines the practicalities involved and how to achieve a successful result.

It contains Chapter 8, 9 and 10.

Chapter 8, 'Writing proposals' gives advice about writing proposals for different contexts, including for research programmes and conferences. Examples are given of successful proposals.

Chapter 9, 'Masters and doctoral dissertations and theses' is about which learning outcomes are expected at masters and doctoral levels, and how progression may be achieved across levels. Examples are given to show how to do this at different levels. Advice is offered about how to structure texts to achieve what examiners are looking for.

Chapter 10, 'How will the quality of your dissertation/thesis be judged?' is about assessment practices and different criteria for judging quality at masters and doctoral levels. It offers practical advice about how quality is assessed in action research, communicability and higher degree texts in order to ensure successful completion.

Each chapter gives practical advice and theoretical resources for producing academic texts for the successful completion of academic programmes.

EIGHT

Writing Proposals

This chapter is about writing proposals for different contexts. When you write a proposal, you say what you intend to do, how you are going to do it, and why. You let your reader see that the plan is feasible, and that you have the capacity to carry it out. This means first planning and designing your project and producing a working blueprint.

The chapter covers the following:

1. What goes into a proposal?
2. How do you write a proposal?
3. How is the proposal judged?
4. Examples of research proposals.

Remember that doing your project and writing your proposal are different things. Designing and doing your project will help you improve what you are doing and offer explanations for it; writing your proposal sets out how you intend to do this. Your proposal will be judged in terms of (1) how well you plan and design your project; (2) how well you communicate the processes involved; and (3) how relevant and meaningful it is for the context you are writing for.

Here is what is involved in writing a proposal.

What Goes Into a Proposal?

You write a proposal for different purposes including:

- Permission to do a research project.
- Getting ethical approval.
- Submitting a paper to a conference.
- Writing a proposal for a book.
- Bidding for funding.

Although the contexts are different, the same principles apply. Your proposal will go to a reviewer who does not know you or your work, so you need to give them relevant information to help them decide whether to allow you to proceed or amend your proposal.

Your proposal acts as the basis for planning and designing your project. It is a practical feasibility study that enables you to take stock of logistical matters as well as your capacity to complete the project successfully. Because your research is about knowledge creation and theory generation, your reader needs to know what knowledge claims you intend to make and how you are going to make them.

Normally a proposal contains two aspects:

1. Planning your research project.
2. Designing your research project.

Planning your research project

Planning involves identifying what you hope to do and why, what resources you need to enable you to do it, and whether you have access to them. It lets you take stock both of availability of resources, and your capacity to do the job.

Think about the following.

What do you hope to do and why?

Be reasonably clear about your reasons and purposes in advance. New ideas will emerge during the course of the project but you need to have a strong sense beforehand about the rightness of your aims.

Getting a picture of the overall shape of your project involves saying what you want to do, why you want to do it, and what you hope to achieve.

Say what you want to achieve

Here are some of the things you may wish to achieve.

- You wish to improve an aspect of your practice, such as developing dialogical management strategies.
- You want to encourage others to evaluate what they are doing.
- You are aiming for systemic influence.

State your reasons

Here are some of the reasons you may have for wanting to take action.

- You wish to develop dialogical management strategies because your current ones appear not to be working well.

- You want to encourage others to evaluate what they are doing because you feel that self-evaluation is important for organisational success.
- You are aiming for systemic influence because you believe that people can beneficially influence one another's learning.

State your purposes

Here are some of the purposes you may have for your action enquiry.

- You feel that encouraging dialogue among employees will lead to stronger relationships.
- You want to encourage others to evaluate what they are doing so that work standards will rise in your workplace.
- You are aiming for systemic influence so that a culture of enquiry will develop.

What logistical aspects do you need to enable you to do your project?

Logistical aspects include the following:

- **Costs:** Are any costs involved? Cater on obvious costs such as travel, postage and technical equipment, and hidden costs such as possibly sending out work. Will you have a contingency fund for unexpected costs?
- **Time:** Will you have time to do your project? Will your family and friends give you space? What about work-life balance?
- **People:** You will involve other people as research participants, critical friends and validation groups. Have you access to them? Will they be willing to help?
- **Permissions:** You must clear all ethical matters before you begin. Will you get permissions? Any possible difficulties? This is especially important when planning to use multimedia, where you will not have control over your visual narratives when they go on YouTube.
- **Resources:** Have you access to resources? These include a library or resource centre, money for books and equipment, a good supervisor, conversations with professional groups, and anything specific to your context. If you are using multimedia, you will need a good computer, camera and recording equipment.

Have you the capacity to carry out your project?

Reviewers want to know:

- Have you access to necessary resources?
- Have you a sense of the overall conceptualisation of your project? Do you understand the issues involved and how they can be addressed?
- Do you know (roughly) where you wish to go and how to get there? Talk about your methodology, specifically about gathering data and generating evidence. Say what kind of knowledge claim you hope to make and how you will test its validity.
- Have you read sufficiently to get started? Which literatures will help advance your thinking? Set out some of your conceptual frameworks such as returning to work for long-term unemployed or the need for child protection.

- Do you have the stamina and commitment to maintain a prolonged study schedule? This means explaining that you really want to undertake this research, and you are aware of the significance of what you hope to do.
- Are you able to undertake independent study? Do you communicate that you have already started your study programme because you are curious and can't wait to get on with it?
- Do you demonstrate critical capacity? Action research and practice-based research programmes usually involve critiquing normative understandings, including your own.
- Can you write reasonably well? You must present a clean, error-free proposal. Your readers will not warm to you if they sense that your texts will need a lot of editorial work.

These are some of aspects involved in planning your project. Now consider designing it.

Designing your research project

Your research is about creating knowledge about a topic or subject area, so your proposal outlines how you will do this. The knowledge is about how you have evaluated and, where necessary, improved some aspect of your practice, and you understand better what you are doing. It is not enough to say, 'I want to improve my practice' because your practice involves thousands of things. Your proposal explains how you intend to create knowledge of this aspect, test the validity of the knowledge, and use it. If you wish to improve your leadership capacity, you improve your conceptual knowledge of leadership as well as your practical capacity as a leader.

Designing a project involves asking practical 'what? which? who? when? where? how? and why?' questions, though not in any particular order: Bolton (2014: 34–5) calls these 'tin openers'. It should be clear that they have informed your thinking to give a sense of coherence and flow to your proposal and communicate your understanding that you are doing research, not just professional activities.

Probably the easiest way to design an action research project is to think of a set of action reflection questions. You should aim to write a proposal that reflects your unique way of doing things, but this set of questions gives you a hook on which to hang your thinking in relation to your own purposes and contexts.

- **What issue do I wish to investigate? What is my concern?** This question lets you identify your research issue and formulate a research question about a specific aspect of practice.
- **Why do I wish to investigate this issue? Why am I concerned?** Spell out the contexts of your research and the values that inspire it. Outline your key conceptual frameworks, and say which literatures you will engage with. Talk about the values base of your research and explain whether or not you are realising those values in practice.

- **How do I show the situation as it is and as it unfolds?** Explain how you intend to monitor your practice and gather and analyse baseline and ongoing data. Say who your research participants will be. Explain how you intend to generate evidence from the data, and what standards you will use to judge the quality of your practice and your research.
- **What can I do about it? What will I do about it?** Outline your options for action, and choose one. Discuss which methodology you will use and why, selection of participants, ensuring ethical conduct, securing permissions.
- **How do I check that any conclusions I come to are reasonably fair and accurate?** Explain how you are going to test the validity of your emergent claims, probably by inviting the feedback of critical friends and validation groups in relation to identified criteria.
- **How do I modify my ideas and practices in light of my evaluation?** Say how you intend to continue working, perhaps in a new direction, using your new knowledge to inform new practices.
- **How do I communicate the significance of my research?** Explain what the significance of your research is for your own education, for the education of others, and for the education of your social and cultural formations.

If you wish, you can use this set of questions to frame your whole proposal. Just make sure you also address the issues in the next section.

The next step is to combine the two aspects of planning (logistical issues) and designing (methodological issues) into a document that becomes your research proposal. Here is how you do it. Examples appear on pages 158 and 160.

How Do You Write a Proposal?

Different institutions have different requirements. Some want a proposal of 400–500 words; some want 1,500 words. A book proposal or a proposal for an international project usually needs more words than, say, a proposal for a local conference. Check the official guidelines in handbooks and on websites to see what is required.

Here is some advice on organising your ideas. Stylistically it is helpful to place each section under its own heading to guide your reader around your text. The same technique is used here. You do not have to organise your proposal in the same sequence of ideas presented here, but you should aim to address them all somewhere.

Who am I?

Introduce yourself. Say where you work, how long you have been working there, and what your position is. Do not tell your life story; tell your reader enough so they get a sense of your professional contexts. Tell them anything special about your workplace: if you work as a health care professional, or if you have special responsibility for running a chain store.

What is this research about and why do I want to do it?

Identify an area of interest. Say that you want to improve some element of your practice, which involves carrying out an in-depth investigation to evaluate what the practice is currently like and how you need to improve it. You may also wish to contribute to policy-making.

Formulate your research question, using the idea, 'How do I improve what I am doing?' Your question should become more refined over the period of your research. 'How do I improve my practice?' could become 'How do I learn how to be a better listener?' It is the permeating theme that guides your research. Your question, 'How do I do this?' at the beginning of your research eventually transforms into your claim, 'I have done this', at the end. Tell your reader that you understand this and will work towards generating a claim to knowledge that is grounded in your research question.

What do I hope to find out from this research project?

Say what your study is about. Say that your theory of practice (your understanding of what you are doing) will constitute your original claim to knowledge. You know that doing research is about generating knowledge, and you feel the knowledge you create will contribute to knowledge of your field. Map out your project in terms of what you see as the possible findings and their importance. This section gives your reader a sense of whether the project is manageable within your available timescale and resources.

When and where will I do the research project?

Draw up a timescale. Times can vary depending on the scope of your project, whether it will last for three months or three years. It can be helpful to draw up a chart to show what will be done when: you may wish to organise your project as cycles of action reflection, as in Figure 8.1.

Say where you will conduct your research. Most people conduct it in their workplaces, but may also use other contexts, such as a library or resource centre for when you do desk research or consult archives. You may also need to go outside the workplace, perhaps if you wish to survey people's attitudes towards a topic. Remember to get permission from any persons responsible for the workplace and its good order (see 'Ethics', page 153).

2014–2015	2015–2016	2016–2017
Year 1	Year 2	Year 3
Focus on	Focus on	Focus on
identifying	data	....
research issue	gathering	

Figure 8.1   Project organised as action-reflection cycles

Who will you involve in your research project?

The focus of your research will be you as you improve an aspect of your practice to try to help others. You will involve other people in the following capacities.

Observers and friends of your project

Identify the people who will observe you as you conduct your research, or gather data on your behalf.

Participants

Identify the people you will work with as research participants. Say that you will ask them to keep a reflective journal and will ask them to let you see it as part of your data-gathering, or give you feedback through interviews and focus groups about whether you are influencing their learning.

Critical friends and validation groups

Identify your critical friends who you will consult on an ongoing basis, and a validation group who will meet on a more formal basis to listen to your progress and summative reports. Explain what kind of schedule of meetings you will draw up.

How will I conduct the research?

Say that you intend to pursue a systematic enquiry into improving your practice, which you will then make public through your report. You will disseminate your findings widely, to contribute to new thinking and practices. Some institutions and conferences expect you to designate a form of dissemination, such as writing for publication in a refereed journal.

Say which methodology you intend to use. Say why you intend to use this methodology, what is special about it, and why no other methodology would be appropriate. Perhaps you will choose a mixed-methods approach, in which case explain which methods you will use. (Remember that 'method' refers to a technique such as tape-recording or triangulation; 'methodology' refers to the processes of generating theoretical understandings through research.)

How will I gather data and generate evidence?

Outline your data-gathering methods, which may include quantitative and qualitative methods. Explain that you need to select appropriate methods and will check availability of technology. This is especially important if you intend to use multimedia. You may also need the help of a specialised technical adviser. Will you have access?

Say what you intend to monitor and gather data about. For example, if you are investigating how you can improve your work as a manager through developing dialogical practices, you would need to monitor how your own thinking is changing, and show how it is informing your changing practice with others. This means you will also have to monitor *their* thinking, and how it is informing their practice. This can be complex, because you cannot directly monitor people's thinking, so you have to ask them to do it themselves, and make their data available to you.

A useful model in this regard is the one cited in McNiff (2013a), which explains how your learning influences your actions, which also influence other people's learning and actions. This in turn raises issues of ethics (see below).

Say how you intend to generate evidence from the data. This involves identifying standards by which the quality of the practice and research will be judged. Because you are doing academic work, it will also involve explaining how you will fulfil academic criteria. Explain how you will use your research to find ways of living more fully in the direction of your values.

How will I test the validity of my claims to knowledge?

As you generate evidence in relation to your research question, you strengthen your position towards making a claim to knowledge, to say that you now know something that you did not know before. The strongest claims are original ones; you say you know something that no one knew before. Aim to show that these claims are not only your opinion, but are grounded in evidence that you have presented to the scrutiny of your critical friends and validation groups.

Say how you will keep a record of these meetings, and all validation matters. Identify your standards of judgement, in terms of academic criteria, and in relation to how your values become the dynamic standards by which you make judgements about the quality of your practice and your research.

How will I modify my ideas and practices in light of my evaluation?

Say that you will continue your research, because the end of this action reflection cycle will become the beginning of a new one. Explain what you hope to have learned through doing the research, and how this will inform new learning. Perhaps you may do things differently, because some elements will not be so successful; say that you will anticipate this. Explain how you see the need for continual professional learning, and how you may contribute to this, perhaps through convening new research interest groups.

How will I explain the significance of my research?

Say how you think your research may be significant. This may be in terms of informing new practices and policies. You also hope to contribute to new forms of theory, by placing your personal theory of practice into the public domain. Say how you will disseminate your findings through publications, conference presentations, blogs and websites, social networking, radio and TV appearances, and exercise your educational influence in the workplace for systemic transformation. You may join networks and professional associations in your field, to influence their thinking, and speak with local government groupings who may learn from you.

Ethics

Make clear that you will observe ethical conduct at all times. Say what this will involve, such as ensuring anonymity where appropriate and making available tape-recorded transcripts to originators. Say that you intend to submit your proposal to the ethics committee and other stakeholders in your institution and secure their permission before proceeding. You will make progress reports available to them on a regular basis, if they wish, and invite their critical comment. Explain that you will draw up an ethics statement for distribution to all participants, and place a copy of this statement as an appendix to your proposal. This section is key, because if you do not spell out how you will observe ethical issues you may not be granted permission to do your research. Also, do not expect a reviewer to assess your report unless ethics statements are included as appendices.

Engaging with the literatures

You must engage with the literatures throughout. Say which literatures you will access and some of your key authors. This means outlining your conceptual frameworks. Also say why you have chosen these literatures: you need, for example, to be familiar with methodological issues to justify using an action research methodology, and substantive subject matters. Show in-depth understanding in all areas.

A note about multimodal and multimedia proposals

The use of digital technology, especially in the production of video narratives, is extending and transforming the forms of representation that educational researchers use (Eisner, 1997). These show, sometimes better than words on a page, how to communicate the dynamic nature of the transformation of values into living practices. The presentation of texts online also carries consequences for how practices may be understood:

… the life-world may be turned into an artifact to be (re)used. That can be done on the spot, by uploading the artifact on the Web or sending it to friends, for example. As a consequence, life lived offline is directly connected to life lived online, for instance in one's YouTube or MySpace profiles which now are 'literally' lived and enacted by means of representations. Life lived offline may become subordinated to life lived online or lived for life online. (Kress, 2010: 9, cited in Yamada-Rice, 2012: 162–3)

How is Your Proposal Judged?

Your proposal serves several purposes, and will be judged in terms of whether it is fit for purpose for different people. These include yourself and your readers and assessors.

How is your proposal useful for yourself?

Your proposal acts as your map to doing your research, in the same way as the route map you draw up for a walking tour. Spend time working on it, especially on formulating your research question, and be clear about what you hope to achieve. Importantly, clarify how your values act as the grounds for your research, and also transform into your conceptual frameworks, criteria and standards of judgement.

Also remember that your proposal is dynamic. The details of your proposal may change. This is acceptable in action research, and to be expected, because the proposal is written for today's contexts, while recognising that those contexts may change tomorrow so the research focus will change too. Your thinking and your research question may be refined as you deepen your analyses and extend your cognitive range through reflection, discussion and reading. Sometimes people discard their first proposal because they see it is not viable when problematics emerge, and begin again.

Your proposal is dynamic also in how words transform into action. It is rather like an organisation's policy statement. Although written as a static text, the meaning of the proposal or the policy statement lies in the intention of the author; these intentions transform into purposeful action. In Arendt's (1958) terms, it is a way of taking your place in the world – for you, the academic world, and your statement of intent to take communicative and educational action. Husserl (1931) says that once something is intentional in the mind, it triggers the actor's capacity to take action in the social world. Said (1997) says that intent carries its entire methodology within itself; you can imagine the future in every beginning. This has implications for Habermas's (2001) ideas about the public sphere where all persons may speak their truth through communicative action. Your research proposal is your entry into the academic public sphere; it communicates that you are capable of theorising your work and wish to have the work recognised as research-based practice. You are also claiming that you are a professional who does not simply react but acts from a specific set of theoretical bases. Your proposal is therefore both about how you are going to improve your subject area and your capacity to theorise what you are doing, and test the validity of your personal theory of practice in the public domain for its possible adoption or adaptation by others.

Your proposal is, in many ways, your passport to a new place. However, like all passports it has to be approved and stamped by a passport office. In your case, this means the reviewers and committees who you hope will approve your proposal.

How is your proposal useful for reviewers and committees?

Your reviewers and assessors will judge your proposal in terms of their expectations, which are grounded in their values, and which in turn inform their standards of judgement. They judge your proposal in terms of certain questions:

- Is the researcher able to undertake a systematic enquiry at an appropriate level?
- Is the researcher able to undertake independent study?
- Is the researcher able to write a good report?

Through reading your proposal they can be confident that you are capable of the following.

Is the researcher able to undertake a systematic enquiry at an appropriate level?

Your reviewer wants to see whether you understand what is involved in doing action research. In relation to action, they want to see whether you understand that action is not just about activities, but is intentional and purposeful, with identified reasons and purposes. In relation to research, they want to see that you appreciate the steps involved, that research involves making claims to knowledge and testing the validity of those claims. In relation to knowledge, they want to see that you have knowledge of your subject area and knowledge of your practice in this area. They need to see that you can articulate the importance of your work in relation to its originality, rigour and significance; that you will be exercising influence, or 'impact' in wider domains; and that you are aware of the need for the dissemination of findings.

Is the researcher able to undertake independent study?

When you register for an award-bearing course, or apply for funding, it is expected that you can undertake independent study. Although your supervisor will be available for advice and support, you have to do your own learning. You are expected to be pro-active in finding data, new ideas in the literatures, and negotiating with critical friends and research participants. Your proposal communicates your hunger to study and your eagerness to get on with it. You would probably explain that you have already begun your enquiry informally and now wish to formalise it institutionally.

A reader will welcome a proposal that is optimistic, thoughtful and focused. Especially they welcome proposals that communicate the researcher's understanding that they need to learn and are willing to put time and energy into creating knowledge. They will not welcome a proposal that communicates lack of self-confidence or self-discipline, and that assumes that this can all be over by the weekend. A proposal is a scholarly document that shows how the researcher grounds their enquiry in knowledge of the literatures and indicates that they need to read more. Your proposal is your statement of intent about how you intend to conduct yourself over the next few years while producing a high quality research report, thesis, article or book, and about your capacity to do it. It is your statement that you can finish what you hope to begin.

Is the researcher able to produce a good text (report, thesis or book)?

The quality of the text of your proposal indicates what the quality of your final text will be like. Think about issues raised in Chapters 5, 6 and 7, about what is regarded as good quality writing and how to achieve it. This means thinking about technique in writing as well as ensuring the communicability of your text in terms of its comprehensibility, authenticity, truthfulness and appropriateness (pages 109–17). Especially it means both demonstrating these criteria and also articulating to your reader that you know that you are doing so. This is a higher-order capacity that the best proposals demonstrate. The researcher states explicitly that they know what they are doing in their writing; this is a form of meta-analysis and demonstrates the capacity for reflexive and dialectical critique. You therefore say things like, 'In this section I explain how I engage with issues of validity ...', and then do it; or 'I have shown how I have reflected on my thinking and have transformed it in light of my reading ...'.

In summary, here are some general dos and don'ts about writing a proposal.

General dos and don'ts

- Write with a reader in mind. They do not know you or your contexts so you must tell them. The only thing they know about you is what they read on the page. Do not expect them to guess: tell them clearly.
- Keep in mind that you have a limited time for this research project. In doctoral studies you usually have 3–4 years full time to complete or its part-time equivalent, usually up to seven years, but aim to get it done in four or five. Have your data gathered in the first eighteen months (full time) or first three years (part-time) and spend the rest of the time composing and refining your thesis. It takes time to sort out the writing; remember that you are writing a book (your thesis constitutes a book and should be about 80,000 words, which is longer than many textbooks).
- Time goes by quickly so get on with it as soon as possible. Start before you are ready. Don't necessarily start at the beginning. Start anywhere and let the text develop through the writing.
- Your reader is on your side. They want you to get your PhD and to publish your book. They are not out to trick you, but they do want to see that you know what doing research and writing a text is about. This is your opportunity to show them.

Writing for your reader

- Write your proposal as if you are writing a travel plan or development plan. Your proposal is an outline document where you state what you want to do in your research (the next three or four years). The purpose of your proposal is to explain to your reader what you want to find out. Many people aim too high: this often means that the proposed research could quickly get out of hand. Keep it small, focused and manageable.
- Make sure your topic(s), research question(s) and focus are all about the same thing. Make sure your reader knows what this thing is; don't leave them to guess. Get to the point and make sure they (and you) know what the point is.
- Don't write quotations in your proposal unless absolutely necessary; they are good for the thesis but not particularly for the proposal. Your proposal should be clear, focused and to the point. It is an action plan, not a draft thesis.

Content of your proposal

- Give the aims of your research project. Keep it short and sweet. Don't be over-ambitious and keep everything manageable.
- Give a rationale for wanting to do the project. This may involve outlining the background and contexts. Explain what is already happening in the field that has inspired you to do this project.
- Explain which methodological approach you will use and why you intend to use it. Give a rationale for its use.
- Do cite appropriate literatures. These may be indicative literatures, to give your reader an indication of the kinds of issues and conceptual frameworks you intend to work with.
- Give information about practical matters, including:
  - Participants: say who your participants will be, how you will recruit them, what your relationship will be with them. Explain ethical issues and how you will safeguard your participants' well-being. Say what sampling methods you have used to select them – perhaps they constitute an opportunity sample?
  - Data: say which data you hope to gather, how you will gather it, how you will analyse it and generate evidence. Say how you will test the validity of emergent knowledge claims.
  - Say what you feel the significance of your research may be, for whom, and why. Explain how this will constitute your original contribution to knowledge of the field.
  - Logistics: say what equipment and/or resources you will need. Say how you are going to fit your project into your busy life. Identify any obstacles to your potential success and say how you are going to deal with them.
  - Timeline: give an estimated timeline for the project. Be realistic.
  - Say how you hope to disseminate your findings. Do you wish to publish your work in refereed journals?
  - Any other practical issues.

Examples

Here are two examples of proposals. The first is a fictitious proposal for a doctoral programme; the second is extracts from a proposal for a real-life conference paper, accepted by the American Educational Research Association. AERA require a proposal of 2,000 words, with each section written according to strict word counts.

Example 1: A proposal for a doctoral programme of study

Title: *Improving my management capacity to develop communities of educational enquiry*

Background Recent debates in the educational research literatures (Furlong and Oancea, 2005; Whitty, 2005) have focused on the problematics of establishing quality in educational action research (Feldman, 2003). Of particular interest are issues regarding the nature of the standards of judgement to be applied to test the validity of, and to give academic legitimacy to, an individual's claim to have generated their personal theory of practice. There are as yet few self-studies by university practitioner-researchers into the nature of their educational and learning relationships and into appropriate standards of judgement in professional education (Russell and Korthagen, 1995), or how to foster inclusional and dialogical practices that will contribute to the development of sustainable communities of educational enquiry.

Purpose   By undertaking a self-study of my professional practices as a university-based practitioner-researcher I intend to find ways of understanding my practice as an educational manager with responsibility for supervising the professional learning of peer academics. A key feature of my enquiry will be to explain how I judge the quality of my practice and my research by showing how my educational values transform into standards of judgement as I research the question, 'How do I improve my management capacity in developing communities of educational enquiry?'

Scope   I will investigate my professional practices as a university-based manager organising and teaching a course for peers, acting as schools-based tutors of novice teachers, with a focus on issues of access and social justice. I will work with six academic staff, tutoring a group of eight novice teachers during the 2015/2016 session, as they seek to encourage the teachers to develop self-efficacy. My enquiries will focus on an understanding of the nature and development of educational relationships between myself and my peers, as they research their practices with novice teachers. These processes will be explored and explained through a negotiated programme of meetings as participants discuss their experiences of articulating the nature and formation of their educational relationships.

Methodology   I will use an action research methodology, which involves enquiring into and explaining the processes of improving practice, with an emphasis on contributing to improving the social context in which the practice is located. This involves systematic action reflection cycles of expressing concerns, producing action plans, acting and gathering data, and evaluating the effectiveness of changing practice. My accounts of practices will be subjected to the critical scrutiny of a validation group, following the procedures recommended by McNiff (2013a). From my database I will generate evidence to show the nature of my educational relationships with colleagues.

Issues of ethics   I will seek the approval of the university ethics committee for my proposal, in relation to how I conduct my research. I will ensure the protection and well-being of myself and my research participants, as set out by Robson (2002), and I will include all records regarding ethical conduct in my data archive and appendices.

Timings My research programme will proceed from spring 2015 to autumn 2019. I will organise my activities as follows:

2015–2016 Desk research to investigate current thinking around peer supervision. Identification of research issue and question, engagement with issues of values, imagination of solution. Round 1 of data-gathering. Interviews and focus groups with all participants to establish base line data. Maintenance of reflective journal. Reading about substantive and methodological issues. Regular meetings with supervisor and critical friends. Progress report 1. Informal validation meeting. Draft writing Chapter 1.

2016–2017 Continued desk research. Round 2 of data-gathering as I implement proposed solutions. Focus on transforming data into evidence. Articulation of standards of judgement. Continuation of reflective journal, encourage participants to maintain reflective journals. Regular meetings with supervisor. Progress report 2. First formal validation meeting. Continued reading. Draft writing Chapters 2 and 3.

2017–2018 Evaluation of implemented solution. Generation of evidence from all data. Maintenance of reflective journal. Progress report 3, and plan for thesis. Regular meetings with supervisor. Second formal validation meeting. Continued reading. Draft writing Chapters 4, 5 and 6.

2018–2019 Writing up of thesis. Regular meetings with supervisor. Third formal validation meeting. Submission of thesis and viva.

References [Include your list of references. The references for this proposal can be found in the main references section of this book.]

Indicative bibliography [You could also include an indicative bibliography, which is a short list of books and papers that you intend to read, and that will inform your study.]

Example 2: Proposal successfully submitted to the American Educational Research Association (abridged): Jean McNiff (2013)

Title: *Writing Action Research for Publication: A New Legitimation Crisis?*

This paper is an account of a three-year action research professional education project conducted in a European university with a group of nine senior nurse educators, supported by myself, as part of a broader institutional commitment to developing research capacity. The project arose in response to local policy recommendations, within an international policy framework that ... A preferred methodology for achieving this would be action research. ... This paper focuses on this critical issue of writing action research for publication, itself part of developments that are increasingly relevant to the international community, including the following:

- Greater interest in practice-based research in universities, given the recognition of Mode 2 forms of knowledge (Gibbons et al., 1994) for generating theory of direct relevance to contemporary social needs.
- Increasing demands for academics to publish their work, within an audit culture where reputation depends on publication (Hyland, 2007).
- Ensuring publication of action research texts within a literary orthodoxy that demands specific forms of academic writing, and … (Gibson, 1993; Herr and Anderson, 2005).
- Danger that the content and form of action research texts become domesticated … .

Consequently, the production of texts that show the processes of realising socially-oriented values through their content and form within a literary culture that prioritises outcomes and analytical forms of expression could be seen as constituting a new legitimation crisis (Habermas, 1975), where ….

The task was made more difficult because:

- learning to do and write action research involved shifts in individuals' self-identity, including: …;
- 'Research' for colleagues from a health care background meant 'scientific research'; intellectual and emotional discipline were required to … ;
- an increasing requirement that texts for publication should be written in English, given that writing in English is now regarded internationally as a form of academic skill (Hyland, 2007); colleagues therefore had to … ;
- It also involved my learning about ….

Methodology and methods   The methodology throughout was action research, a process of enquiry in action on action for action (e.g. Schön, 1995; Reason and Bradbury, 2001; Noffke and Somekh, 2009; McNiff, 2013a). Our group of ten (nine university-based colleagues and myself as supporter) constituted a designated university research group. The project took the form of an action enquiry, with four 3-day meetings across the year, online support between meetings, and a developmental focus over the years: year 1 focused on … .

We regarded our work together as an action enquiry. We systematically documented our practices, learnings and reflections, which in turn required adopting specific attitudes and practices, including:

- A dialogical relational approach: talking through ideas and emerging understandings within the safe space of our group, while recognising the need for both empathy and critical support;
- Patience with self and others while experiencing episodes of ontological insecurity as part of identity formation and transformation and engagement with new forms of knowledge;
- Determination and commitment in the processes of producing texts.

We developed strategies for practising writing and boosting confidence: individual research presentations to colleagues for critical feedback; individuals sent me online draft writing for comment on conceptualisation, form of expression, and editorial support in English; online video communication; … .

Our data took the form of tape and video-recorded conversations and presentations; videoed conference presentations; reflective journals; individuals' draft writing for professional research portfolios. We built a collective knowledge base comprising spoken and written texts that showed ... .

I made my data public in the form of my learning journal, draft writing, critical commentary of personal progress in learning about contextualisations of ... .

Findings, outcomes and results The project ends in December 2014, and a seminar is planned to show peers and institutional managers the outcomes, and explain the significance of the work, for different constituencies. These include the following:

- At a personal level, academics may move from a one-dimensionally-constituted identity (Marcuse, 1964) of either researcher or practitioner, ...
- Professionalism is reconceptualised as ... .
- Institutional improvement is seen as the dialogical interaction of individuals within ... .
- Educational improvement is seen as commitments by all to contribute to a dynamic relational culture that enables and supports the intellectual, emotional and spiritual growth of all. Cross-disciplinary, inter-professional learning becomes a normative institutional practice whose focus is the well-being of the service user.

These insights are communicated through our books and journal articles, currently in process, to be made available at our end-of-project conference, written by individuals and collectively as a group, to show ... .

SUMMARY

This chapter has considered what is involved in writing proposals for different contexts. It has outlined what is involved in deciding the content of a proposal and writing one that reflects the action steps you intend to take. Examples of worked proposals are given, with advice about how you can adapt these to your own circumstances.

REFLECTIVE QUESTIONS

- Are you reasonably confident about what goes into a proposal for different contexts? Have you considered issues of what you need to do and what you wish to achieve? Have you articulated your reasons and purposes?

- Have you given all the information your reader needs to see what the proposed research will involve, and whether you have the capacity to carry it through?

- Have you explained how your proposed research will be useful for others and yourself? Have you communicated that you are able to do the work, so your reader will have confidence in you and your proposed research?

RESEARCH EXERCISE

Choose a type of publication and write a proposal for it. This could be for a research programme, a conference presentation, or an assignment. Include the necessary detail to let your reader see that you have anticipated what is involved and that you are capable of carrying out the project.

Chapter 9 now addresses issues of how to write masters dissertations and doctoral theses.

NINE

Masters and Doctoral Dissertations and Theses

This chapter is about writing masters and doctoral dissertations and theses. Masters-level work is becoming increasingly common as a form of professional accreditation, and is often compulsory as evidence of continuing professional development. A doctoral thesis is the highest form of academic accreditation, so writing one takes considerable commitment to hard work, reading and time. The challenge for action researchers is how to fit the process stories of action research within the orthodox structures of academic writing.

The chapter covers the following:

1. What are the contents of an action research masters and doctoral account?
2. How do you structure your text?
3. What do examiners want to see?

Masters and doctoral level work is the province of universities whose task is to ensure quality as set out in national and international frameworks. These frameworks provide guidelines for what a work contains in the form of learning outcomes, and its assessment in terms of nominated criteria. In the UK the Quality Assurance Agency for Higher Education (QAA) publishes documents such as the *Framework for Higher Education Qualifications* (QAA, 2008), setting out the criteria and standards that higher education providers are required to meet. This kind of quality assurance exists in most countries; international agreements such as the Bologna Process ensure comparability of standards and qualifications.

This chapter considers the outcomes of higher degrees and therefore what a dissertation or thesis should contain; Chapter 10 considers how outcomes are assessed.

What are the Contents of an Action Research Masters and Doctoral Account?

The learning outcomes for higher degree work are fairly standard across higher education institutions, and take the form of descriptors. Each descriptor refers to a particular level, premised on the assumption that there will be progression from masters to doctoral level in terms of these descriptors. In the UK, Level 7 refers to masters work and Level 8 to doctoral work.

Descriptors are often organised in terms of domains, including:

- **Knowledge and understanding**

  This includes aspects such as subject knowledge; use of data and evidence; capacity in research and development; understanding of ethical issues.

- **Cognitive skills**

  This includes aspects such as capacity in analysis and synthesis, self-reflection and evaluation.

- **Practical skills**

  This includes elements such as awareness of context and use of learning; use of resources; communication and presentation skills; demonstration of research and social responsibility.

Table 9.1 is an example of this form of progression in relation to the two domains of 'knowledge and understanding': the advice given is adapted from several QAA documents.

Advice is given about what achievement of these skills involves: for example, in relation to the same area, Level 7 masters candidates will be able to:

- deal with complex issues both systematically and creatively, make sound judgements in the absence of complete data, and communicate their conclusions clearly to specialist and non-specialist audiences;
- demonstrate self-direction and originality in tackling and solving problems, and act autonomously in planning and implementing tasks at a professional or equivalent level;
- continue to advance their knowledge and understanding, and to develop new skills to a high level.

Level 8 doctoral candidates will be able to:

- make informed judgements on complex issues in specialist fields, often in the absence of complete data, and be able to communicate their ideas and conclusions clearly and effectively to specialist and non-specialist audiences;
- continue to undertake pure and/or applied research and development at an advanced level, contributing substantially to the development of new techniques, ideas, or approaches;

Table 9.1 Examples of criteria for different levels of achievement at Level 7 and Level 8

Area to be examined	Level 7	Level 8

Generic area: Knowledge and understanding	Candidates will demonstrate:
	
	• a systematic understanding of knowledge, and a critical awareness of current problems and/or new insights, much of which is at, or informed by, the forefront of their academic discipline, field of study, or area of professional practice;
	• a comprehensive understanding of techniques applicable to their own research or advanced scholarship;
	• originality in the application of knowledge, together with a practical understanding of how established techniques of research and enquiry are used to create and interpret knowledge in the discipline;
	• conceptual understanding that enables the student:
	
	  o to evaluate critically current research and advanced scholarship in the discipline;
	  o to evaluate methodologies and develop critiques of them and, where appropriate, to propose new hypotheses.
		Candidates will demonstrate:
		
		• the creation and interpretation of new knowledge, through original research or other advanced scholarship, of a quality to satisfy peer review, extend the forefront of the discipline, and merit publication;
		• a systematic acquisition and understanding of a substantial body of knowledge which is at the forefront of an academic discipline or area of professional practice;
		• the general ability to conceptualise, design and implement a project for the generation of new knowledge, applications or understanding at the forefront of the discipline, and to adjust the project design in the light of unforeseen problems;
		• a detailed understanding of applicable techniques for research and advanced academic enquiry.

and will have:

• the qualities and transferable skills necessary for employment requiring the exercise of personal responsibility and largely autonomous initiative in complex and unpredictable situations, in professional or equivalent environments.

(Compiled from various online QAA documents, including QAA, 2008)

The criteria for examination of works looks something like the following (see also pages 54–7).

Criteria for examining masters dissertations and doctoral theses

• The work contains a claim to knowledge and makes a contribution to knowledge of the field. At doctoral level the claim should be original (see below).
• The work shows the candidate is able to undertake a study in an appropriate and professional manner (sometimes couched as 'the candidate is able to undertake an educational enquiry in an appropriately critical and balanced fashion').

- The work demonstrates understanding of relevant contexts.
- The work is written in a form and style appropriate to higher degree level standards.
- The work contains material of peer-reviewed publishable merit (not necessarily for a masters level dissertation).
- The work is error-free and technically accurate with a full bibliography and references.

Sometimes an examiner is asked to respond to specific questions, such as:

- Does the work demonstrate that the candidate has an understanding of the field of research?
- Does the work show that the candidate has satisfactorily designed, undertaken and reported on an investigation in the specified field of research?
- Does the candidate present the thesis in a manner and level appropriate to the field of research?
- Is the literary standard of the work appropriate?

Most examiners would look for the following in a masters dissertation:

- A clear statement of the knowledge gained or generated through the research.
- Engagement with literature in a critical and focused manner.
- Demonstration of analytic, comparative and critically reflective skills.
- Gathering and analysis of material and interpretation of results.
- Justification of methodologies, techniques and processes.
- An error-free document, with a full bibliography and accurate references.

In a doctoral thesis, they look for all the above and in addition:

- An explanation for an original and significant contribution to knowledge and understanding in the field.
- Demonstration of capacity for independent research.

General expectations

The points above should appear somewhere in the dissertation or thesis, as set out in Table 9.2, whether throughout the text or in specific places in a more focused way. The left-hand column indicates the expectation and the right-hand column describes what it would look like. This is where action research accounts, with a focus on personalised narrative accounts, differ from more impersonal traditional social science accounts.

Here are two examples, from Alex Sinclair and Maria James (introduced on page 51), to show progression in action. Alex and Maria are senior lecturers in education at St Mary's University, Twickenham.

Alex Sinclair

Here is the introductory paragraph from Alex's masters dissertation (Sinclair, 2008).

Table 9.2 Some criteria for action research dissertations and theses

Research aspect regarding content	How it is achieved
Research aim.	The work begins with a clear articulation of the aim of the research, and its reasons and purposes.
Research question.	A clear question and articulation of the research aim and its importance.
Claim to knowledge and demonstration of testing validity. In doctoral studies the claim represents an original contribution to the field.	In masters studies you show that you have engaged with aspects of knowledge of the field. In doctoral studies you say you know something that was not known before, and initiate validity tests to show the claim is believable.
Contexts; description of grounds for the study.	Background and contextualising issues, including historical, social, cultural and political influences; also personal and institutional contexts – anything relevant to frame the study and show its importance for the field.
Articulation of values that inform the research.	Values are embedded in the research; transform into criteria for judging quality of practice and for generating evidence from the data; provide reasons and purposes for the research.
Your positionality as researcher.	You explain whether this is first, second or third person action research, outsider or insider; why you have chosen this positionality and what its effects may be on the research.
Explanation of conceptual and theoretical frameworks.	Conceptual frameworks refer to issues identified as main themes for the text such as discrimination in the workplace, forms of leadership, environmental issues. Theoretical frameworks include preferred methodology, data-gathering and analysis, linking formal systems such as content and rhetoric. Rationales for these should be given so the reader is clear about their place in the text.
Critical engagement with the literatures and with own thinking.	Critical engagement means appreciating what key authors are thinking; developing arguments; critiquing arguments and suggesting alternatives; engaging with own thinking and showing willingness to critique and find a better idea or positioning.
Explanation for choice of criteria and standards of judgement.	Explanation for choice of criteria to judge elements of the research, such as quality of practice and research, aspects of validity of data and evidence, authenticity of researcher's account; standards identified to judge how well the criteria have been achieved.
Participants and ethics.	Explanation for who you identified as research participants and ensured their safety and well-being throughout; your positioning in relation to participants.

(Continued)

Table 9.2 (Continued)

Research aspect regarding content	How it is achieved
Story of action undertaken; story of empirical research within the action.	You tell the story of what you did in the research; how practice became the research; how you investigated what you were doing and tried out different strategies; how you succeeded (or didn't) across a specific time and came to provisional conclusions about the effectiveness of what you did.
Data and evidence.	You tell how you: gathered data and generated evidence; conducted validity checks to test the authenticity of the evidence and the rigour of methodological procedures; emphasised evidence as key part of offering explanations, not only descriptions; analysis of data.
Discussion.	A specific discussion about the findings of the research; general discussion of issues runs through the work as arguments that emerge from critical engagement with the literatures and with own thinking.
Articulation of significance of the research.	Potential significance of the research for different constituencies: for yourself, others in the social and organisational world, knowledge and theoretical base of the wider field.
Conclusion.	Tie the text up neatly, even though the research may still be in progress.

Research aspect regarding form	
Clear structure and cyclical form.	The work has a clear structure, which is explained to the reader. The research story demonstrates a cyclical form with transformational potential communicated to the reader.
Narrative form.	A story of attempts to improve learning to improve practice.
Voice.	Mainly active voice; mainly first person singular or plural.
Explanations for choice of medium of communication.	Explanations offered for choice of medium of communication, whether print, digital, multimedia or other; choice of data-gathering media also offered, e.g. social networking media, spoken or printed texts.
Explanations for choice and form of stories.	Explanations for whether a story is a backstory or the main story; whether linear or circular; whether first, second or third person; whether main story or embedded.

In this research paper I am offering an account of my action enquiry to date. My enquiry has focused on exploring my understanding of how I have developed from a commitment to propositional knowledge, while teaching as a secondary school science teacher, to a commitment to dynamic transformational forms of knowledge, following a move to my University College, undertaking the role of science lecturer to BA Initial Teacher Training (ITT) students. My research has been on how I encourage independent enquiry amongst my students with a particular focus on how I can develop this through a virtual learning environment (VLE). My original claim to knowledge is that I have come to understand how a VLE can help students develop the skills of independent enquiry and how discussion forums play an important part in this. Throughout this paper my wish is to demonstrate that I am contributing to a new epistemology of educational knowledge (Schön, 1995) and in particular that it has been possible for my students to have learnt with me as I gain a better understanding of how I can best develop my practice. In this way I believe I am working towards an epistemology of symbiotic practice. (Sinclair, 2008: 1)

In 2014 he produced the following for the introduction to his draft doctoral thesis:

The focus for this research originates from my growing concerns for the health of our planet and the well-being of its inhabitants, both in the present and in the future. With the global human population recently reaching 7 billion inhabitants the effect this is having has been well charted; resource depletion, the numerous and complex effects of anthropocentric pollution including that of global warming and all against a back drop where the difference between the world's richest and poorest is phenomenal.

Orr (1992) argues that most of Western modern education has been designed to assist the industrialisation of the planet by its conquest over all things natural. Little regard, if any, is given to the 'health of natural systems, an awareness of the delicacy, complexity and interconnectedness' (Braungart & McDonough, 2002: 26) with Western society's primary focus being the speed at which a product is produced and consequently received by the customer. It is this disconnection from nature, where the true symbiotic relationship we have with our planet is misunderstood, and an inability to comprehend the consequences of our actions that has led Orr (ibid) to label most students leaving educational institutions as ecological illiterates. By inference, contemporary learning institutions now have the potential to produce graduates who are not only ecologically illiterate, but also 'able to exploit others and the environment more efficiently and effectively than their predecessor' (Sterling, 2001: 45). Because of this, Sterling argues (2003) that a new value should enter education, that of the well-being of the Earth. (Sinclair, 2014: 1)

Maria James

Here is the introductory paragraph from Maria's draft PhD thesis, 2012:

> This thesis is an explanatory account of how I have generated my living theory of practice. In the beginning, in respect of this work, I started to research my practice, in order to make sense of it in the understanding that my practice is my purposefully intentional action which has in-built assumptions about reasons for and purposes of the action. I offer this thesis as an explanation of how I have come to understand my professional life as teacher-educator and Religious Education (RE) specialist. Throughout, I have asked how I can legitimately be a Christian teacher-educator and my primary claim to knowledge is that I have developed a new epistemology of practice that I term theopraxis (James, 2007). I understand this theopraxis to be a morally committed and thoughtful practice in the light of my belief in my God and it is the development and generation of this that constitutes the focus of this work.

Here is the introduction from her successful doctoral thesis (James, 2013).

> This thesis is an explanatory account of how I have generated my theory of practice as a professional teacher-educator in a University College of Education and as a Religious Education specialist. My intent in undertaking my research has been to make explicit my understanding that my practice is purposefully intentional action, and to clarify embedded assumptions about the reasons for and purposes of this action. Throughout, I have asked how I can legitimately be a Christian teacher-educator, seeking validation for this through the writing and publication of this thesis.
>
> My main claim to knowledge arising from my study is that I have developed a living theory of practice that I term 'theopraxis' (James, 2007); that is, a morally committed and thoughtful practice in the light of my belief in my God.

In both accounts it is possible to see the development of capacities of knowledge synthesis and explication, and a strong rhetoric that carries the reader along, as well as increasing confidence of researcher and scholarly voice and authority in subject matter.

The question now is, how do you structure your text to achieve the same standards?

How do you Structure your Text?

You structure your text so it shows your research design and methodology. Most institutions require dissertations to be written according to established structures, but you can be creative within the given structures and by moving them around.

Examples of accepted ways of structuring masters and doctoral texts include the following.

Murray (2002) gives a generic structure for a thesis written from an orthodox social sciences perspective as this.

- **Introduction/Background/Review of literature**
  - o Summarize and evaluate books, articles, theses, etc.
  - o Define the gap in the literature.
  - o Define and justify your project.

- **Theory/Approach/Method/Materials/Subjects**
  - o Define method, theoretical approach, instrument.
  - o Method of inquiry.
  - o Show links between your method and others.
  - o Justify your method.

- **Analysis/Results**
  - o Report what you did, list steps followed.
  - o Document the analysis, showing how you carried it out.
  - o Report what you found.
  - o Prioritize sections for the thesis or for an appendix.

- **Interpretation/Discussion**
  - o Interpret what you found.
  - o Justify your interpretation.
  - o Synthesize results in illustrations, tables, graphs, etc.

- **Conclusions/Implications/Recommendations**
  - o For future research.
  - o For future practice.
  - o Report issues which were beyond the scope of the study.

(Murray, 2002: 116–17)

Davies (2007) suggests the following, applicable for social science texts but that can be adapted for more project-based studies, especially what he calls 'SPSER' forms: 'situation, problem, solution, evaluation, recommendation'. This fits within an action research frame.

1. Prelims.
2. Introduction of the topic.
3. Literature review.
4. Research aim(s).
5. The methods used.
6. Research findings.
7. Discussion.
8. Conclusion.
9. References.

(Davies, 2007: 211)

McMillan and Weyers (2010) say that a basic structure shows movement from the general (the introduction) through to the specific (the main body) and back to the general (the conclusion).

- The introduction should contain 'a brief explanation of the context of the topic; an outline of the topic as you understand it; an explanation for how you plan to address the topic ... – in effect, a statement of intent' (p. 222).
- The main body should contain an analysis of the topic according to the approach (methodology) you have decided on;
- The conclusion summarises the entire work in terms of a restatement of the research question, the evidence you have presented in support of your views, and a statement of your overall viewpoint on the topic.

(Adapted from McMillan and Weyers, 2010: 223.)

These kinds of frameworks and templates are helpful, and many major research associations and journals favour them too. The disadvantage for action researchers is that they reflect largely the assumptions of scientific and social scientific enquiry, mainly of externalist researcher positionality, cause and effect, linear form and definitive conclusions. Action research, however, usually adopts an emergent cyclical form and is presented as ongoing narrative inquiry, without assumptions about cause and effect or linearity. An action research story is one of discovery and creation; you do not know what is going to happen until it does (see Popper, 2002: xi–xii). You therefore cannot take action until you know what is happening. The kind of underpinning epistemology of these stories is one of faith in the unfolding moment (Bohm, 1987). Stories have an emergent form and fractal shape; each piece links with others – a Gestalt – where the whole becomes more than its parts through dynamic interaction.

However, speaking from experience, it is not so difficult to adapt an action research story within the given macro-structures, though you need to be strategic. This means finding ways of getting your own way tactfully, what MacDonald (1987) refers to as 'creative compliance'. A main strategy is to recognise and not openly flaunt established rules, and then produce a work that others will admire and accept. Take for example the 1968 moment when Dick Fosbury introduced 'the Fosbury Flop'. By introducing the technique he changed the history of the high jump event forever, and thousands followed him to success. You can do the same, not by challenging the core rules and principles (in the high jump it was still necessary to get over the bar and observe protocols) but by working within the rules to develop innovative ways of telling a story. It is also important to identify an appropriate examiner (see Chapter 10).

You can fit an action research story into established structures such as those above, which gives something like this (Table 9.3).

Table 9.3 Placing action research aspects within an established structure

Traditional research linear structure	Action research narrative structure
Title: Write the title.	**Title:** Write the title.
Abstract: Write the abstract.	**Abstract:** Write the abstract.
Introduction, background, research question Write an introduction. Say what the background to the research was in terms of a hypothesis to be tested. Write the research question. Explain the methodology and methods used.	**Introduction, background, research question** Write an introduction. Describe the focus of the research and issue to be investigated: 'What issue did I wish to investigate? What was my concern?' Explain the methodology and methods used. Describe background and contexts: 'Why did I need to investigate this issue? Why was I concerned?' Give reasons for the project in terms of the values base of the study. Outline the contexts.
Methods, methodology, data, participants, ethics Explain all aspects of conducting the research, focusing on collecting and analysing data. Say who your research participants were, and why you chose them. Issues of ethics.	**Methodology, methods, procedures, data, participants, ethics** Explain what methodology you used and why; say how you gathered data, who your participants were, how you ensured good ethical conduct. Say what you did to find new ways of working to encourage improvement in the social situation you were in. Tell the story of practice; explain how this became a research story. Issues of ethics.
Results, findings Outline results. Analysis of data in order to generate evidence. Produce quantitative and qualitative evidence; explain how you have tested its validity.	**Results, findings** Say what happened when trying out new ways of working. What worked and what didn't; offer opinion about why it worked, or didn't. Produce quantitative or qualitative evidence; explain how you have tested its validity.
Discussion, critique Discuss findings in relation to evidence; explain relevance as a contribution to the field; accepting or refuting established theory.	**Discussion, critique** Discuss findings in relation to the evidence; explain relevance as a contribution to the field (original for doctorates), for research, practice and theory; contributing to new thinking and practice, and new communities of enquiry.

(Continued)

Table 9.3 (Continued)

Traditional research linear structure	Action research narrative structure
Conclusion, summary Summarise main points, revisit research question; conclude by restating the importance and significance of the research for the field.	**Conclusion, summary** Summarise main points, revisit research question; conclude by restating the importance and significance of the research for the field, and your continuing learning.
References Give a full list of references, paying attention to academic conventions.	**References** Give a full list of references, paying attention to academic conventions.
Scholarly aspects Engage throughout with the literatures. Do a literature review. Develop arguments from drawing on key concepts in the literatures; offer critique and different conceptualisation where appropriate.	**Scholarly aspects** Engage throughout with the literatures. Do a literature review where necessary, and possibly at intervals throughout the text. Develop arguments from drawing on key concepts in the literatures; offer critique and different conceptualisation where appropriate.
Reflexive critique Optional.	**Reflexive critique** Compulsory. Demonstrate critical and dialectical reflection at all points, i.e. reflection on own learning, on potential influence in wider domains.

Important aspects include:

- Writing at different levels.
- Ideas about originality and critical engagement.
- Need for literature reviews.

Writing at different levels

Your text tells interwoven stories working at the following different levels.

- Description: You say what you did: in terms set out in Chapter 3, this is knowledge-telling.
- Explanation: You say why you did what you did and what you hoped to achieve, that is, you set out your reasons and purposes, with the intent of helping your reader understand what you are saying: this is knowledge-transformation and shows your rhetorical skills.
- Analysis: You bring your critical capacities to bear on analysing your descriptions and explanations as the basis of theory generation (knowledge analysis).
- Synthesis: You say how your actions, reasons and purposes combine to help you theorise your practices (knowledge synthesis).
- Explication: You make clear to your reader how you have described, analysed, synthesised, communicated and explained all aspects of doing and writing your research. This gives you a research text that helps you theorise your writing practices.

Ideas about originality and critical engagement

Make sure you are fulfilling the criteria of making an original contribution to knowledge of the field and demonstrating critical engagement.

Originality   Originality is a defining feature of doctoral work. Phillips and Pugh (2005) set out a range of definitions, including:

- carrying out empirical work that hasn't been done before;
- making a synthesis that hasn't been made before;
- using already known material but with a new interpretation;
- trying out something in Britain that has previously only been done abroad;
- taking a particular technique and applying it in a new area; ...

(Phillips and Pugh, 2005: 62)

Something is being done for the first time. In action research, the 'something' is this:

- You know how and why you have improved an aspect of your practice.
- In doing so, you have generated your personal theory of practice, for which you claim validity.

Critical engagement   Action research emerged from critical theory and other earlier theoretical traditions whose aim was to critique normative assumptions.

An action enquiry therefore problematises discourses, practices and ideas, including your own normative assumptions.

Literature reviews

Literature reviews are important for contextualising research, to show the current state of the field of enquiry. When studying your own practice you show the relevance of key texts for your own topic and contexts, and incorporate them into your thinking as appropriate: how do the literatures of leadership help you understand and extend your leadership practices? You critique or develop them according to what you find through studying your practice.

You should include all the above in your dissertation or thesis, while addressing issues of what you write and how you write it to achieve the criteria for masters and doctoral degrees. However, your reader or examiner is not simply looking for the mechanical fulfilment of criteria, but wishes to see how you have engaged thoughtfully with your own thinking and how you demonstrate capacity to problematise issues, that is, not simply take things for granted, as follows.

What do Examiners Especially Want to See?

Here are some elements that examiners really want to see, set within a widely-adopted action research structure.

Title and abstract: Job to do – Your title and abstract communicate the main aspects of the research

Make sure you – outline the topic clearly. Summarise the key features of the dissertation, including claims to knowledge. Any claims made should be fulfilled in the thesis. The abstract makes clear what the original contribution to knowledge is, and outlines the research contexts. Most abstracts are between 150–400 words, which means focusing on what people really need to know (try writing your abstract in six words: see page 94).

Chris Glavey works as an educator at the Marino Institute of Education, Dublin. Here is part of the abstract from his doctoral thesis (Glavey, 2008).

This thesis offers an explanatory account of my living theory of educational leadership in fostering and sustaining student and young adult leadership processes in educational and community settings. Grounded in my research to address my concern for the marginalisation and voicelessness of young people in schools and within their local communities, I explain how I have developed educational processes to help them to develop their leadership abilities and provided them with opportunities to express these abilities in contributing to a good social order in educational and community settings. My practice is rooted in my respect for the uniqueness, the 'natality' (Arendt, 1958) of each person, and their capacity to contribute to a just and inclusive social order, and my thesis accounts for how I have attempted to live these values throughout my daily work.

Conceptualising my work as praxis, and drawing on Groome's (1991) concept of shared praxis, I demonstrate how I have nurtured communities of shared praxis as sites for educative and social transformation. I explain how I have developed a living theory of educational leadership appropriate to encouraging the growth of such communities and I define my understanding of spirituality and liminality as these have contributed to my emerging epistemology of practice. ... (Glavey, 2008)

Introduction: Job to do – Your Introduction introduces the research and the text

Make sure you – write your claim to knowledge (your original contribution to knowledge of your field in doctoral studies) at the beginning. Define your field (horticulture, retail, nursing) and say what your original contribution is (your claim to knowledge) and its significance (your work will contribute to knowledge of your field). Explain how this involves ontological, epistemological, methodological, practical and socio-political issues. Explain how you have tried to live your values in your practice. Comment on your capacity for reflective explanation and theoretical analysis (meta-cognition). This demonstrates your capacity for reflexive critique (awareness of the transformation of your thinking) and dialectical critique (awareness of the influences acting on you – see Winter, 1989). Also comment on your capacity for agency in influencing other people's thinking. Explain how your text stands as your personal theory of practice, and the importance of its narrative form. Outline your methodology, and explain how it is communicated through the form of the text. Your introduction should relate directly to your abstract.

Aims of the research: Job to do – Identify your research issue, or area of concern, and formulate a research question

Make sure you – explain that the research is more than problem-solving. It is about problematising and asking about what can improve (starting with your own understanding). Beware easy assumptions that everything can 'be improved'. Some things cannot be improved; some people don't want to improve their situations; most don't want to 'be improved', though they may wish to improve themselves with your help. This means interrogating your own preconceptions about how social change happens: perhaps it begins with changing yourself.

Also consider:

- What is it possible to achieve?
- Can you do anything about the issue? Will new situations be sustainable?
- What may be the possible benefits and losses?

Show you are realistic. Questions such as, 'How do I stop the violence in my neighbourhood?' are probably too big, although you can influence people at local level and small acts can lead to systemic change (Crawshaw and Jackson, 2010). Be prepared to say that some issues are irresolvable, and you have to walk away; and that sometimes a 'solution' may generate new problems. Enabling people to critique means they may run risks and may get silenced: say this, while pointing out the importance of critique:

I take criticism so seriously that, even in the very midst of a battle in which one is unmistakably on one side against another, there should be criticism, because there must be critical consciousness if there are to be issues, problems, values, even lives to be fought for. (Said 1991: 28)

Your research question: Job to do – Formulate a realistic, achievable research question

Make sure you – take care when using first-person action research, which focuses on the 'I'. Check out your relationship with others. 'I' am part of a social situation (which is about people together) in which 'we' work collaboratively. 'I' can become 'we' when 'we' share the same values commitments. Each 'I' focuses on their own learning while influencing the learning of the other 'I's. Each person holds themselves accountable for how they are with the others. Check your research is not about serving the interests of 'me'. It is about how 'I' can promote the other's well-being and flourishing. A collective of 'I's becomes greater than a collection of individuals.

Why is this an issue? Why am I concerned? Job to do – Explain why you wish to investigate this area

Make sure you – show that the idea of realising one's values in practice can be problematic. Ask:

- Why values?
- Which values?
- Whose values?

Why values?

Discussions about values often transform into discussions about action. What kinds of action? Unintentional? Purposeful and intentional? What kind of intent – to control, emancipate or persuade?

Which values?

Values are what we believe in so we try to turn them into practices. Explain the problematics of this view. Values are grounded in discursive practices (talking about values); how do you turn abstract principles into social practices?

Whose values?

Some people maintain that their values are better than other people's. Also look at contradictions, when people espouse values but don't live them (see Schön, 1995; Schön and Rein, 1994). Make sure you engage with these issues. What about values pluralism? Perhaps the capacity to negotiate values should be a main criterion in action research. Also your values can change through the course of the enquiry. Make all these matters clear.

How do I show the situation as it is and as it develops?
Job to do – Gather and analyse data

Make sure you – explain how you monitored practice, gathered data and generated evidence to ground your knowledge claim. Also consider:

- Which data are relevant?
- How do you ensure that you represent people fairly?
- How do you generate evidence from the data?

Which data are relevant?

Aim to gather data relevant to your research question. If you want a social situation to improve, you have to begin with yourself: you cannot improve another person, though you can arrange conditions to enable them to improve themselves. Your data shows how you do this, and how your research participants respond to you. The data is in the nature of their responses.

How do you ensure that you represent people fairly?

How do you ensure ethical conduct: matters of confidentiality, negotiating access, and doing no harm. This involves more than issuing ethical statements and securing permissions, more how you portray yourself and others. Do you represent people in ways that reinforce stereotypes? Explain how you use language to challenge the reproduction of culture. Explain how your capacity for criticality informs your choice of data. Do you gather only those data that reinforce the rightness of your own position? An experienced examiner asks, 'Where is the evidence to show that everyone agreed?' Provide disconfirming data; show the processes including episodes of dissent. Do not filter them through a sanitising lens: life and research are not like that. Examiners warm to an author who explains that the research was difficult. They raise their eyebrows when the story has an entirely happy ending.

How do you generate evidence from the data? Job to do – Show that you know the importance of the processes involved

Make sure you – explain that evidence is in those pieces of data that directly show the processes involved in transforming a research question into a knowledge claim. Your evidence shows the realisation of your espoused values in practice (or their denial), and how the values emerge through the practice as the means by which you assess progress (your standards of judgement).

What can I do? What will I do? Job to do – Outline what you did to address your research issue

Make sure you – explain how understanding the problematics of taking politically-oriented action influenced what action you took while respecting others' values, opinions and cultural, social and political positioning. Explain that processes of social and cultural evolution begin in the mind, so changing surface-level practices means first changing the deep-level thinking that informs those practices, which is easier said than done. We are born into social, political, economic and cultural systems, underpinned by an epistemological system, which we usually accept unproblematically. Foucault (1980) also explains how we internalise rules so that we learn to supervise and regulate ourselves.

What do you choose to learn? According to Habermas (1975: 15), humans cannot *not* learn in processes of social evolution. When you take action, what kind of learning do you encourage? How do you do this?

Much learning can be mis-educational (Chomsky, 2000): it does not generate emancipatory or inclusional knowledge. How do you encourage people to think freely and creatively?

How do I ensure that any conclusions I come to are reasonably fair and accurate? Job to do – Test the validity of emerging knowledge claims

Make sure you – justify your claim that your learning and actions are morally good, and that your research is rigorous. Explain how you engage in validation processes, which involve your responses to public critique. This raises questions:

- What counts as good in social practices?
- What counts as good in research practices?
- What counts as good in assessment practices?

What counts as good in social practices?

Good social practices can be understood in terms of the realisation of ontological and social values in relation to the flourishing of the other. This view of 'the good' is grounded in relation to the natural order and its sustaining energy, a key characteristic of which is its capacity for self re-creation – that is, appreciating that whatever happens in one part of a system influences all other parts. Life goes on, unless disrupted or destroyed. The purpose of life is more life. In terms of knowledge creation, 'passing on' knowledge (see page 6) contributes to the healthy evolution of the entire system. The energy that sustains living evolutionary processes is inclusional because it works for all, and relational because everything is embraced within the flow of its force-field: see Feynman's idea that scientific enquiry is 'the pursuit of understanding of some subject or some thing based on the principle that what happens in nature is true and is the judge of the validity of any theory about it' (Feynman, 2001: 240). The question becomes, 'What kinds of values and practices will sustain life for all? How should people be towards one another?' Your work reports on these ethical dilemmas.

What counts as good in research practices?

Research practices are usually recognised as 'good quality' when they demonstrate the researcher's capacity to undertake a systematic enquiry and make it public (Stenhouse, 1983) with social intent, and generate new knowledge and theory. You show the validity (truthfulness and verifiability) of your claim to have done this. Researchers who wish to experiment with creative forms of representation, such as multimedia work, must still show the methodological rigour of their research: explain to your reader how you have done this.

What counts as good in assessment practices?

Some people see assessment practices as good when all parties reach inter-subjective agreement about the validity of claims and the quality of the research. This can be problematic for action researchers in higher education settings where 'objective' criteria are preferred, whereas action research practices are grounded in 'subjective' criteria and standards. Can you show how you negotiated expectations?

How do I modify my ideas and practices in light of my evaluation? Job to do – Show how your learning informs new ideas and practices

Make sure you – say how you intend to develop your practice and research in light of the learning from your evaluation. Also celebrate what you have done, state its potential significance for the learning of yourself and others, and set out some of the implications. Remember that you do not need to reach happy endings in action research, only constantly new beginnings.

SUMMARY

This chapter has outlined the main issues involved in writing a masters dissertation and a doctoral thesis. It has given advice about the descriptors and learning outcomes appropriate for the different levels, and indicated what is required to achieve them. It emphasises that examiners are looking for aspects that go beyond the achievement of outcomes to show how the candidate has conducted meaningful research and produced a text of such a quality that the award is justified.

REFLECTIVE QUESTIONS

- Are you confident about the differences in level for the award of masters and doctoral degrees? Do you know what the different descriptors refer to and how they can be achieved in practice?

- Are you clear about the need for achieving nominated criteria, especially about making an original contribution to knowledge of the field and critical engagement? Have you written a text that shows how you are contributing to knowledge of the professional field as well as producing knowledge of personal practice?

- Have you cited appropriate references to other works, and offered literature reviews where appropriate? Can your examiner see that you have read widely and eclectically and are not simply name-dropping? Have you read every text you have cited?

- Have you read your work with an examiner's eye?

RESEARCH EXERCISE

Write an outline plan for your masters dissertation or doctoral thesis. Write a meta-reflection to accompany it, showing how you have demonstrated awareness of what you need to do to produce a quality text that examiners will approve.

So, now you have written your doctoral thesis, how will it be judged? This is the focus of Chapter 10.

TEN

How Will the Quality of your Action Research Dissertation/Thesis be Judged?

This chapter is about how your dissertation or thesis will be judged. It outlines different assessment frameworks for judging quality in (1) higher degrees, (2) action research and (3) the communicability of texts, and how you can achieve specified criteria. It discusses procedures for submitting your doctoral thesis, conducting your *viva voce*, and the importance of finding the right examiner. It also suggests how you can contribute to developing the field.

The chapter looks at the following questions and issues:

1. How is quality in a dissertation or thesis judged?
2. How is quality in an action research text judged?
3. How is quality in the communicability of texts judged?
4. Procedures for examining higher degrees.
5. Suggestions for future development.

How is Quality in a Dissertation or Thesis Judged?

A dissertation or thesis is judged in terms of the following criteria (see also page 167 above).

- Scholarly texts should contain accounts about knowledge creation and should contribute to knowledge of the field.
- They give an account of an enquiry in an appropriately critical, original and balanced way.
- They show improvement in the practice being described, or explain what may have hindered progress.
- They demonstrate critical engagement with the writer's own thinking, with the thinking of other research writings in the field, and, where appropriate, from works of literature.

- They contain material worthy of peer review.
- The story they tell follows a 'golden thread', so it is possible for a reader to see the story woven through the text in a systematic way.
- The work is error-free and technically accurate, with a full bibliography and references.

Additionally, Sharples (1999) says that a text should:

- not present unwarranted belief as fact;
- provide justification for ideas, by reference either to the publicly observable world or to an acknowledged authority;
- reference the sources of ideas;
- not selectively ignore facts, but offer all the information that is relevant to an argument;
- acknowledge the limitations of an argument;
- present the text in a form that is designed to assist, not mislead, the reader. (Sharples, 1999: 165)

Further, Graf (2003) says that when you make an argument (which is what a dissertation, thesis, article or book does) you:

1. enter a conversation just as you do in real life. You begin your text by referring to the prior conversation that you are entering: unless you do this, what you have to say won't make sense to your readers;
2. make a claim as soon as possible;
3. remind readers of your claim periodically;
4. summarise the objections you anticipate will be made (or that have in fact been made) against your claim;
5. say explicitly why you think what you're saying is important and what difference it would make to the world if you are right or wrong. Imagine a reader over your shoulder who asks, 'So what?' or 'Who cares about any of this?';
6. write a meta-text that stands apart from your main text and puts it in perspective;
7. remember that readers can process only one claim at a time, so resist the temptation to try to squeeze in secondary claims that are better left for another time;
8. be bilingual: avoid Academicspeak when you can but if you do have to use it to say something, try also to say the same thing in conversational English too;
9. don't kid yourself. If you couldn't explain it to your parents the chances are you don't understand it yourself (paraphrased from Graf, 2003: 275–7).

Other authors offer similar sets of criteria, to show that you should produce an original text where you:

- make a claim to knowledge and show its significance for your field;
- demonstrate the validity and originality of your claim by showing your critical understanding of the processes involved;
- explain that your claim is about improvement in learning, practice and research, within your context;
- explain how and why the practice has improved, or not;
- communicate your ideas in an appropriate form;
- communicate the significance of your claim through an appropriate form of language that qualifies it to enter the public domain;
- ensure that the text is error-free and technically accurate with a full bibliography and references.

A key criterion (not always articulated in assessment schedules, but noted in Graf above) is that the work should demonstrate rhetorical validity: it should contain a meta-text that tells you how to read the core text (this highlights the importance of encouraging academic literacy and writing capacity for higher education staff and students).

Now look at how quality in action research is judged.

How is Quality in Action Research Judged?

An action research dissertation or thesis is judged in terms of two sets of criteria:

- Criteria for judging the quality of research, spelled out above.
- Criteria for judging the quality of action: this involves judging whether the research shows the demonstration of the espoused values and purposes of the researcher.

These two sets of criteria form two parallel, complementary and interweaving stories (Figure 10.1) moving continually towards openness and criticality, representative of the unconstrained visions of Sowell (1987) (page 13). This in itself generates new criteria: does the text show the interweaving of the researcher's awareness of the need for quality in action research? Does the text show the researcher's awareness of the need to explain how quality is understood in terms of openness and criticality, and for what purposes?

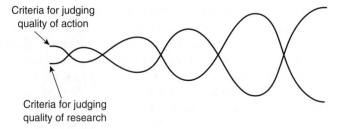

Criteria for judging quality of action

Criteria for judging quality of research

Figure 10.1 Interweaving criteria for judging quality in action and research

Now consider how quality in the action of action research is judged.

Many authors have produced criteria for judging quality in action research (for example, Feldman, 2003; Bullough and Pinnegar, 2004). A well-established typology is in Winter (1989). Winter says that action research needs to show the following:

- **Improvement**: You try to live your educational values of, for example, justice, freedom, inclusion and independent thinking in your practice.
- **Learning**: You learn from doing the action research, with and from others.

- **Collaborative enquiry**: You take other people's ideas into account, while taking responsibility for your influences in learning.
- **Risk**: You appreciate that nothing is certain. You go on the journey nevertheless.
- **Reflexive critique**: You deconstruct your thinking in light of new learning from experience.
- **Dialectical critique**: You understand how you and your circumstances have been influenced by history and culture.
- **New beginnings**: You understand that the end of one action reflection cycle will become the beginning of a new one (adapted from Winter, 1989: 46–55).

My own view, argued since the 1980s (McNiff, 1984, 1989, 2013a) is that values should be seen as having potential to transform into living practices. Thus the value of freedom is demonstrated through the exercise of freedom; the value of happiness is shown when people are happy. Values on the page remain abstract principles until they are realised in the world. An abstract principle such as justice (as in Rawls, 1971) cannot be realised simply through being written: real people must engage with the value if it is to become real. Values transform also into the criteria we use to judge the quality of our practices. The words 'friendship' and 'peace' become yardsticks by which we judge whether we are acting in a friendly or peaceful manner. These wider practices, as MacIntyre (1985) says, are characterised by their internal goods: friendship is demonstrated through dialogue and listening; peace is demonstrated by people working together amicably. A value does not realise itself until it is given away by the individual into the world.

Jean Flood, coordinator of Mission in the Economy, in Liverpool writes about 'Real Christmas: Read All About It' (see www.missionintheconomy.com; see http://youtu.be/wAxD5qcmnt8 for the video of this project). Jean is one of a group of chaplains I work with, all of whom are researching their practices using an action research approach. In her account she tells how she and colleagues decided to create a living crib in Liverpool City Centre, in an effort to bring the Church to the real world. Through working with our research group she hopes to turn this practice account into a research account.

As noted earlier, these days a note of caution is required in some first-person action research accounts. While the 'I' may be the focus of action research in that the 'I' takes responsibility for actions, the research should not be about the 'I' as the centre of enquiry (as I have written in other texts). First there cannot be a centre (see page 93): in relational cultures the idea of 'centre' disappears and the dynamics of relationships remain. Second, in some contemporary texts the 'I' has become 'me': the story is all about 'me'. I think this is awful, and denies the very values that the text claims to be fulfilling. In my thinking, the 'I' is realised only through the 'you', as Buber (2002) says: the self is conceivable only in relation to others (see also Levinas, 1998). I see the realisation of the value of relationship as a main criterion for judging quality in action research.

Now consider how the communicability of texts is judged.

How is Quality in the Communicability of Texts Judged?

Two sets of criteria are helpful. The first is from Habermas (1976) in relation to knowledge claims, as follows.

- Is the claim comprehensible? Does it make sense to the reader?
- Is it truthful? Is the researcher telling the truth? Do they provide a firm evidence base against which to test the claim?
- Is it authentic? Does the researcher demonstrate their authenticity by showing, over time and through interaction, that they have committed to living as fully as possible the values they explicitly espouse?
- Is it appropriate? Does the researcher show that they understand how historical and cultural forces form a normative background to the claim?

Here is the original text from which these ideas are drawn:

I shall develop the thesis that anyone acting communicatively must, in performing any speech action, raise universal validity claims and suppose that they can be vindicated (or redeemed). Insofar as he *[sic]* wants to participate in a process of reaching understanding, he cannot avoid raising the following – and indeed precisely the following – validity claims. He claims to be:

1. uttering something understandably;
2. giving (the hearer) something to understand;
3. making himself thereby understandable; and
4. coming to an understanding with another person.

The speaker must choose a comprehensible expression so that speaker and hearer can understand one another. The speaker must have the intention of communicating a true proposition (or a propositional content, the existential presuppositions of which are satisfied) so that the hearer can share the knowledge of the speaker. The speaker must want to express his intentions truthfully so that the hearer can believe the utterance of the speaker (can trust him). Finally, the speaker must choose an utterance that is right so that the hearer can accept the utterance and speaker and hearer can agree with one another in the utterance with respect to a recognized normative background. Moreover, communicative action can continue undisturbed only as long as participants suppose that the validity claims they reciprocally raise are justified.

(Habermas, 1976: 2–3)

Linking with the ideas of Habermas, a second set of criteria comes from Foucault (2001), who speaks about *parrhesia* (commonly understood as 'speaking one's truth'). This involves demonstrating:

- frankness: the speaker believes what they say and communicates the conviction of their commitment to others;
- truth: the speaker knows what truth is and can communicate it to others;
- courage: the speaker accepts the risk of telling the truth;
- criticism: the speaker exercises critique towards self and others;
- duty: the speaker accepts the responsibility of telling the truth.

In relation to these two sets of criteria, you need to show that you have:

- **Conducted rigorous research**: you test the validity of your ideas within a disciplined methodological and epistemological framework.
- **Engaged in scholarly enquiry**: you test the validity of your ideas against the ideas of people in the literature.
- **Told the truth**: you go through rigorous validation procedures, to test the validity of what you are saying: you do not expect people simply to take your word for it.
- **Developed confidence in your personal knowledge**: you believe your claims are worthy of merit.
- **Displayed courage and tenacity**: you get your claim validated and legitimated through informed debate.
- **Exercised provisionality**: you believe that you are right, but you acknowledge that you may be mistaken.
- **Lived your values in practice**: you are prepared to stand up for what you believe in.

Keep your examiner in mind

Throughout, keep your examiner in mind. Remember that they expect to see that specific criteria have been achieved and will look for the following:

- You have fulfilled the criteria for an academic report (see above) through the commensurability of the content and form of your text. Examiners will expect to read an action research text or at least a largely qualitative research one (that can still contain quantitative data and analysis), not a scientific one.
- You tell the story in a way that is comprehensible, authentic, truthful and appropriate for its context; you demonstrate courage through speaking your truth in spite of potential fall-out.
- You make explicit how you have achieved certain validity criteria, as follows.
  - You claim content validity for your work through giving descriptions and explanations for improvement in your workplace.
  - You show the processes involved in influencing this improvement, what you have done and how you have done it. You claim process validity for your work.
  - Your dissertation or thesis shows that people have come to respect one another and have developed dialogical practices. You can claim democratic validity for your work.
  - Your text shows how you have encouraged and enabled people to take responsibility for their own decisions in future, so you can claim catalytic validity (Lather, 1991) for your work.

Make sure you explain what you mean by your terms, so your reader will see the significance of what you are doing.

You meet examiners' expectations by explaining what you have done: these explanations need to work at the highest level of communication (at the level of explanatory adequacy). You write these explanations into your text at every opportunity. In a generic way you show that you have engaged with:

- your own thinking;
- the thinking of others;
- the thinking of the social formation of which you are a part.

Engaging with your own thinking

Explain how you have reflected on and tried to improve your learning and actions. Do not pretend that you got everything right, or that everything went well. It is important to outline the uncertainties or how you got side-tracked. Show how you made sense out of chaos. Quote from your reflective diary, and give comments from your critical friends to show how you learned through interaction and how this led to new learning. Be brave: say that you sometimes had to change your mind because your data showed you things you would rather not have seen (disconfirming data).

Engaging with the thinking of others

This means engaging with the ideas of colleagues and key theorists in the literature. Aim to engage with the literature throughout, perhaps by providing mini-literature reviews. Explain how you have been inspired by the ideas of others, and are testing the validity of your ideas in relation to theirs. Remember that 'the literature' refers to all kinds of books, scholarly papers and newspaper reports, and visual and oral communications through film, video, and radio (see Collins, 2010; Andrews et al., 2012).

Engaging with the thinking of the social formation of which you are a part

A major focus in your research report is dialectical critique (Winter, 1989), where you locate your action research within its social and cultural context. This means understanding and analysing the different social, economic, political and cultural forces that have shaped the context. For example, in formerly colonised countries you would comment on how previous colonial regimes have left a legacy of inequality and oppression. These have strengthened your emancipatory intent. In contested spaces you would comment on the struggle for competing rights, and show how you have developed inclusional practices in response.

You also need to show how your thinking has developed within specific contexts. Bourdieu (1990) says we are born into a *habitus*; we buy into the cultural and social context with its normative behaviours and epistemologies. Our thinking is influenced by the epistemological traditions of our culture, and by cultural expectations that are outcomes of the thinking of people who have also been influenced by those cultural expectations. Some of the best action research accounts are those where the writer comments on how they have freed their own thinking so that they and others can create new futures. For example:

- Zola Malgas (2008) developed a new critically-oriented in-house staff development programme.
- Willem Louw (2011) found ways of improving the service delivery and relevance of a psychology training clinic.
- Josephine Bleach (2013) shows how she contributes to educational well-being through an Early Learning Initiative.
- Odd Edvardsen (2006) explains how he has helped people in rural areas to cope with landmine injuries.
- Marianne Olsen (2014) shows how she enables students from privileged backgrounds to work with and learn from people in contexts of significant deprivation.

You can anticipate examiners' questions and deliberately insert appropriate sections of text into your account, as follows:

Question: Does your work contain a claim to knowledge and do you show its significance for your field?

Answer: You should be able to say:

The unit of enquiry (what you are studying) is your claim to know your practice. Through doing your action research you can claim to have improved your practice by improving your learning. You know something now that you did not know before. Your claim is original because no one else has improved your practice or made the claim. You also know how you have done this: you have developed your own epistemology of practice.

Question: Do you demonstrate the validity and originality of your claim by showing your critical understanding of the processes involved?

Answer: You should be able to say:

You demonstrate the validity and originality of your claim by showing how you experienced emotional and cognitive dissonance when your values were denied in your practice. You took action to address the issue, to try to live your values more fully. You systematically monitored the situation and gathered data to show how things developed, and you generated evidence whose validity you tested against identified criteria and standards of judgement, and against the critical feedback of others.

Answer: You should be able to say:

You claim that you have improved your practice by improving your learning about how to live your values more fully than before. You are moving towards what you understand as the good. You can show that you have inspired others to investigate their practices and to think for themselves and make independent choices. If you have not succeeded you can say why: possibly your context constrained your efforts. Mzuzile Mpondwana (2008) shows how he works with communities in a South African township to try to encourage quality relationships in spite of external constraints; Gerrie Adams (2008) shows how he challenges external constraints to move from being a transmitter of knowledge to a mediator of learning.

In addressing these criteria, you are demonstrating an improvement in knowledge, skills and research capacities, as follows.

You can claim an improvement in knowledge

You know and can articulate:

- understanding of your values;
- the reasons and purposes of your research;
- your subject knowledge;
- what counts as evidence, and particular standards of judgement;
- issues of context, and how this may help or hinder your efforts at improvement.

You can claim an improvement in skills

You know and can articulate:

- how to take political action in your workplace;
- how to influence your own learning and the learning of others, and inspire them to improve it;
- how to monitor and research your practice;
- how to negotiate, delegate, be personally effective, and plan strategically;
- how to do research and tell the story;
- how to evaluate and negotiate your criteria.

You can claim an improvement in research capacity

You have developed capacity in the following:

- undertaking independent enquiries and bringing them to successful completion;
- the sustainable renewal of practice, and influencing organisational learning;

- research capacity; you know what is involved in doing research;
- explaining how and why research should be understood as good quality, especially in terms of its originality, rigour, significance and impact.

You have done all these things, and can say so, as your original claim to be contributing to knowledge of your field.

If appropriate, you can also ask your examiner to judge your report in terms of your own standards of judgement in relation to those aspects that you consider most meaningful for your practice. For example:

- Whether your text shows your capacity for transforming your thinking, so that you can claim transformational validity for your text.
- Whether it manifests its underlying logics and values through its form, so that you can claim that it shows formal validity.
- Whether it uses a narrative form, so that you can claim that it shows narrative validity.
- Whether it shows processes of deconstruction through reflexive and dialectical critique so that you can claim that it shows reflexive validity.
- Whether it is transformational and catalytic so that you can claim that it shows catalytic validity.
- Whether it shows methodological rigour so that you can claim that it shows methodological validity.

These ideas are developed below.

Now consider some procedures for assessing masters and doctoral texts.

Procedures for Assessing Masters and Doctoral Texts

This section is about how masters and doctoral texts are examined and accredited. It is in two parts:

- Examining and accrediting masters degrees.
- Examining and accrediting doctoral degrees.

Examining and accrediting masters degrees

Many universities offer taught masters level programmes in action research. Given that many professions now require masters certification as evidence of ongoing professional learning, action research has become a popular strategy. Most universities embrace action research at masters level, and often package it into a form that fits well with the modular structure of programmes. The knowledge created at masters level is not required to be original. For some, it is sufficient to show engagement with others' ideas, and perhaps a reworking of those ideas, and not explain how the work generates theory. Personally I disagree with this position. I have supervised many masters programmes, and have always insisted on participants explaining how they generate their theories of practice through studying the practice: see, for example Aston (2008); Jackson (2008); Nugent (2000): see also masters reports at www.jeanmcniff.com/theses.asp.

Masters programmes in Europe are referred to as second cycle study programmes, following common arrangements in the European Higher Education Area. Assessment is based on the European Credit Transfer System (ECTS), with different modules often carrying different weightings. You can accumulate credits and trade them in across participating universities. Most universities accept equivalence for entry to programmes, including schemes such as The Accreditation of Prior (Experiential) Learning. This encourages cross-disciplinary studies through knowledge transfer.

A typical masters programme lasts for one or two years and is usually organised as four to six modules followed by an extended module that counts as a dissertation. Assessment is usually conducted by the module or programme supervisor(s) and may then go through an institutional moderation process to ensure quality and robustness of assessment. There is normally no *viva voce*, though there may be for an MPhil, which is a higher-level degree.

The masters programmes, and occasional discrete modules I have taught in the UK and internationally have taken the broad form shown in Table 10.1.

Table 10.1 Structure of a typical modular masters programme

Module	Title and content of module
1	Research methods and forms of enquiry: core module, usually compulsory.
2	Selected from a menu: options such as leadership, management, life story, collaborative enquiry, business, art history, classical studies … a wide range spanning most disciplines.
3	Frequently a 'free' module is offered, such as independent study. This means that the candidate may study an option they are especially interested in.
4	Personal choice from menu available, or depending on institutional provision and/or requirement.
5	Also personal choice from menu available, or depending on institutional provision and/or requirement.
6	Preparation for dissertation: core module, usually compulsory.
7	Dissertation, usually between 10,000 and 20,000 words: this carries greater weighting than modules.

Examining and accrediting doctoral degrees

Studying for a doctorate is different from studying for a masters. A full-time doctorate usually lasts for three or four years, whereas a part-time programme usually has a minimum of three and maximum of seven or eight years. It took me eight years to get my PhD because I took a year's suspension and a year's extension, given that I was working full-time as a deputy head teacher and had little time to study or write. Many part-time doctoral candidates find it hard to juggle work and study. If you meet someone with 'Dr' in front of their name, you know they have earned it.

Nowadays there are many doctoral programmes, including traditional PhD and part-taught disciplines-based professional doctorates, such as the EdD (Doctor of Education) and DProf (Professional Doctorate) (see Murray, 2002; Costley and Stephenson, 2009). Professional doctorates suit some people better than PhDs: for a PhD you are expected to engage almost totally in independent study, with negotiated contact hours with your supervisor, whereas in a professional doctoral programme you are supervised for modules. All doctorates demand the same amount of work and all should command the same level of prestige. A PhD thesis is usually about 80,000 words in length, whereas a professional doctoral programme requires module assignments of about 4–10,000 words and a thesis of about 40,000 words or less. For all doctoral theses, detailed criteria are issued to examiners, who are also expected to write a full report according to guidelines supplied by the institution.

Action research is popular on taught doctoral programmes. As with masters programmes, it is a valuable form of professional education, and it is possible to use the doctoral experience as a form of professional learning through studying aspects of personal practice (Evans, 2010). It is also easy to build in multimedia and multimodal forms of representation to supplement the core written work (Beardshaw Andrews, 2012), and many universities give the option of performance such as dance or music as part of the accreditation process.

Examining a doctoral thesis

A doctoral thesis is usually examined by an external examiner from another university and an internal examiner from the home university. Neither examiner should have had substantial previous contact with the candidate. Both examiners read your thesis and compare notes prior to the *viva voce* examination, which is a core aspect of most doctoral examinations. The viva enables your examiner to pursue any aspect they are interested in or they may have picked up from reading your thesis.

A *viva voce* examination is an oral examination, during which you defend your thesis. You stand up for what you have written and justify why you have written it. Most vivas last for about one to two hours, and take the form of a critical conversation. The examiners ask questions about your action (substantive issues about ideas and practices) and your research (epistemological and methodological issues). The aim is not to catch you out with trick questions, but to ask you searching questions that give you an opportunity to show what you can do. Often examiners ask you questions that enable you to show that you have addressed the university criteria, and many actively wish to engage in a detailed conversation about a particular topic.

The outcomes of the examination usually take the form of:

- Pass without modification (rare).
- Pass with minor modifications: which could include corrections of typographical or grammatical errors, and possibly some minor re-writing or revisiting of chapters. You could have somewhere between three weeks or six months to make the revisions.
- Pass with major modifications: this means revisiting areas of the thesis, including themes and concepts that may be lacking in discipline or depth. Usually examiners give detailed advice about what needs to be done to bring the thesis up to standard.
- Don't pass: in which case you are recommended to resubmit, within a negotiated time.

Many universities allow a candidate one chance of resubmission. If this is not successful the candidate may not resubmit but must accept another option offered by the institution, such as an MPhil degree.

You and your *viva*

The *viva voce* is a core part of the examination, and you can prepare for it by practising with your supervisor and colleagues.

Here are some commonly asked questions, which refer to the criteria, and the kinds of points you should include in your responses. The responses are idealised, and you should always respond in your own creative way, but these ideas show the kind of answers examiners are looking for.

Question: 'Tell us about your thesis.'   This is a frequent 'settling down' question. The examiner also wants to see whether you understand the requirement to make an original claim to knowledge, and that you can articulate the significance of your original contribution to your field.

Your answer could include the following:

- 'My thesis contains my original claim to knowledge.' Explain what you mean by this. Say why you chose a narrative form and why you positioned yourself as the author.
- 'My claim is that I have generated my personal theory of practice' or 'my personal theory of educational leadership' or whatever aspect of practice your thesis deals with. Explain how theory generated through action research is different from traditional propositional theory. Say what your job is, and what your practice involved. Briefly outline what you did during your action research. Explain how you have improved your practice (or not), so that you are confident in testing the validity of your claim in the public domain.
- 'My claim is that I have developed an epistemology of practice.' You explain that you know what you are doing and you know how and why you are doing it. If you give this answer, you should be confident about issues of epistemology, because your examiners would probably pursue this line of thinking.

- 'I show how I have generated evidence against which I test the validity of my knowledge claims. I test their validity in relation to identified standards of judgement. I can explain how my values have transformed into my criteria and standards of judgement.' You must show that you understand the importance of testing the validity of knowledge claims. Say what your criteria and standards of judgement are: 'I show how I have realised the value of social justice as a living practice.'
- Link everything you say to the literature wherever possible. Cite names and dates.

Question: 'What has doing your research meant for you?' Your examiner wants to see what you have learned, and how this will inform new learning and practices. They want to see if you demonstrate critical engagement with your own thinking.

Your answer could include the following:

- 'I have learned to become critical. I have developed the capacity for reflexive critique (Winter, 1989) by deconstructing my previous assumptions, and the capacity for dialectical critique by deconstructing other people's assumptions.' Explain what you mean by this, and how you have changed your thinking.
- 'I have a deeper understanding of processes of social and cultural transformation.' Say what you have learned through learning how to become critical.
- Link everything you say to the literature wherever possible. Cite names and dates.

Question: 'What are the main findings of your research?' The examiner wants to see what you have found out through doing the research, and if you can comment on its originality, rigour, significance for knowledge creation, and any effect you think it may have had on other people.

Your answer could include the following:

- 'My main findings are that I have contributed to new thinking and new practices.' Say what these are, for example that you have introduced new forms of communication, or have encouraged people to become more critical of what they are doing.
- 'I have learned to exercise my educational influence so that our workplace is a more open society (Popper, 1945).' Explain what you mean by 'educational influence' and how you have achieved this.
- 'I am aware of the significance of action research for improving practice through knowledge creation.' Explain how you have improved practice through knowledge creation.
- Link everything you say to the literature wherever possible. Cite names and dates.

Question: 'Please speak about the experience of writing the thesis.' The examiner wants to hear if you are aware of what writing a PhD thesis involves, and whether it is all your original work. They want to hear that you are aware that you have the capacity for independent study and 'writing knowledge'.

Your answers could include the following:

- 'I developed a regular writing schedule.' Explain your awareness of the need for maintaining a research focus.
- 'As I wrote, I tried to show, through the form of the text, how I was generating my personal theory from within my narrative of practice.' Outline the form that your narrative took, and say why you used this form.

- 'I consulted the literatures at all stages, incorporating the ideas of key theorists within my own theory of practice.' Outline who your key authors were and what you found attractive about what they had to say. Be prepared to engage in a discussion of their ideas. Your examiners know these things.
- Link everything you say to the literature wherever possible. Cite names and dates.

Question: 'How will you disseminate your work? How will you develop it?' The examiner wants to see if you appreciate that you should now publish the work in a range of ways, and if you are still passionate about intellectual engagement.

Your answers could include the following:

- 'I have learned the importance of speaking my truth. I will continue to do so through making my work public.' Say how you intend to continue challenging established orthodoxies through writing for publication, and presenting your work in public places such as conferences.
- 'I have learned the importance of writing, and of multimedia forms of representation. I intend to produce video narratives of my ongoing research into my practice, and make them public through web-based publishing.' Say that you intend to contribute to new e-journals and develop documentaries and other visual forms.
- 'I intend to move my research into a new phase where I investigate the following issues ...' Say what you intend to do now, and how you will do it.

These are only some questions you could be asked, but they give a flavour of the kind of answers that will earn you a doctorate.

Finding the right examiner

A dilemma that candidates and supervisors often face is how to find the right examiner for the task. It is usually the responsibility of the main supervisor, in consultation with the institution, to identify and approach a potential examiner. It is essential that at least one of your examiners is familiar with and sympathetic to the principles of action research, even if they don't do action research themselves.

I worked for some years at a university (not in the UK) that did not have a tradition of action research, and where I had sole responsibility for the supervision of several doctoral programmes. My strategy was to arrange for the internal examiner to take responsibility for questions about the subject area of the thesis, while negotiating an external examiner from elsewhere who had in-depth knowledge of methodological issues. The strategy worked and all candidates succeeded, and the university now has a thriving tradition of action research. Doctoral achievement is a political game, and you need to be strategic. Fortunately, now that a new generation of doctoral researchers (including you) is emerging, the pool of examiners will also enlarge, and in future candidates will not experience so many difficulties. This gives you another reason to succeed.

Suggestions for Future Developments

Here are some ideas about how you can influence the development of the field through succeeding in your dissertation or thesis.

I have said throughout that you need to stay within the parameters of established criteria and other conventions, while working creatively within them. My advice to candidates is the same as that offered to Willem Louw, introduced in Chapter 5, who writes to me in an email:

When my supervisor commented on my text being too personal and not scholarly enough and that the style of writing would not be acceptable to examiners I showed him some of your books. His response was: once you have made a name for yourself, you can write in any style you like, but until then, I had to follow convention. [Continued in Chapter 11]

Yes. Get the degree and then do what you like.

However, regarding creative working within the parameters, as part of getting the degree you can also request a negotiation of the criteria with your examiners (see above page 194), or you can ask your supervisor to do so on your behalf. For example:

Peter Raymond was a primary classroom teacher and headteacher for 21 years, and is now a senior lecturer in teacher education at York St John University. He takes as a main criterion of quality for his doctoral studies whether his undergraduate students implement in practice their understanding that creativity is something you do, not only something you have. He writes:

> The practice I am investigating lies mainly in my teaching in and leading of a final year module called 'Creativity and Communication in Primary Education'. The aim is to encourage and help student teachers to challenge their own and others' perceptions of creativity and to see creativity not as an object but as a form of practice – more of a verb than a noun. In doing so student teachers are asked to develop what I have come to call 'living definitions' of creativity; living in the sense that they evolve and change through an ongoing engagement in critical dialogic reflection and also in the sense that they become drivers of student teachers' professional practice – the living definitions become affective definitions. (Raymond, 2014: 3)

These kinds of innovative criteria go into the knowledge base and begin to influence the literary canon. It is a gradual process of introducing change: once a new criterion is accepted through the legitimation of the degree it is there to stay; it will not go away. It sets a precedent, as in common law legal systems: it is written into the record.

This slow work of words is a major strategy for influencing processes of change. It is also why it is so important to create a public knowledge base of masters and doctoral accounts to make precedents known to others who may come after. It is a long revolution (Williams, 1965): once change is accepted, people change their thinking and practices. This is why you should aim to be successful, and write up your work. Look at your power: look at what you can do for the future.

These ideas are developed in Chapter 14. Meanwhile, here is a summary of the main points in this chapter.

SUMMARY

This chapter has considered how the quality of your dissertation or thesis will be judged. Several aspects will be judged: the quality of your practice in your workplace; the quality of research conducted; and the quality of text produced. Throughout the production of your text, keep your examiner in mind and give them what they are looking for. Especially give the meta-text, which is a critical commentary on the quality of the research and practice, and how this quality may be communicated through writing. Further issues are considered such as the need for selecting the right examiner and for negotiating new criteria for judging the quality of your work.

REFLECTIVE QUESTIONS

- Are you clear that your work will be judged in relation to different aspects and criteria, including the quality of your practice in the workplace, the quality of your research, and the quality of text you have produced? All these aspects contribute to the assessment.

- Have you articulated in your work how the research will be useful for different people? Have you explained that the research will continue, even though the dissertation or thesis is now complete?

- Are you confident about examinations procedures? Do you know what to expect, and do you know who to ask for further information?

RESEARCH EXERCISE

Write a critical analysis of a text you have written; comment on its content, style and the effectiveness of your communication.

So now your formal studies are complete, or even if they are still in process, it is time to think about writing for publication. This brings us to Part IV, where advice is given about writing for academic and professional journals and possibly for writing a book.

PART IV

Writing for Publication

This Part is about writing for publication in academic and professional journals and as books.

It contains Chapters 11 and 12.

Chapter 11, 'Writing for academic and professional journals' gives practical advice about how to write an article for journal publication, including what to write and how to write it, and procedures for submitting the article.

Chapter 12, 'Writing your first academic book' does the same in relation to book writing. It outlines what you need to know about writing a book, how to get it published, and how to sell it.

Practical advice and theoretical resources are offered throughout, to help ensure that your text will be noticed by editors and other decision-makers and accepted for publication.

ELEVEN

Writing for Academic and Professional Journals

This chapter is about getting published in academic and professional journals. Different people have different reasons for doing this: they may like writing articles or it may be an institutional requirement or even a condition of tenure. In your case, be as clear as possible about why you wish to write for journal publication, whether for career prospects or to contribute to scholarly debates about a particular topic. Many people think it is difficult to get published, but this is not necessarily the case. The advice here is to approach the task in a systematic way, learn what it involves, and see it as a research project where you ask, 'How do I learn to write for academic and professional journals?'

The chapter is organised as follows:

1. Before: planning and getting ready.
2. During: writing the article.
3. After: what to expect and do after submitting.

The next chapter is about writing books and more extended texts. The difference between writing articles and books is similar to the difference between travelling to do a presentation by train or car. You put the same amount of time and effort into both, but with a car you can carry everything you need, whereas with train travel you can pack only so much into a suitcase, so you need to be more selective in word and deed. Writing articles calls for this kind of disciplined selection, as outlined now.

Before: Planning and Getting Ready

This section is about planning and getting ready to write. It contains the following ideas:

- Questions to guide your preparation.
- Finding and storing ideas.
- Developing habits and routines.

Questions to guide your preparation

These questions act as your main guiding principles:

- Why have you chosen to write an article?
- Are you sure your article matches the needs of the journal you target?
- What do you want to say?
- Why do you want to say it?
- Who do you want to say it to? (This means also thinking about how you want to say it.)

Why have you chosen to write an article?

Be clear about why you wish to write an article rather than, say, a book. Is it an institutional expectation or a condition of tenure? Many academics write articles as a sign of prestige, to establish themselves with their peer community: 'Success is seen as largely measured by recognition and, in turn, the process of acquiring recognition as dependent on the capacity to write papers valued by one's colleagues' (Hyland, 2007: 19). Being clear about why you wish to write will help you decide whether to go for a 'top' journal with high impact factor (difficult because of the standards expected, and the long lists of already accepted articles) or one with not such a high impact factor, which may be quicker and easier but less prestigious. Being clear about your reasons will help you decide which journals to target.

Are you sure your article matches the needs of the journal you target?

Make sure the content of your article matches the requirements of the journal you target. This means researching the field. First identify one or two journals in your discipline you think may be appropriate for your article. Look up the 'About this journal' section on the journal website and read the 'Advice to authors'; note carefully what the editors say they want. Note word lengths and other structural requirements. Look up as many articles as possible from the journal(s) and read them. Read what the abstracts say. Is there a common theme? What kinds of articles are published – methods-based articles, literature reviews, narrative accounts, policy debates? Note how the authors structure their papers and develop arguments. Decide how best to communicate your messages according to the way the articles are structured.

While some people like to target specific journals and write for them, others prefer to write the article and then look for an appropriate journal. Decide for yourself what works for you, but make sure your product meets the market need.

What do you want to say?

Be clear about what you wish to say in the article; this means making sure you know what your topic is and that you know enough to write about it in a succinct, authoritative manner. You have only 6–7,000 words to get your message across. Can you do it? Writing an article means staying on task and focusing on one topic only, while demonstrating extensive knowledge of related issues and literatures. This takes discipline and discernment. Are you really prepared to leave out anything extraneous? Or would a book be better for your and your readers' needs?

What is the issue? What is the concern?

Make sure you have a topic you really wish to write about. An action research article deals with matters arising from current practices, or offering different angles on issues in the literatures, or lessons from experience. Action research articles are usually practice-based, though some articles offer strong conceptual frameworks and resources to support action researchers in different settings. Be as clear as possible about what the issue is. Write it down as bullet points. Write an abstract: you will have to do this anyway. If you cannot write a 150-word abstract stating what the main issue is, you need to rethink and focus more closely.

Why do you want to say it?

Why is it important that you say it? Is the topic in your field? Is something lacking in current thinking or policy? Have you found a new way of doing things? Have you generated new ideas from your research so want to get critical feedback from readers? Have you an exciting model to share, or an idea from your thesis? A thesis should generate a range of articles, on different topics, one at a time. Some authors write a series of articles related to the same topic, though using different words, materials and examples. You can do the same.

Who do you want to say it to?

This means thinking about how you want to say it. Be clear about who your audience is, and write for them; this also helps you decide which journal to target. Keep your reader in mind, and write about your topic in a way that catches their attention. Adapt your style of writing to their needs. Are they your peers, in which case you would adopt a form of expository writing? Or early career researchers, when you may use a more pedagogical voice? Are you exploring an idea or theme, so developing experimental writing? Are you explaining something, which means adopting a discursive or thematic form? Aim always to write in a style appropriate to your reader's needs: remember AIDA – get their Attention, attract their Interest, arouse their Desire, inspire them to Act (to read your work).

Here is a comment by Willem Louw (see Chapter 10) on his earlier efforts to write journal articles. His experiences appear to be shared by many. He continues his email:

> My challenge to myself became one of learning to write in an academic way that did not kill the passion of the project for me (disconnect me from my values). How I wrote determined whether I would get stuck in self-doubt or not.
>
> My experience (and I am certain that I am not unique) is that whenever I read a published article, I found that the clearly articulated arguments and neat conclusions made my own text appear infantile and impotent and this was a hard demon to face. The articles were often very inspirational, but they only added to my own sense of not being good enough to write about this project, as I would read a piece of highlighted text from a respected action researcher, and then look at a paragraph of my own writing on my computer screen – and then the familiar despair would set in. Keeping my own 'truth' in focus was my only salvation. I had to move away from trying to play in the orchestra of an international research debate to becoming the conductor of my own research concert, where all the big names play their instruments (arguments) to a piece I composed. I had to direct them (scholarly and respected authors) to play softer on this theme and with more tempo and vigour on another. I wrote the themes of my concert piece from my heart and set it to beautiful music by using the talent of accomplished musicians.

Finding and storing ideas

Sometimes people ask, 'Where do I find ideas?' Here are some ideas.

How do you find ideas?

You can find ideas virtually anywhere. As noted, it is important to develop a constant alertness to new ideas as part of a creative habit (Tharp, 2006). Once you are in a mentally receptive mode you will not need to go looking for ideas: they will arrive thick and fast. You will hear ideas in conversations and presentations, in books, blogs and films, and on radio and television. Rowlands

(2005) claims, 'Everything I know I learned from TV', and cites themes of loneliness in *Sex and the City*, obligation from *Buffy the Vampire Slayer* and modernity and morality from *The Sopranos*. Lisa from *The Simpsons* becomes an Übergirl (pp. 250–2). Ideas are everywhere: your job is to be alert to them and keep a record of them before they flit away.

Where do you store ideas?

Ideas come and go quickly so store them as soon as possible. Keep a list of ideas as you go: keep a notebook handy, or use the tape recording function on your mobile phone (get an app that transcribes as you speak: many are free to download) and file them later on your computer or in a journal. On my computer I have a collection of files with one or two sentences about a theme, and I add to this over time with references to papers and other resources when I come across them. You can collect ideas from notes you write at meetings and conversations, and turn them later into an article. Aim to have several articles on the go at the same time, and keep them organised in files on your computer. Add to them when you have another idea, and keep a list of relevant papers and resources. Draw up a chart or desk chart to keep you on track, as in Table 11.1.

Get into a routine: Develop the habit

Look at writing for publication as part of your capacity building as a researcher and writer. Many universities require doctoral candidates to start writing articles for publication as soon as they begin their formal studies. Although this can be daunting, it is good training in the discipline of doing research. Writing and writing for publication is not done after the research event when the data-gathering and analysis is done: it is part of the event, and, in many ways, it is the event. Build in writing from the start and regard it as a job of work to be done conscientiously and regularly.

Here are the main processes involved in writing the article.

During: Writing the article

This section contains two main points:

- Organising yourself.
- Writing your article.

Table 11.1 Chart to show a record of writing activity

Article title/theme	January	February	March	April	May	June
Month						
Writing for publication	Initial literature search; identify journal(s)	Main ideas noted: links thought through	Section 1	Sections 2 and 3: further reading around writing for publication	Complete first draft. Send to critical readers	Act on feedback from readers; edit and revise
Developing cosmopolitanism		Ideas formulated	Some draft writing	Need to do more reading around cosmopolitanism and related areas. Wrote rough draft in two days. Important theme for different constituencies	Shelve for the time being	Visit to inner city organisations: revived interest in issues of cosmopolitanism. Submit to selected journal
Practitioners' right to research	Issue at work that sparked idea of right to research	Interviewed participants to see what they are doing as researchers	Awareness of conflict between right to research and duty to protect		Begin editing, revising and refining	

Writing is as much about organising yourself and your resources as about having inspiring and creative ideas. It is possibly one of the hardest things to do yet it is imperative, so that you can channel your creativity. It means deciding on and sticking to a schedule; sorting out mental and physical clutter; taking care of yourself; getting your work-life balance right; and many other routines. It means committing to writing regularly, not finding excuses not to write, and developing a positive frame of mind and speech. It is so easy to blame, to say, 'I haven't got the time to write'. Stern (2014b) points out that writing is part of doing research, which is part of your everyday job. You don't say, 'I haven't got time to do my job', so why say, 'I haven't got time to write', if writing is part of the job? Physical organisation, which implies doing things systematically, stems from an organised mental attitude that sees things in good order. There is a lot of wisdom in the principles of Feng Shui, tuning into the natural universal order of harmony in emergence. You are part of this order, so anything you can do to strengthen the relationship between you and your environment will greatly contribute to the sense of well-being necessary for writing fluently and achieving flow (Csikszentmihalyi, 1990).

Here are some ideas about what you can do to achieve this at a practical level.

Organising your academic research time

The advice offered in Chapter 7 applies here, as well as the following, which is about organising your academic research time to accommodate writing. As an academic/researcher you are possibly allocated research time, though many colleagues I know say they use this time to catch up on other jobs, or simply to relax. While relaxation is essential, don't use the need for relaxation as an excuse not to write (but do make dedicated time to relax and take your exercise, even if it is a walk around the block). Aim to set aside an hour or so for thinking, reading and writing during the working day. Aim to write in short bursts: it is amazing how much you can get done on a train or bus journey, and tablets are great devices for writing two or three sentences at a time. Carry your voice recorder with you and transfer the contents to your computer or tablet when you get back to your desk. Record conversations with colleagues and use excerpts from the conversations to go into your text (make sure you ask their permission first).

Set yourself writing goals and identify specific times to write. Murray (2005) recommends making a mental or written note to the effect, 'By 5pm tomorrow I will have written the Introduction to the paper'. You can take advantage of postponed meetings or quiet days and write for two hours, and you can set aside one hour a day depending on other routines. If you are serious about setting aside a specific time, put up a 'please do not disturb' sign or close your door.

Organising writing support

Enlist the help of friends and colleagues to give you critical feedback on your writing and ideas. Email your original writings and ask them to respond. Use social networking as a way of sharing ideas and getting critical feedback; this way you can form an Internet-based collaborative community of inquiry. Form a study or reading group with colleagues, to read and comment on ideas from texts. When appropriate, aim to write collaboratively; this can be facilitated by dedicated writing retreats, with structured times around writing, and timetables to achieve specific tasks. However, note that these work for some and not others; not everyone can adapt to such strict routines, and many need flexibility to allow for thinking time and reflection.

Read at every opportunity: read eclectically and keep notes on anything that interests you. Type relevant quotations direct onto your computer to create a resource bank, and remember to record the page number. Buy used books from Internet stores and charity shops at a fraction of their original price.

Be your own best support by deciding when you do your administrative work and when you do your writing. Keep them separate so you come to your writing with an uncluttered mind and can focus on the job in hand. Sometimes you have to force yourself to write, but also make space for watching television or strolling around the park.

Organising your work area

Here are some specific strategies for organising your work area when writing.

- Set up a conceptual space (in your head) for thinking and writing. Try to keep it clear of clutter.
- Set up a physical space (on your desk) for your resources, so you can access them readily. Identify a number of key texts and have them handy for reference and for inspiration.
- Set up a writing space (in your house or office or garden), where people will leave you alone. Turn off the emails, resist the urge to find out what's on TV tonight, and write.

Keep your work area pleasant. Put some flowers on the table (but not near the computer), and keep your space fragrant. Aim to feel good about your space to let it work for you.

Organising your thinking

Marshall your thoughts through gathering together jottings and field notes (Clandinin and Connelly, 2000 refer to data as field texts). Use notes from conversations and meetings as data. Look through your emails and tweets and use those as data too (and get permission to use them).

Draw up an outline plan for your article. You can do this in several ways. Write a PowerPoint presentation of your article. Make a list of points as a blueprint and use this as a writing plan: write the section headings as 'A', 'b' and 'c' headings, or use numbers and indents. When I prepared the manuscript of this book to send to the publishers I adopted the following strategy:

A heading: plain bold type, centred on the page
B heading: plain bold type, with space below, ranged left
C heading: italics bold type, with space below, ranged left
D heading: italics bold type, no space below, ranged left

Using this stategy, the outline plan for this chapter is as follows (I have also used numbers and indents, to show how it is possible to use systems together if you wish):

Chapter 11 Outline plan

1 Planning and getting ready

1.1 Questions to guide your preparation

1.1.1 *Why have you chosen to write an article?*
1.1.2 *Are you sure that your article matches the needs of the journal you select?*
1.1.3 *What do you want to say?*
1.1.4 *What is the issue? What is the concern?*
1.1.5 *Why do you want to say it?*
1.1.6 *Who do you want to say it to?*

1.2 Finding and storing ideas

1.2.1 *How do you find ideas?*
1.2.2 *Where do you store ideas?*
1.2.3 *Get into a routine: develop the habit*

2 During: writing the article

2.1 Organising yourself

2.1.1 *Organising your time*
2.1.2 *Organising writing support*
2.1.3 *Organising your work area*
2.1.4 *Organising your thinking*

2.2 Writing your article (this could form an embedded action research cycle)

2.2.1 *Before: Preparing to write the article*
2.2.2 *During: Writing the article*
    2.2.2a *Act 1: Planning and drafting*
    2.2.2b *Act 2: Composing*
    2.2.2c *Act 3: Editing, revising and polishing*
        Editing
        Revising
        Polishing
2.2.3 *Act 4: Submitting your article*

3   After: what to expect and do after submitting your article

3.1   Making revisions

Summary

Reflective questions

Research exercise

Here is the same outline plan presented in graphic form.

Table 11.2   Outline plan for Chapter 11 in graphic form

'A' heading	'b' heading	'c' heading	'd' heading	other
1 Planning and getting ready				
	Questions to guide your preparation			
		Why have you chosen to write an article? *Are you sure that your article matches the needs of the journal you select?* *What do you want to say?* *What is the issue? What is the concern?* *Why do you want to say it?* *Who do you want to say it to?*		
	Finding and storing ideas			
		How do you find ideas? *Where do you store ideas?* *Get into a routine: develop the habit*		
2 During: writing the article				
	Organising yourself			
		Organising yourself *Organising your time* *Organising writing support* *Organising your work area* *Organising your thinking*		
	Writing your article			

'A' heading	'b' heading	'c' heading	'd' heading	other
		Before: preparing to write the article During: Writing the article		
			Act 1: Planning and drafting *Act 2: Composing* *Act 3: Editing, revising and polishing*	
				Editing *Revising* *Polishing*
		Act 4: Submitting your article		
3 After: what to expect and do after submitting your article				
	Making revisions			
Summary Reflective questions Research exercise				

If you are doing a conference presentation, use it to try out the ideas, and keep a record of the feedback from listeners. Try out any strategy you think will help you focus, and then stay focused for the time you are writing and submitting your article.

Writing your article

This section contains three main points:

1. Before: preparing to write the article.
2. During: writing the article.
3. After: submitting the article, and afterwards.

At this point the text moves into a new mini-action enquiry, like the embedded spin-off cycle in Figure 4.3. It is symptomatic of the iterative cycles and embedded structures of action research.

Before: preparing to write the article

Having decided what you wish to say, how you would like to say it, why you wish to say it and who you are going to say it to, now decide on a structure for your article (see also Chapter 12). Again, it can help to look through existing articles to see how they are written and what the Editorial Board expects and will accept.

Most articles include specific aspects:

Aim: 'In this paper I explore ideas about ...'; 'The aim of this paper is to ...'

Main argument: 'In this paper I argue that action research ...'; 'The main argument in this article is that ...'

Literature review: 'The literatures about research say that ...'; 'Many authors maintain that ...'

Method/methodology: 'I used an action research approach throughout ...'; 'Action research was the preferred methodology because ...'

Contribution to knowledge of the field: 'This paper contributes to debates about ...'; 'An original idea of this paper is that ...'

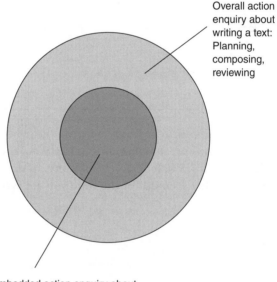

Overall action enquiry about writing a text: Planning, composing, reviewing

Embedded action enquiry about writing an article: Planning, composing, revising

Figure 11.1 Embedded writing practices

Here are two different structures for articles I have had published in recent years. For the first (McNiff, 2013b), I adopted a more traditionalist social science framework, while writing action research content into the structures. You can find this article at www.jeanmcniff.com/writing.asp. The structure is as follows:

Title: 'Becoming cosmopolitan and other dilemmas of internationalisation: Reflections from the Gulf States'
Introduction
Cosmopolitans and locals
Denying cosmopolitanism
The research
   Methodology
   Data
Reflecting again
Assumptions of normative discourses regarding the export of knowledge
   Assumptions about the creation of knowledge
   Potential cultural imperialism
   Cultural and epistemological mnemocide
   Issues regarding the ethics of methodology
Possible implications of the research

Another article (McNiff, 2012) follows a more traditional action research structure, where I explain how I have used the questions of an action enquiry as section headings (see www.jeanmcniff.com/writing.asp).

Title: 'Travels around identity: Transforming cultures of learned colonisation'
Introduction
My contexts, my concerns
Why am I concerned? What do I want to do about it?
   Dominant story 1: Practitioners cannot do research or generate theory
   Dominant story 2: Research should be value-free
   Dominant story 3: Concepts, including identity, are abstract objects of enquiry and should be communicated as such
Writing new stories
   Ireland
   South Africa
However …
   Staying with identities formed from the past
   Staying with the image of coloniser and colonised
   Staying with the image of 'I'm just a teacher'
What about my own identity?
Developing trust
Negotiating identities
   Engaging with the dynamics of self-perception
   Researching practices
   Development of critical capacity

(Continued)

The best advice, as always, is to look at the journals and see what kind of articles they publish, and then develop the same or similar style, while writing your own content.

During: Writing the article

Organise writing your article into acts: (1) Planning and drafting; (2) Composing; and (3) Editing, revising and refining. The fourth act is when you submit it. A fifth act is when you get reviewers' responses and usually need to do a little reworking. The sixth and final act is when the article is published and you actually see it online and in a journal.

Act 1: Planning and drafting First plan your text by producing lists of notes, network diagrams and mind maps, or whatever strategy works for you. Working with these ideas and your notes and diagrams, begin to draft out your article. Write in stages and according to the structure you have identified. Give each section a heading, and use the heading to guide the content.

Turn the notes into sentences. At this point you move into composing, where you begin to produce a rough text.

Act 2: Composing The aim of composing is to produce a complete working (but not necessarily well-written) draft. Composing, says Sharples (1990: 90), is about designing text: 'It is primarily the way we create and structure text to achieve an effect on the reader'. Further, composing is an active process of expanding your working notes and communicating with yourself as you produce a text that you hope will communicate ideas to others. Homi Bhaba comments: 'In a way, writing to me is the staging of an idea, and I use that term with its full theatrical and operatic and dramatic possibilities, in the way in which the concept might be the armature or the architecture of the idea' (Bhaba, 2003, in Olson and Worsham, 2003: 37). As you write, reflect on what you are writing, and come up with new ideas and new forms of expression. The first draft of the *Cosmopolitan* article began life as a completely different text, with a different title. I was never at ease with the first attempt: it just didn't feel right. I sent it away nevertheless, and the reviewers' comments confirmed my felt sense: it was not right. This also was the experience of Raymond Chandler, when he wrote his novels. He tells how he spent months working on a text only to scrap it. Having written 233 pages of the book that was eventually to become *Farewell, My Lovely*, he wrote in his diary: 'This story is a flop. It smells to high heaven. Think I'll have to scrap it and try something new' (quoted in MacShane, 1976: 85). He did, however, return to it and revised it substantially so that it went on to become the best seller that it was.

I was fortunate with the *Cosmopolitan* article, because one of the reviewers was extraordinarily thoughtful and kind. They sent me detailed critical feedback, which meant that, acting on their advice, I changed my thinking about what I was trying to say, so I revised the whole thing. What was eventually published was significantly different from the original, even to the title.

Act 3: Editing, revising and polishing The editing, revising and polishing stage of producing a text often takes far longer than drafting or composing, which can be done fairly quickly. This is the stage when you need to go through the text for its overall meaning and ensure it communicates well. Each component of the process is essential for the overall integrity of the text, as follows.

Editing Editing refers to the technical activities of correcting spellings and grammatical and typographical errors, and changing words for better words. It can be done at different levels: at the level of words, where you check that every word is used and spelt correctly and punctuation is accurate; at the level of sentences, where you change the order of words to make the text read more easily or turn passive into active voice; and at the level of paragraphs, where you ensure that link words such as 'furthermore' and 'therefore' join paragraphs and ideas seamlessly. Editing may be done sentence by sentence while composing, or at the end, when you have produced a draft text. This is my preference. I tend to write a first draft reasonably quickly, but spend ages editing. I also produce far too many words in my first version, and go through the text later, taking out redundancies. My best lesson in this regard came from an editor who commissioned a book of 50,000 words and I produced 60,000. She rejected the manuscript until it was down to the required length. Her advice then was, 'Make every word earn its keep'. I have heeded this advice since. The rejected 10,000 words were modified to go into another text, so nothing was wasted. You learn your craft through experience and hard work. Writing seldom comes easy to anyone.

Revising Revising is a more complex process where you look at the text through new eyes. It can be useful, if possible, to leave your draft work for a few days or weeks before revising, because this gives you the necessary distance to revisit it as a stranger. You put yourself in the shoes of a reader whom you do not know and who does not know you or your work, and write for them.

Achieving distance also helps you see the difference between lower and higher levels of revising. At a lower level you go through your existing text section by section and change sentences and paragraphs to make the text hang together more coherently. Higher level revising means actually changing the text, taking out pieces that do not belong and moving pieces of text around so that new, more profound meanings emerge with greater clarity. It is the enactment of the dialogue between yourself and your text, where the meanings in the deep structures of your mind emerge through the syntactical order of the text.

Polishing Now polish things up, checking you have chosen the best word for the job, eliminated every 'very', and ensured that the rhythm of the sentence is easy on the ear and the cadence immaculate. Richard Rorty is a great polisher. He says, 'I'm conscious of striving after turns of phrase and that kind of thing. I spend a lot of time polishing things up' (Rorty, 2003, in Olson and Worsham, 2003: 179). I do too. I like to turn in a text that pleases me, and I hope pleases the editor and eventual reader. To ensure that the text reads well, a great technique is to read it aloud or listen to the voice in your head, so you can hear the text for yourself. If a sentence does not ring true, change it; if an article rings false, follow your instincts and change it or throw it out.

As part of your general editing, revising and polishing, send your article to friends and colleagues for critical feedback. A support group or retreat can be valuable for helping you produce a high quality text (see below). Check that you have drawn on appropriate literatures in developing your arguments and have supported your arguments throughout. Check that your paper makes a useful contribution to the field.

Make sure the article is error-free and has a full list of references, all of which are in the text. Proofread your manuscript several times: if your proofreading it not particularly accurate, try pointing a finger at each word, or read the text aloud and put a dot over each word when you have read it. This sounds laborious but can pay huge dividends. Your text now has the appearance of a polished piece of work.

Then, having produced the best text you are able to produce, prepare to submit it. This also calls for knowledge that you learn through experience.

Act 4: Submitting your article Most journals require articles to be submitted through an online system, and these systems can sometimes be tricky to navigate. You need to ensure that you remain anonymous, because your article is going to be sent to at least two reviewers as part of a blind review process. Take out all reference to yourself, and hide any detail that could identify you.

This means anonymising yourself at the level of the text (take out your name for any texts you have authored in the list of references and substitute it with 'Author'), and at the level of the online submission system (go to the 'preferences' section of your computer and ensure that the 'security' button is on). If you don't hide all information about yourself, the journal editor or administrator will return your article and ask you to anonymise it.

Before submitting your article, write an abstract and produce several keywords. The journal's 'Advice to authors' tells you how many words to allow for your abstract, and how many keywords to choose. The abstract is a focal part of the article and serves several functions: it tells your reader what the article is about; locates your article in the wider literatures; and, from your perspective as author, forces you to focus on the central meanings of the text. Try writing the abstract twice: once before you begin to write, to plan what the article will say. Put this abstract away until you have completed the text. Write the abstract a second time when you have written the article without looking at the first one, and summarise what you have written, and then compare abstracts. If they match, your article has integrity. If they are widely divergent, check what you have said in the article and make sure it is what you meant to say. Meanings often change during the course of writing, and often the action of writing itself generates new ideas and meanings.

Then, when you are satisfied that it is the best you can do, hit the button and submit it.

After: What to Expect and Do after Submitting your Article

Once they receive it, the journal editors will send your article to at least two reviewers, and the editor will read it too. Reviewers are usually asked to read and respond as quickly as possible, and usually within four weeks. Sometimes this is not possible and the time extends. You should get a response from the journal editor within eight to twelve weeks. If you don't hear from them in this time, drop them a brief, courteous email to ask where your article is in the reviewing system. Editors tend to be sympathetic to such emails and do their best to move the process on, and you should receive feedback in a reasonably short time.

Reviewers send their responses back to the editor, who reads them and makes a decision about whether or not to publish your article, or ask for revisions prior to possible publication. Reviewers' responses may vary: one may think your article is excellent while another may wish to reject it altogether. The journal editor has the final say. They then communicate their decision to you. The decisions usually take three forms: accept, reject or revise. It is rare that an article will be accepted as it is in the first round of reviews. Recommendations for revision can vary, from revising a few paragraphs or ideas, to revising the entire article (I have experienced both). Reviewers and editors usually send advice about what should be changed, giving reasons for decisions; sometimes the advice can be extensive. Take this as a good sign: they would not bother giving you detailed advice if they didn't think your piece had merit. While you may disagree with the reviewers' perceptions, you also want to get your work published in the journal, so it is the same advice as when writing a dissertation: stick with the rules, play the academic game, and get published.

Making revisions

Work with reviews by being prepared to make alterations and act on any advice given. Do not ignore it. Journal editors know what they want to publish: this is why it is important to target the right journal initially, and make sure you write according to its style and approach. Write back to the editor, thanking them and saying you will make the revisions according to the recommendations, and that you will return the revised article as soon as possible. Analyse the reviews and note carefully any specific points they make. Then, acting with these points, make the revisions. Spend time doing this, and make sure you address each and every point the reviewers have raised. Do this as soon as possible.

Draw up a list to note what you have done in accordance with the recommendations, and send this as a cover letter when you resubmit the article. Check everything thoroughly, go through security on your computer, and send your article away again. If you have addressed every point, and produced a decent article, you may be pleasantly surprised how quickly the article will appear in print, often within a few months.

These days, most articles are published online before appearing in paper form. For online journals the online version becomes the final version. Print-based journals will send you offprints for free, which you can distribute as you wish. Journals also encourage you to disseminate login details for the online version to your colleagues via social networking or websites. It is in your interests to market your article in as many ways as you can.

After publication, try not to delay writing and submitting a new article. Many people have multiple articles out for review by different journals at the same time. Develop the habit of writing articles, and work at it as a practice. You may be surprised at how much easier it gets with practice.

The world of publishing is changing and online journals are booming, some good, some not so good. Many publishing houses offer fast online publication for a fee. It is your choice whether to go down this route or not, and to check whether you are staying true to your initial purposes of getting published in academic and professional journals.

This chapter has given some general advice about writing for academic and professional journals, but the best strategy, as always, is to do it yourself. Nothing substitutes for practice: work at your craft. Find every opportunity to write and promote your ideas. Yes, it takes effort and time but the rewards are that you can potentially influence global thinking through one of the most prestigious forms of academic publishing. Don't wait: just get on and do it.

SUMMARY

This chapter has outlined how to write for publication in academic and professional journals. Advice has covered matters of finding and writing for a journal that is right for your article, and deciding what you want to say, why you want to say it and who you want to say it to. It has also outlined what you need to do in the 'before', 'during' and 'after' phases of writing your article. It explains how to submit your article to your targetted journal, what to expect then, and how to work with the journal editor to ensure successful publication.

REFLECTIVE QUESTIONS

- Are you clear about what you wish to say in your article, why you wish to say it and who you wish to say it to? Have you got good ideas about what could go into your article that will make reviewers and editors wish to publish it?

- Are you confident about what you need to do before writing, in terms of planning and preparation? Are you reasonably good at organising yourself and your time?

- Will you stay focused during the writing phase? How will you ensure this? How will you negotiate time and space to write while coping with the demands of other work?

- Will you be prepared to edit and revise your work, prior to submission, to ensure that you produce your best product? Are you clear about how to submit your article online?

- Are you prepared for recommendations for revision, and see these simply as part of the job rather than rejection? Will you factor in time for revisions and resubmit your article as soon as possible?

RESEARCH EXERCISE

Draft an article for an identified outlet or journal, with a view to writing it up and submitting it for publication.

So now you are under way with articles, consider a book. This brings us to Chapter 12.

TWELVE

Writing your First Academic Book

This chapter is about writing your first academic book (and then your second and third). Writing a book is different from writing an article and involves specific skills: the chapter explains these differences, and how you can develop expertise. It contains the following.

1. What do you need to know about writing a book?
2. What do you need to do to get a book published?
3. How to sell your book.
4. Self-publishing, print on demand.

This issue is especially relevant if you wish to turn your thesis into a book. Most publishers would not accept a thesis in its original form, so this chapter gives advice on what to do to get it published. Writing a book is long-haul stuff: you have to be ready to spend time, energy and commitment, but it is definitely worthwhile.

What do you Need to Know about Writing a Book?

Writing a book involves knowing the following:

1. Advantages and disadvantages of writing a book.
2. Practicalities of writing books for publication.
3. Turning your thesis into a book.

Advantages and disadvantages of writing a book

Here are some of the potential advantages and disadvantages of writing a book.

Advantages

These include:

Greater scope and flexibility Instead of writing within a word limit of 6–7,000 words as for an article, you now have the freedom to write 60–70,000 words. This freedom can be awesome: you can develop themes and ideas and write about things that are important for you.

Editors welcome you Book editors are always on the lookout for authors who have something interesting to say and who can turn their ideas into books. Once you catch their eye they will encourage and support you. However, this brings obligations including delivering the book on time and ensuring its quality.

You achieve status Being an author can enhance your standing in your peer community. People say, 'Oh, you're *that* John Smith', and ask for your autograph in your book. Friends and family celebrate you – 'This is my mum's book!'

A wonderful sense of achievement Writing a book can bring the very best sense of achievement. You spend months of your life in highs and lows, tied to your desk, and often feel like giving the whole thing up. But you don't, and you finally receive your book, published, which makes it all worthwhile.

Disadvantages

These include:

Time Writing a book takes a long time. First-time authors should cater on at least a year's writing time, possibly more. Many experienced authors take six months to several years, depending on topic and length of the book. How long you take depends on your writing strategies and degree of self-discipline. Time for thinking, reading and writing is time away from family and fun, so consider the pros and cons before you sign the contract.

Money Producing your manuscript may cost more than you catered on. Paper and cartridge ink cost a lot, and you will never get recompensed for your time. The average sales of an academic textbook count in a few thousand, so do not expect a high income even from a high-selling book. However, books can bring in considerable secondary income through invitations to do presentations and consultancy work. Most authors probably do not write books for the money but for the excitement of working with ideas and seeing them in print.

Energy Writing can be exhilarating when you are on song and exhausting when not. Sometimes the writing just does not flow, and you lose a sense of well-being. Learn to develop coping strategies for the difficult times.

Need for solitude Solitude is important at times (Stern, 2014a) and especially for thinking and writing. Many writers need to avoid company when working. P.G. Wodehouse would leave a party he was hosting to go and tap away at his typewriter. Time spent thinking is as important as time spent on writing. This means negotiating priorities with your partner, family and friends, which is sometimes not possible.

Status of books in the academic community Different kinds of books occupy different positions in academic communities. Scholarly and philosophical monographs are usually seen as prestigious whereas textbooks tend to be deemed useful but not especially academic or prestigious.

Practicalities of writing books for publication

The general advice in Chapters 5, 6 and 7 applies to writing academic books. Also note the following.

Write for an identified audience

Identify your target audience and tell them the book is written for them. You can do this in different ways, including:

- Say who the book is written for:
  'This book has been written for those workers, both professional and non-professional, who provide services to people in community, organizational, or institutional contexts' (Stringer, 2007: xv).
- Say what the book is about:
  'This book is an inquiry into values in higher education' (Harland and Pickering, 2011: 1).
  'This book is about writing university assignments at degree level' (Crème and Lea, 2008: 1).
  'This book presents the complex and shifting field of applied linguistics as "a surface that can be dealt with"' (Hall et al., 2011: xvii).
- Say why it is written:
  'Qualitative researching is exciting and important. It is a highly rewarding activity because it engages us with things that matter, in ways that matter' (Mason, 2002: 1).
  'The aim of *Writing for the Market* is to show you how and what to write for today's market' (O'Reilly, 1994: 1).

Style of writing

Here are some additional everyday dos and don'ts.

Do
- Use the principles of AIDA – *Attention* (get your reader's attention with your first line); *Interest* (secure their interest by explaining what they will get from reading the book); *Desire* (evoke their desire to read it); *Action* (they want to read the book).

- Make your book interesting: let the passion rip, but keep it disciplined and don't let it run away with you.
- Be critical. A critique of established ideas can be a unique selling point for a book, which an editor would welcome. Just make sure it is unique and not a rehash of someone else's idea.
- Keep to the point. Make sure your arguments are relevant and keep them under control.
- Write in a form of language your reader will understand. Don't try to write in 'academic' language – write as you speak. Tell a favourite story but don't labour it, and use it only as illustration. Use 'I' selectively – the book is about the topic, not about you.
- End chapters on a note of high closure: keep your reader wanting more.
- Begin and end your book with a high-impact sentence. Make it interesting. Lee Child is not the only author who can write page-turners.

Don't
- Don't try to be too clever. Stay with ordinary language, even when experimenting with new ideas.
- Don't try to be funny or use trite language – a book I reviewed included: ' … this book will lead you gently by the hand as we meander through the chapters …'. This kind of language grates.
- Don't try to make connections where there are none, or labour analogies. If ideas fit together, fine. If not, don't force them.
- Don't name drop, especially out of context. If you cite a text, make sure you have read it.
- Don't confuse or mislead your reader with inaccurate statements. Check your facts.

You learn how to write through practice and through listening to readers' critical feedback. Aim to become your own best critic, and always re-read your text as if you were another person. This takes time, patience and tenacity.

Turning your thesis into a book

Most publishers are not interested in publishing a thesis: they want books about issues. If you wish to get the thesis published as it is, go for self-publishing (see below) or put it on a website.

You can, however, adapt aspects of your thesis for a book. For example:

- Write themes and original ideas into your book.
- Explain how your ideas are original contributions to knowledge of the field, and their significance for moving the field forward.
- Include examples of good practice from which other people can learn.
- Regard your masters or doctoral studies as preparation for a future life-time of writing.

Maria James (see pages 51 and 172) writes in personal correspondence:

I have read books on academic writing but have found it difficult to apply the techniques they recommend. Writing is a personal thing through which we make ourselves vulnerable and open to critique, so I imagine 'how to do' texts fail in some way because everyone has to discover their best plan. Throughout my academic career I have found how powerful writing can be: the pen is definitely mightier than the sword.

What do you Need to Do to Get a Book Published?

Here is what you need to do to get your book published.

Find a publisher

Look at books in the library or on the Internet. Identify the different publishers and check which books they publish. Make a list and match your book with their kinds of books. Search the website to find the right editor: different subject areas give the names of editors. If you cannot find one, write to the central email address and ask them to send you the information. When you have a contact email address, send the editor a short email asking if they would be interested in reading a proposal from you, and outline the key features of your book, including:

- What you would like to write about.
- Type of book, whether textbook or secondary reading.
- Summary of what your book covers.
- What makes the book distinctive: why would readers buy it?
- What its special contribution would be.
- Your writing background and institutional position if you have one: show you are qualified to write the book.
- Offer to send a sample chapter if required.
- Your contact details.

You can do this without making initial contact, but checking with the editor first shows good manners and professional respect.

Write to several publishers to gauge their level of interest. You may get responses from all. If from only one, work with them. If from none, check whether you have been clear and have pitched your approach appropriately, and do it again if necessary. Seek advice from experienced colleagues. Keep trying until you get an answer. Do not give up. Do not give up.

Writing a proposal

Write a proposal and send it to your identified editor. In some cases an editor will approach you and invite you to write a proposal.

Most publishing houses have guidelines on their website, and give detailed guidance on how to draw up a proposal. The Sage website gives advice about publishing books, at www.uk.sagepub.com/publishWithSage.nav. Advice about writing proposals is at www.uk.sagepub.com/repository/binaries/pdf/proposal_guidelines.pdf. You are asked to give information about:

- Proposed author, title and date.
- Type of book: is it a core textbook, a supplementary book or a reference work?
- Identified audience.
- Synopsis of the book: topic, length, sales pitch.
- Table of contents.
- Pedagogical features such as list of chapter objectives, case studies with questions, boxed conclusions, annotated further reading, companion website.
- Digital resources: usually for textbooks.
- The market: will your book be appropriate for courses? What is the state of the market?
- Competing titles: what are the strengths of your own book compared with others in the field?
- Writing plan: when do you intend to complete sections and deliver the manuscript?
- Your CV: who are you and what can you offer?
- Reviewers: if possible, identify one or two people who could review the book.

Be prepared to spend time on writing the proposal. This tells your editor how serious you are about writing and whether they will be able to work with you. Aim to pitch your idea strongly to your editor, as you do in *Dragon's Den*, so they will buy it and in turn sell it to their editorial board, and ultimately to their customers (your readers).

Working with your editor

Work with your editor always, and listen to their advice. They are experienced people who know the competitive world of publishing and what will sell. If they feel your book has promise they will spend time with you. Many editors are happy to talk through ideas and suggest improvements, so welcome their advice: they know what they are talking about. However, if they are not interested, don't chase. I have had proposals rejected, and in hindsight saw why. Book publishing is a business, so respect your editor's expertise and write a book that they will want to publish.

Here is how you can work with your editor throughout the process of writing your book.

- Draw up a writing schedule for them and yourself. Be realistic about time. Producing a book usually takes longer than you think; allow for contingencies such as spraining a wrist or moving house.

- Keep to the schedule. If your delivery dates change, let your editor know so they can reschedule. Publishing schedules are tight and planned, involving different departments including copyediting, proofreading, typesetting and printing. A delay in one part can mean an overall delay in production, with implications for what goes into catalogues and the final publication date. Play fair with your editor and maintain a professional working relationship. Respect them as much as they respect you.
- Stay within your word limits. Books are budgeted for in terms of numbers of pages, so do not exceed the agreed limit. If you do you may be asked to edit down.

Once submitted, your editor will take your proposal to their editorial board. They may recommend that you proceed immediately, or suggest amendments. Take these ideas seriously and implement them. The board is also experienced and knows what will sell. Sometimes you may need to wait for a decision, but most publishers respond within a month or so. They want you to write your book as much as you do.

Once you have agreement to publish, here is what you do.

Writing your book

Draw up an action plan for writing. Organise it into phases as outlined in Chapter 7. Be honest about whether you tend to procrastinate, so decide whether you do or don't want to do this project. If you do, get on with it. If you don't, don't pretend that you do.

Organise your action plan into phases, to include:

- planning;
- drafting;
- composing;
- editing and revising;
- checking protocols.

Planning

This has probably included drawing up and submitting the proposal. Once you have permission to go ahead, do the following.

Keep records Keep a notebook from the start, and write down any and all ideas as they come to you. Cross them out once you have dealt with them. If appropriate, keep a second notebook for key sources and references. Note all references in this book or on your computer as you go. Do not leave this until the last. Keep a writing diary from the start. Record events and your reflections. Give everything a date so you can refer back if necessary.

Draw up a plan of your book Use your proposal as your guidebook. Think about what you want to say, who you are going to say it to, and how you are going to say it. You already have an overall picture and shape of your book in your head and a sense of the main ideas, themes and conceptual frameworks. Decide on whether you will use case study material, and where it will come from. Organise your computer: create a folder for your new book and allocate folders within the main folder to hold files related to useful papers and resources, draft chapters, references and correspondence.

Revisit your title   Your title shows what the book is about. Most writers have a working title that then changes slightly during the writing phase. Negotiate this with your editor.

Map out chapter headings, contents and word lengths   Map out chapter headings and provisional contents and decide what goes where. It can be useful to divide your book into parts, each containing specific chapters. This mapping process clarifies and strengthens the overall structure of your book. Study the contents pages of books you have found useful, and put yourself in the shoes of the author. What did they want to say? How did they want to say it? If appropriate, adapt these structures to your own text and see if it flows organically. You may find while drafting and composing that you change the chapters around a little, but the overall structure should stay the same. Doing this will give you a sense of word lengths, and you can write the numbers into your plan to keep yourself on task. You can initially do a simple division of the agreed total length of manuscript to arrive at word lengths for individual chapters: a total of 65,000 words divided by eight chapters gives you roughly 7,500 words per chapter with sufficient remaining for lists of references and preliminary pages (prelims). Remember also to include figures, tables, prelims and references in your total word count, and adjust accordingly.

Drafting

You now move to the drafting stage. The aim is to produce a reasonable working draft in a specified time, so mark a date by which to complete this phase and aim to stick to the schedule. Everything you read in Chapter 7 about planning for the production of texts applies here. Now also you need to plan for what you are going to write. Remember that this is a book about action research, so you ground your book in your knowledge and experience of action research. You could write:

- A textbook on how to do action research (dozens are now available).
- The story of what you have done in your action research: draw on your dissertation or thesis for ideas. Emphasise the significance, not only activities such as data-gathering.
- Ideas about specific aspects of action research (issues about data, story, writing).
- Critical commentaries on action research.

Whichever topic you choose, structure it so that your reader can follow your argument. Some textbooks adopt a specific structure that broadly follows the lines of an action enquiry, the same as is visible in an article, for example:

- Research issue and research question – background to the issue: reasons for writing the book; aims; how the reader will benefit; what they will learn; why you are authorised to write (your experience, your knowledge of the field); why you wish to write.
- Contexts for the research issue: its values base; what is happening at the moment in relevant contexts; where the gaps lie; how your book will help fill the gaps; contribution to the field.
- Data to show the reality of the issue: issue in action; what the literatures say; what they don't say; how you are contributing to the field.
- Action taken: what you and colleagues have done about the issue; how you have done it; methodologies and methods used.
- What has happened as the result of actions taken; what changes have taken/ should take place?
- Significance of what you and colleagues are doing: how you are modifying practices; how you will develop new practices.
- Contribution to knowledge of the field: what other people will learn from reading your book.

Remember at all times to link the idea of action research with issues of knowledge: make sure your book is about doing research, not only about practices.

Composing

Composing is where you begin putting the book together: you begin to design and produce text. Work out your own strategies for doing this. You could do the following:

- Jot down your chapter headings on sticky notes and stick them, in order, down the side or along the top of a large piece of paper.
- Jot down ideas for each chapter, each on a sticky note, and stick them under the chapter headings. Rearrange them into a rough order. This gives you the outline of an overall working text.

You could try a similar strategy using paper and pen or a white board, where you can add or erase ideas for chapter entries. You can draw mind-maps and spider diagrams, to help conceptualise the overall structure and contents of your book.

Points to bear in mind when drafting and composing:

- Remember this is not a novel: it is an academic book. You have room in a novel to develop the story, starting perhaps with a backstory, which then builds up to and ends with a denouement of some kind. In an academic book you say right at the beginning what the denouement (findings) is, and then tell the story that led to it (the backstory). The villain gets their comeuppance in the first paragraph, not the last.

- Make everything interesting. Build up to a lively conclusion and end the book on a high. When you read the book yourself in the editing stage and come across anything that slumps, take it out, shorten it, or add anything that keeps the pace moving and consistently engages your reader's interest.
- Each chapter should end on a note of high closure. The work of Dickens is exemplary here: he wrote novels for newspaper serialisation so had to end each chapter on a high to keep his readers interested and wanting to know what comes next, similar to episodes of *Coronation Street* and other soap operas. Study the work of novelists and look at the techniques they use to keep the pace going. Hemingway said that he would end the day's work knowing what he was going to write the following day, which enabled a smooth transition and no break in the text.
- Stay within your word limits (see above).
- Use personal anecdotes and real-life stories where appropriate. Quote from novels and any other relevant text. Let your reader see you are eclectic, and aim to build a reputation for being a credible, authentic and knowledgeable writer, someone people will want to read.
- Use real-life case studies where appropriate. Always get permission to do so, acknowledge your sources, and recompense them in some way for your use of their words (give them a copy of the book on publication).

Editing, revising, polishing

You now move into the editing, revising and polishing stage. As noted in Chapter 7, this requires close editing to ensure technical matters such as accuracy in spelling, punctuation and grammar; and to check that all your references are intact and correct and you have your facts straight. Revising can take a low-level form of revising words, sentences and paragraphs, and also a higher level form of revising chapters and moving text around to ensure the integrity of the book. This is where sticky notes and PowerPoint presentations or a similar strategy can be helpful, because you can move the points you make on the notes around on your board, and mirror the process in the writing of your text. This stage can also take time. You can produce a first draft in a matter of weeks, where virtually anything goes and you over-run word limits with abandon, but when revising you begin to look at the text as a disciplined work that is going to go public and that someone is going to read.

Revising is when you revisit ideas and make sure they are in the right place; when you check you have linked paragraphs with appropriate link sentences. Before computers this would often involve scissors and paste; with computers it is a matter of cutting and pasting material across chapters. A word of caution: keep all previous drafts in a folder, because you may find you have unintentionally deleted an idea when revising and need to find it again in earlier drafts. Also keep your text updates on several memory sticks. We all know what it means if a computer crashes or is doused with a cup of tea.

Some people take revisions to considerable lengths. Raymond Chandler would write an introduction, then, when he reached the end of a novel, would re-write it. This is, in my view, an excellent strategy and something I try to do;

it enables you to map out your broad vision at the beginning of your book, to some extent let the book write itself, and then go back in light of refined learning and re-write the now transformed vision.

A further form of revising comes from seeking the critique of colleagues and readers. Ask as many people as possible, whose opinion you trust, to read and give you a critical response to individual chapters or the entire book, and act on their advice. This helps you gain new insights into ideas or reconsider existing ones.

Checking protocols and ethics

Part of your polishing is to check you have carried out writing and publishing protocols, such as ensuring that you have all necessary permissions. You must secure, in writing, permissions from other publishers to use any figures, diagrams and models in your text. Sometimes you can negotiate their reproduction for free but usually you have to pay, so be sure you have arranged everything before you hand your book to your publisher. You may have to send them a copy of agreement from the original publishers. Also secure permission from any case study contributors, get their written permission, and acknowledge their contributions in your Acknowledgements page. Never infringe copyright in any way, and ensure copyright of your own materials by writing the copyright symbol – © – together with the current year at the foot of your work.

Once you have revised and polished your text, and ensured everything is in good order, go ahead and send your book to your editor, as per their instructions.

Karen McArdle is Director of Research and Knowledge Exchange and Reader in Adult Education at the School of Education, University of Aberdeen. She is writing a book called *Freedom Research*. In a presentation at the 2014 Value and Virtue in Practice-Based Research conference, she outlines her overall vision.

FREEDOM RESEARCH

Freedom Research is underpinned by an argument that the conventions of traditional approaches to research in education may be confidence sapping and constraining to the developing researcher. If ethics, values and virtues are clarified and brought to bear on the research process, then the researcher may be liberated to research with freedom, creativity and innovation.

Underpinning the book are the following ideas:

- the linking of concepts of freedom and research;
- the linking of ethics, values and virtues to the full range of research choices made by the researcher, not just methodological choices;

(Continued)

- the reinstatement of (old fashioned) virtues to a research context;
- attention to creativity, impact and innovation in a research context, as a product of values clarification.

This book seeks to topple some of the much-loved conventions of research in education studies. Ethics is rarely considered in research methodology except for links to research methods. This book integrates concepts of ethics, values and virtues to each stage of the research process, showing how they underpin all of our choices. The book seeks to be accessible and confidence building for researchers, providing a challenge to research orthodoxy, whilst promoting coherence, integrity and validity in research in ways that are more exacting and sophisticated than is usually the case in methodological texts. (McArdle, 2014)

What then?

The production phase

Your book goes into the hands of the production team who will look at it for content, form and appearance. Your editor will read it, because they are primarily responsible for placing it in the public domain. It then goes to a copyeditor and proofreader (sometimes the same person), who checks everything in the text for different aspects and sends you questions, usually electronically, about various matters such as the meaning of a possibly ambiguous sentence or a missing reference or page number. Their job is to check the text for accuracy and that it holds together as a book. They will send you a list of questions about details, and you must respond to them by a specified date so that production remains on schedule. Work carefully and considerately with your copyeditor. They do a complex job for your benefit.

Once the working manuscript has been agreed, it goes to the typesetter, who typesets the text and sends you the typeset copy for checking. At the same time you may produce an index. You may prefer to ask a professional indexer to do this job, in which case the production manager appoints an indexer whose fee is paid out of your royalties. If possible, opt to do the index yourself; an index is an invaluable piece of the book that contributes to its educational nature. You know your book better than anyone and you will be able to pick out nuances and categories and show your reader how to find them. Readers use the index to help them search for and cross-reference items. If well done, an index can show a potential reader what the book is about at first glance. Once you have done the index and checked the copy, you send the book back to the production manager and the book goes to press.

Now you wait, anywhere between two and six months, for the book to be printed. The production team liaises with your editor, and they alert you to a publication date. While this is happening, you get on with your next manuscript, and wait patiently for the golden morning when there is a nice thud on the doormat and you open the package to see your book. It's a brilliant feeling that you always remember and that makes it all worthwhile.

It is relatively straightforward to write and produce a book, albeit a lot of hard work, time and commitment. The thing now is to sell it.

How to Sell your Book

Do not leave selling your book only to the publisher and sales team. You can do a lot too. Again this takes energy and commitment.

Promoting your book

Writers tend to be somewhat retiring when it comes to promoting their work but in this case put your reservations to one side and celebrate it as much as possible without being a nuisance. Here are some strategies you can easily develop.

Work with your marketing department

Your marketing department will send you various documents asking for information about you and your book. They use this information to draw up promotional material including flyers and website alerts. Work with the department closely and willingly, and send them whatever information they need on time and as fully as possible. Give them lists of people who may wish to put information on course reading lists, or who may review the book for journals and websites. The marketing department will also ask you for a list of people to whom they could send an inspection copy for possible adoption on courses.

Develop your own marketing material

You can also develop your own marketing material and find ways to promote your book. These include the following:

Create a companion website: Many books have companion websites, and you can create one if appropriate. Your publisher may offer advice and technical support; enquire if this is available. You may already have a personal or institutional website. Put information about your book in a prominent position. Ask your institution to promote it on the institutional website.

Update your personal/institutional profile: Make sure your own profile is updated on personal and institutional websites, and include a sentence such as 'Most recent book ...' with your list of publications, or to begin this list. You can also put this as part of your email signature.

Use e-alerts: you can send e-alerts with text messages and emails, and send information to your networks. You can also send flyers and other promotional material to networks but be careful not to overdo things and get a reputation as a nuisance.

Start a blog: If you have a website, start a blog. If you have participated in a blog before, you know that they are time-consuming, so check whether you will have time to maintain it regularly. If you can do it, a blog can be a marvellous forum for disseminating information and inviting feedback and reviews.

Share by social media: Use social media to promote the book. Send flyers and cover photos; send emails. Develop a following for the book, but avoid positioning yourself as a 'guru' (to be avoided at all costs).

Wikipedia: write a page on Wikipedia about yourself and your book. Include ideas as set out in the 'proposal' section above, about what the book contains, what contribution it makes to the field, and how it will help readers get the knowledge they need.

Tell the librarian: tell your institutional librarian about your book and ask them to buy in several copies.

Get endorsements if you can: ask your marketing department if it is possible to get endorsements from two or three people whose work is known and respected in the field, and for these to be put on flyers and possibly on the back of the book. Be prepared to supply information about potential endorsers.

Take flyers to conferences: if possible, ask for flyers to be placed in conference packs. Your marketing department will create and supply promotional material so ask them for what you need. If you give a talk, distribute the flyers among the audience, or leave them on tables around the venue so people can pick them up and read them later. You never know who may be interested.

Talk about it: celebrate your book by talking about it and talking it up. You thought it was a good idea, and you have spent all this time and effort in producing it, so now is not the time to hide your light. Let is shine, graciously and joyfully, and do your best to persuade people to buy it.

Many people these days opt for self-publishing, which can be a great way to go if you know reasonably what you are doing and are prepared to work at it. I set up my own publishing business in the 1990s and have published five books. They have sold well by academic book publishing standards, usually about 3,000 copies each, which has brought in a reasonable income though again it means hard work. When you self-publish you are responsible both for writing your text, producing it and disseminating it. Just setting up the operations of selling, probably through a website facility, takes an enormous amount of time, let alone advertising through mailing lists, finding endorsements and through personal letters. Packing and posting comes on top of this. These days I write for top publishers, and am careful to negotiate my own publishing activities with them, so that we do not encroach on one another's fields and interests. If I have an idea for a book I check with the publisher(s) whether they wish to publish it; if they do, fine, and if not, I check with them that they will be comfortable if I publish it. Many famous authors have self-published and been highly successful – Mark Twain, Beatrix Potter, Virginia Wolff, James Joyce. Print-on-demand technology now makes short-run books easy to produce and reasonably inexpensive, so you don't need to cater on laying out huge sums of money initially. It is also nice to see money going into your account from your own labour. It is satisfying to wrap a book for sending and think, 'I did this. I made this myself'. You can also produce e-books, which saves you packing and posting (see below).

If you decide to self-publish, make sure the books themselves are high quality in design and feel. I am reasonably proficient at some production elements such as copyediting, but fairly useless at typesetting. I typeset a book once but it looked really amateurish, so from then on I have given a manuscript over to a professional typesetter. I also arrange for a graphic designer to produce an attractive cover: the cover often sells a book. Costs for good designers can be high, but it is worth it in terms of producing a book that looks professional and that you can be proud of. Self-publishing means you have overall control of your book from start to finish, but it also means you are entirely responsible for what goes into the reader's hands. They pay good money so they rightly expect good value. Their reviews on the Internet can make or break you, so you do need to be vigilant about the overall quality: retail is detail. Look after the details and the product will look after itself.

You can also produce e-books, and set up a dedicated website and blog for advertising and selling. The production process of electronic books is different than for printed books, but they demand the same level of professionalism in production. If you wish to make publishing a business you must be prepared to do it properly, which means possibly giving up day jobs and devoting your time to publishing. If, like me, you do other things such as institutional part-time work, as well as writing, you may prefer to work with the more established publishers who know what they are doing and have the marketing expertise to produce and sell your book for you. As noted earlier, writing a book will not bring you in a lot of direct income, but it does generate secondary income in terms of invitations to do consultancy work and keynote presentations. This in itself can involve the excitement of travel and meeting new people, and the encounter with different cultures, which can give you abundant material for your next book. Life means choices, so choose well and good luck with it all! Ignore the prophets of doom who say that printed books will disappear; books are with us, and here to stay.

In summary, writing and producing books can be exhilarating, fun and professionally fulfilling. It means hard work and commitment, but if this is what you wish to do, do it. You can attend face-to-face or online courses to learn the trade, and link with support groups for advice and support, or start your own. Working for yourself is risky but has other benefits such as independence, control of your life and talent, and being able to say what you wish, with only your reader as your best judge. The validity of your work comes through people's willingness to continue to buy the ideas and products. Gone are the days when self-publishing was simply vanity publishing; it is serious business and part of your overall commitment to making your ideas public for use in the world.

SUMMARY

This chapter has set out some of the practicalities of writing and producing books. It has made the point that book writing and publishing is undertaken for commercial success as well as for disseminating ideas, so requires commitment and stamina. Self-publishing can be feasible provided you are prepared to put in the work. Writing and producing books can be rewarding, personally and commercially, so commit to the process and go for it.

REFLECTIVE QUESTIONS

- Are you clear about your reasons for wishing to write a book? What have you to say that no-one else has said before, or that you can say better? Why do you wish to write a book and not, say, an article? Have you considered the disadvantages as well as the advantages?

- Will you find a publisher for your book? How will you do this? How can you be reasonably confident they will be the right publishers for your project?

- Are you reasonably efficient in drawing up action plans, observing deadlines, staying with approved proposals and guidelines, and other possible constraints? Will you check all protocols and ethical matters?

- Will you continue to be enthusiastic for promoting your book? Have you thought about producing accompanying web-based resources? Are you prepared to work with the publisher's marketing department?

- Have you thought about the pros and cons of self-publishing, and the amount of work involved?

RESEARCH EXERCISE

Visit the website of a publisher in your field and take a look at their proposal guidelines. Draw up a proposal for a book, with a view to submitting it to the publisher.

If you have thought through all these things, go ahead and write your book, with verve. By doing so, you reinforce the significance of your work as a writer who is able to influence what counts as research and who counts as a researcher. These matters are considered further in Chapter 13.

PART V

The Significance of your Text

This Part is about the potential significance of your text for the ongoing professional learning of yourself and other people.

It contains Chapters 13 and 14.

Chapter 13, 'The significance of your action research text' speaks about how your text has potential for influencing new thinking and practices for individuals, groups and social formations, and therefore has potential for influencing policy formation and implementation.

Chapter 14, 'Some implications – what next?' reinforces the case for why higher education needs action research and its texts, and how your writing practices can contribute to a reconceptualisation of what counts as educational research and its uses in the world.

These chapters emphasise the need for writing to be seen as an activist practice that has potential for personal and social transformation.

THIRTEEN

The Significance of your Action Research Text

So now you have written it, this text that has taken weeks, months or even years of your time, countless books, papers and conversations, and a vast amount of thinking. Has it been worthwhile?

Yes. Here is why.

Your text is your means of placing your action research, and your knowledge claims, in the public domain. You are saying you know that you are making an original contribution to your field, you know the importance of that contribution and you can justify your knowledge. The key question for this chapter therefore becomes, 'In what ways is your contribution significant?'

However, it is one thing making your knowledge public; it is another getting it taken seriously, and this is largely down to you. First you need to produce a quality text that people will read; second, you have to explain why your knowledge claims should be legitimated as significant, for whom, and why legitimacy is important. You cannot expect other people to celebrate your work as an original and important contribution unless you do so first.

The word 'significance' implies 'meaning'. Your contribution is meaningful in many ways and for many people: for yourself, the wider community, and for the future, and these are linked: the personal transforms into the social, which then transforms into the political. This transformational process is imbued with your spiritual energy, and with cosmic energy.

Your contribution is significant for *what* you say, *how* you say it, and *that* you say it. Now that you are making your work public, you are also making a case for why your knowledge claims should be legitimated, in these terms; and this is also how the chapter is organised.

1. The significance of *what* you say.
2. The significance of *how* you say it.
3. The significance of the fact *that* you say it.

Furthermore, *what* you say, *how* you say it, and *that* you say it is meaningful for new learning: for yourself, for others, and for posterity; so each section contains ideas about the significance of your capacity to speak at these different levels of transformation.

The Significance of What You Say

In Chapter 10, the concept of *parrhesia,* or free speech was identified as a criterion for judging the quality of a text (see Foucault, 2001). Free speech implies speaking frankly and truthfully. This is a necessary practice, but it can be dangerous because sometimes people do not want to hear the truth, which often amounts to criticism, so they try to silence the speaker. Speaking freely is therefore linked with issues of power, and, given that most people with position power are also those with privilege, it is linked with financial and social capital. Foucault's stated intent was 'not to deal with the problem of truth, but with the problem of the truth-teller, or of truth-telling as an activity: ... the importance of telling the truth, knowing who is able to tell the truth, and knowing why we should tell the truth ...' (2001: iii). Foucault's main concerns were how the individual is able to create their own identity through reflecting critically on what they and others are doing.

These themes appear in the work of other key authors, such as Said (1991) and Chomsky (2002). They also speak of the dangers of lack of critique to public well-being, including the closing down of the capacity to think for oneself and understanding how people's thinking can be manipulated. Developing the capacity for critique means interrogating discourses for hidden strategies of control.

Doing action research involves this: learning how to understand what is going on in social situations and why, and how to challenge normative practices and contribute to improving the social order.

Here are some ideas about the significance of your contribution in different spheres.

The significance of what you say for your own education

You have given your reasons and purposes for doing your action research. These link with your ontological and spiritual values, and transform into social and political practices. You look back at your life and claim it as worthwhile. Reflecting on these issues, and drawing on some of Marx's unpublished notes written in 1844, Bernstein (1971) says we are twice affirmed through our productive lives: first, when we 'produce' or create our own lives; and second, when we contribute, through our own, to the life of another.

You can claim your life as worthwhile in relation to your ontology of being, your relationship with yourself. You understand yourself as a person whose existence and capacity to speak is their contribution on earth (Arendt, 1958). Only you occupy your place on earth, so you need to occupy it well (O'Neill, 2008). You are able and willing to engage with your sense of being (Tillich, 1973). You value those things that give your life meaning, while rejecting mis-educational (Chomsky, 2000) influences that aim to persuade you not to commit to being more than you are.

To note: this chapter contains excerpts from assignments written as part of their masters studies by members of staff from what was, in 2008, St Mary's University College and is now St Mary's University, Twickenham. All achieved their masters degrees with distinction, and some have gone on to doctoral studies. They also actively write for publication.

One of those lecturers, Rita Moustakim, a senior lecturer concerned about issues of immigration and 'asylum seekers', writes (2008):

Driven by the desire to improve my learning and confronted with injustice directed at others, I felt I had to take purposeful action to effect change for the greater good of society. I can relate to Blackburn (2001), who uses the term 'deontologi-cal notions', stemming from the Greek word *deontos*, which means duty. I con-sider the struggle for social justice to be a duty which cannot be denied. I desired to be active and engaged in making a difference for good, in particular in relation to supporting involuntary migrants who I considered to be a group marginalised by society. ... In order to clarify why I was concerned and how my values came to act as my living standards of practice and judgement, I shall first explain my rea-sons for being.

I believe we all have an innate purpose in life. I do not feel it is by chance that any one of us is here or remains here for a given length of time. I consider that my reason for being, in part, is to speak on behalf of others who for whatever reason are unable to speak for themselves. I also consider it my duty to support all people, as I am a citizen of a wider world and not just in relation to my current and immedi-ate situation. I can relate to the work of Freire (1973) who suggests there is an indivisible solidarity between humans and their world, and that they are not just in the world, but with it. We cannot live or work in isolation; each one of us has needs and difficulties and, however insignificant they may appear in relation to another's, at the time for us, they may be all encompassing. I feel compelled to support other people not for self-serving purposes but as purposeful action which is part of a wider reason for being.

(Moustakim, 2008: 7–8)

You show how you engage with issues of epistemology. Foucault (2001) says that, because we have the capacity to tell the truth, we also have an obligation to tell it. You can do this because you have learned to deconstruct your own and others' thinking.

Julie Pearson, a senior lecturer in Physical Education (see also page 120), writes about her processes of becoming critical (2008):

I have realised through my research that I have been schooled in certain ways of thinking and have reproduced the practices I have come to view as the 'norm' and for which I have been rewarded [as a professional educator]. ... I understand now that my traditional form of pedagogy not only raised the value of the 'norm' (Derrida, 1981), but also devalued me as a professional educator and as a facilitator of change. I was failing myself alongside those I was supporting (past, present and future). Now, however, since beginning to become more critical of my epistemological stance, and of my practice, I no longer view myself as more knowledgeable than those I teach, or as a member of a 'specialised class' (Chomsky, 2000). I now position myself alongside the students I teach, becoming part of the teaching and learning process. I have moved from a knowledge-getting process (Bruner, 1966: 72) towards knowledge creation, allowing for the interaction and creative encounters between people (Elliott, 1998) in order to progress and improve. In a constructively critical manner, I have begun to challenge the process of learning by challenging my own practice (Schön, 1995).

(Pearson, 2008: 2)

You are telling your research story from your commitment to criticality, demonstrating its authenticity, rigour and scholarship. You have worked perhaps within cultures of oppression, yet did not give in, through your commitment to life (Frankl, 1959; Todorov, 1999). Foucault was obsessed with death (Miller, 1993); you are obsessed with life.

The significance of your contribution for the education of others in your contexts

Drawing on the renewable energy of the universe, you bring your learning to your relationships with others. You exercise your educational influence in their learning out of your own generosity of spirit, because you understand that the world is sustained through the capacity of all to contribute freely and to ask for nothing in return. Your contribution is to share your knowledge so that others can learn from it and develop it. This is not interfering or 'intervening', but of helping them appreciate their capacities for original critical thinking and political action. It is not about 'doing projects', but a life-long commitment to working with communities who have come together, willing to share their common goals, on an equal footing, and rooted in their self-knowledge as free people of equal worth.

Sometimes making one's contribution to others' learning can be painful. King, Mandela and Gandhi were silenced for advocating justice. This has not stopped their global influence. Chomsky and Said have been vilified for critiquing policies that aim to control the public mind (Chomsky, 2002; Said, 1994). This has not stopped their voices being heard. Through your capacity for knowledge creation, you are enabling people to think for themselves.

You are showing how it is possible to enable people's self-determination for self-development (Young, 2000). This can have implications for how the public sphere can be re-thought, and new understandings about economics developed, which could be a major contribution from your research. Dominant understandings are that the public sphere works as a system of market exchange, where what is exchanged is consumer and social goods (Heilbroner and Thurow, 1998). Gift cultures work like this, the idea that if A gives B a present, B must reciprocate with a better gift. Gift cultures perpetuate the superiority of some over others, where the capacity to pay entitles one to entry into the society. Legitimacy is achieved by virtue of what you can offer. Currently, Britain's policy on immigration is to accept those who have market capacities such as key skills or sufficient money to support themselves. This kind of integration works in terms of legalistic regulation (see Habermas's 2001 *The Inclusion of the Other*). People are included because of external rules and regulations, but this is not a sustainable form of inclusion. Sustainable forms come from free people thinking and speaking freely. What matters is not capacity to pay but capacity to learn and grow.

You are therefore contributing to sustainable forms of living, through freedom for all; and this carries conditions. Sustainability as freedom can happen only when people agree to it. John Hume, former leader of the SDPI in Northern Ireland, famously commented that decommissioning begins in the mind, not with the laying-down of arms. Social freedom begins in the individual mind, and grows through relationships of influence. This has implications for a new form of public sphere: social goods are in people's learning, and exchange mechanisms are in the sharing of critical stories, an economy of shared understandings, grounded in a commitment to freedom (Sen, 1999). The unit of currency is a willingness to show how people hold themselves accountable for what they do. Freedom for all is built in to the regulation of society, a shift from a legalistic view to a relational view, where the structures of society take the form of permeable boundaries that enable all to enter one another's dynamically evolving spaces through the sharing of their personal knowledge for public transformation.

Alex Sinclair (2008), a senior lecturer in Science (see page 171), writes about the significance of his research:

The significance of my research can also be thought of in terms of developing new forms of theory and how I am generating my own living theory of practice. In this way I am contributing to the debates surrounding the nature of education and pedagogies and what constitutes knowledge. By encouraging my students to learn independently I am asking them to make their learning explicit. In turn they will be developing their own living theories around their practice and hopefully developing a critical approach towards reflection and critical thinking. In this way it may break the cycle of socialising teachers as unthinking implementers of normative theories who may be able to pass on these necessary skills to the children they subsequently teach. I hope that it has been possible for my students to have learnt with me as I gain a better understanding of how I can best develop my practice and that I am working towards an epistemology of symbiotic practice.

(Sinclair, 2008: 17)

The significance of your contribution for the education of cultural and social formations

A social or cultural formation refers to groups of people who share a common social or cultural heritage. These groups do not simply come into existence, as if their heritage was the way things have always been. Cultures, including their knowledge systems, emerge, and are frequently different from one another. The knowledge systems of industrialised societies work in terms of 'this' or 'that', a traditional Aristotelian logic that excludes contradiction, whereas in the intellectual traditions of indigenous societies, things tend to be seen as in relation, connected through an underpinning philosophy of inclusion (see Brown, 2004 on African philosophy and Reagan, 2005 on non-Western educational traditions).

Cultures emerge through people interacting with one another through speech and action. The problem is, as Habermas (1976) explains, these knowledge systems often detach themselves from the people who created them, and become reified, things in themselves, so people lose touch with their own systems. They say, 'That's the way things are because that's the way things are,' forgetting that this is the way people have made them, or they have made themselves. They also forget that what is made can be improved. Nothing is static, least of all culture. Look at a photo of yourself taken 20 years ago, and see how culture changes. You also have a hand in cultural change. By following dominant thinking you contribute to reproducing the existing culture; by changing your thinking, you can contribute to new, improved cultures.

New ways of thinking and acting have entered the cultural formation of educational research, for example, through action research. You are contributing to cultural transformation through enabling all voices to be heard in your organisation. You are showing what it means to develop culture as 'a concept that includes a refining and elevating element, each society's reservoir of the best that has been known and thought ...' (Said, 1994: xiii). You have become a cultural entrepreneur; you have cultural capital because you have what counts in cultural affairs.

This is where you can have real educational influence. You have something of worth to contribute. You have encouraged new cultures of inclusion (Cahill, 2007), through developing practices that include the other as the grounds for social action. Inclusion begins in the mind, when people deconstruct their own thinking around what counts as 'me' and 'the other'.

Mark Cordery (2008), a senior lecturer in IT in education, writes:

Prior to becoming a teacher I was a research scientist engaged in medical and veterinary microbiological research. My initial training saw me working within a scientific research paradigm using a positivist empirical approach to planning, collecting and presenting data and developing theory. The precision of this approach and its well defined use of numerical data and statistical analysis worked very well with the bacteria, viruses and blood samples with which my research was concerned. The precise nature of this research paradigm positioned the researcher outside the research forum as an impersonal observer. When I moved into the field of education I found, and indeed I used, many of these research methods applied to the classroom situation. In my own professional development as a primary school teacher I was encouraged to 'cross the threshold', a process for which I was required to submit bland statistics to 'demonstrate the progress' of the children in my class and to prove my worth as an educator.

Through my studies I have begun to realise the need to embrace a more emancipatory, empowering research methodology, which goes beyond generating theory through propositions which determine relationships between variables and begins to seek answers to the question 'How do I improve the process of education here?' (Whitehead, 1989) and thus makes me a living participant in my own research as I strive to generate my own living theory of practice.

(Cordery, 2008: 8–9)

You show how you have deconstructed your thinking. Mr Incredible (of *The Incredibles*) says, 'When everyone is super, no one will be.' You have decentred yourself, so you no longer see 'here' as the centre, because there is no 'here'; 'here' is someone else's 'there', so 'here' and 'there' become meaningless. You have destablised your thinking, destabilised fixed categories; you have destabilised the very idea of 'category'. 'Identity' is not a fixed category; it is a living, creative process, in company with others and as part of the natural order.

The Significance of How you Say It

You have chosen to tell your story in your unique way and from your decision 'that I must understand the world from my own point of view, as a person claiming originality and exercising his [or her] personal judgement responsibly with universal intent' (Polanyi, 1958: 327). This has considerable implications for yourself, others, and your social formation.

The significance of how you tell your story for your own education

Through telling your story in your own way you communicate how you have given meaning to your life. You show how you have moved from not living fully in the direction of your values, to realising your potentials for educational influence. Through your written and visual narratives you show the processes you have engaged in, as you struggled to create your own identity.

You are communicating how you are reconceptualising educational theory as within the practice, and not only as words on a page. You are showing the validity of your knowledge claims through the living practice. You give an account of yourself; you can show that 'there is a relation between the rational discourse, the *logos*, you are able to use, and the way that you live' (Foucault, 2001: 97). You can show 'the relationship between one's way of life and knowledge of the truth. ...', the 'idea that a person is nothing else but his [*sic*] relation to the truth, and that this relation to truth takes shape or is given form in his own life ...' (p. 117). Feynman noted (2001: 240) that 'what happens in nature is true and is the judge of the validity of any theory about it'. You are showing, through the way you live and present your story that your way is the judge of the validity of your own theory of practice.

The significance of how you tell your story for the education of others

Now that you have told your story, you are encouraging others to do the same, so that their stories can be legitimated in the public domain. Your story contributes to the public knowledge base, through contributing to new epistemologies.

We have said throughout that traditional forms of research and practice are grounded in traditional logics and epistemologies – the idea that 'this' is separate from 'that', and everything works in terms of cause and effect – 'If I do this, that will happen'. It is the basis of modernist forms of thinking, where things are seen as stable – stable categories, roles and social structures. Gray (2002) points out that this is the basis of many social ills, because many people pay more attention to fitting others into the structures than to seeing them as people. It is also the basis of traditional institutional epistemologies, including those of modern research universities. This has serious consequences, given that the university is still one of the highest bodies for legitimating what counts as knowledge and who is seen as a knower.

You are changing this. Your action research is part of the New Scholarship (Boyer, 1990), different from traditional scholarship, and grounded in new fluid and transformational epistemologies. Schön (1995) says that the new scholarship requires a new epistemology, through action research, and you are showing how this can be done. Communicating these fluid forms requires new dynamic forms of representation (Eisner, 1997), and you are showing this, too.

The significance of how you tell your story for the education of social formations

Through telling your story in your own way, you are contributing to the transformation of the university. Given that the university is also one of the most powerful bodies for influencing cultural development, you are contributing to new forms of culture. The spread of the culture can be influenced through new forms of global communication such as e-journals and multimedia representations, such as those from Margaret Riel (referenced in Chapter 1).

Many stories are told about the dangers of globalisation, that it is about profit over people (Chomsky, 2002) and strengthens the divide between the haves and the have-nots. You are contributing to new forms of globalisation, through the free exchange of free ideas. Some studies (for example, Perlmutter, 2000) explain how the media are policed in order to control the public mind; and how the Internet provides new open forms which reduce the control of thought-police (although the thought-police also patrol the Internet, though perhaps with more difficulty). It is possible to create new virtual networks of communication, informed by new dynamic epistemologies that confer public legitimacy in new ways. The Internet provides virtually unlimited freedom of communication; whereas previously it was possible to challenge existing forms only through subversive pamphlets and secret meetings, now it is possible to do so through the informal networks of cyberspace. It is said that social networking has contributed to the election and dismissal of Presidents.

However, this kind of social freedom can be achieved only if you have intellectual freedom, and this is the hardest thing of all, as we now consider.

The Significance of the Fact that You Say It

Perhaps the most significant aspect of making your account public is that you are able to tell your story of personal emancipation and are claiming the right to speak, because speaking frankly and truthfully to oneself and others can happen only in a context where one is permitted to do so. Often, external and internal mechanisms of control prevent this. External mechanisms can be visible – censorship, thought control, punishment for whistle-blowing (Alford, 2001), production of standardised texts – while more subtle forms are invisible – propaganda (Marlin, 2002), and diversion of attention from things that really matter through promoting a culture of entertainment and trivialisation (game shows, reality TV). It is then a question of becoming sufficiently critical to combat the influences of these external forms.

It is much more difficult, however, to combat the influence of internalised forms, because it is then a question of deconstructing the mode of thinking while using the same mode of thinking. This is at the heart of the matter, as Bourdieu (1990), Butler (1999), Said (1994) and others explain.

We considered earlier Bourdieu's (1990) idea of the *habitus*. We are all born into an existing culture with social and epistemological norms and standards. We grow up using a particular form of thinking, without thinking about it.

Bourdieu uses the analogy that a fish does not know it is in water. Most people go through life without realising that they are using a particular form of thinking, and that there are other ways.

Butler (1999) illustrates this by drawing on Kafka's (2003) *Before the Law*. The story tells how people wait before a Gate, knowing there is someone behind who will tell them what to do and how to think. Most traditional epistemological systems work like this. They reinforce their legitimacy by perpetuating the mythology that someone is behind a Gate somewhere; this 'Someone' knows the Law. People come to internalise the Law and the Gate. This is of course nonsense, because there is no law and no gate. The only gate that exists is the one we create in our own minds through believing the stories, in the same way as we create things that go bump in the night. But mental images take on their own fearful reality; the monsters under the bed become very real. Dislodging the stories can be difficult and scary, because it means actually changing the way you think, and once you have done this there is no going back. You make your eyes different (Polanyi, 1958: 143) and you cannot then unchange them.

This has consequences for your own education, for the education of others, and for the education of social formations.

The significance of the fact that you speak for your own education

Changing your eyes can be difficult, because you have to learn to see things new, like learning to trust again after emotional trauma. Warren distinguishes the 'arrogant eye' from the 'loving eye':

When one climbs a rock as a conqueror, one climbs with an arrogant eye. When one climbs with a loving eye, one constantly 'must look and listen and check and question.' One recognises the rock as something very different, something perhaps totally indifferent to one's own presence, and finds in that difference joyous occasion for celebration. One knows 'the boundary of the self,' where the self – the 'I', the climber – leaves off and the rock begins. There is no fusion of two into one, but a complement of two entities, *acknowledged* as separate, different, independent, yet *in relationship*; they are in relationship *if only* because the loving eye is perceiving it, responding to it, noticing it, attending to it. (Warren, 2001: 331, emphasis in original)

Changing perceptions involves making conscious decisions, the first of which is to stop thinking that you can't do it and begin to believe that you can. Frankl (1959) tells of how prisoners of war refused to believe they would inevitably die in captivity. For many people, committing to life means hard intellectual and emotional work.

It can also bring awesome consequences. In olden times, people killed the messenger who brought disturbing news. Things are not so different today. If you challenge the status quo you are positioned as a radical, a lefty, a troublemaker, or mad. These concepts are social constructions, as Foucault (1979) explains. Chomsky (1996–98) says that Aristotle would have been called a dangerous radical in his day, and Socrates and Jesus were simply killed off for speaking the truth and encouraging others to do so – 'inciting' in the language of power. We should recognise the language of power for what it is.

Yet you need to keep at it, not be lulled into a sense of complacency, where you simply apply other people's knowledge to your practice and reproduce the status quo. Your job is to disturb the status quo (Havel, 1990). This means turning yourself into a public intellectual, and insisting on your intellectual engagement. This also brings consequences. Said (1994) speaks about the differences between traditional academics and intellectuals: traditional academics tend to focus on traditional scholarship, saying more of the same about existing practices; whereas intellectuals engage in innovative forms of enquiry, generating original knowledge of their own practices. Being an intellectual can also be lonely, because intellectuals automatically place themselves on the outside. Intellectuals are never part of an in-group, because their job is always to critique, and never get drawn into a culture of consensus.

Julie Pearson (2008), mentioned earlier, comments on these processes:

I now realise through my engagement with my Masters studies that I have always been capable of learning and generating new theory, but that I have been previously silenced by the systems in which I engaged and unwittingly served. I have moved from being a traditional academic to being an intellectual (Said, 1994); rethinking assumptions and generating new critical knowledge.

I believe that if given opportunities to work in environments where learning can be shared and experiences are valued, colleagues may also be motivated to improve their practices; learning through action and new informed action. By encouraging colleagues within the teaching profession to undertake their action enquiries, I hope to demonstrate the opportunities for research and change within practice. I wish to engage in research which explores and directly informs practice. I view my role as a professional educator to facilitate opportunities for people to use their own voices (Glavey, 2008) and to express their experiences and understanding of primary education and help to deconstruct authoritarian voices that speak for or on behalf of others. I hope that, as I have, colleagues may transform themselves from being submissive conformists to being active change agents in their own lifeworld (Fullan, 1993). The more individuals I can assist to increase their self confidence, skills or knowledge alongside my own, the better I believe the quality of educational experience will be for the people we teach.

(Pearson, 2008: 18–19)

As a practitioner, you need also to become a public intellectual. Granted it may be scary, but you should have courage and faith in your capacity to speak your truth. Polanyi says: 'In spite of the hazards involved, I am called upon to search for the truth and state my findings' (Polanyi, 1958: 299).

He also says that we are born into a world for whose making we are not responsible, yet which determines our calling. This brings us to the next section.

We are speaking about validity and legitimacy. There is a big difference between them, though both are interrelated. Validity means that a thing does what it says it does: 'It does what it says on the tin'. Your claim, 'I have improved my practice' means that a reader can expect to see improved practice and an explanation from you on how it has improved. A knowledge claim must demonstrate its validity, or believability. It then transforms into a truth claim.

Legitimacy has nothing to do with telling the truth, and everything to do with establishing how the truth may be told and who will tell it: '... who is able to tell the truth, about what, with what consequences, and with what relations to power ...' (Foucault, 2001: iii). Granting legitimacy means granting legitimacy to the validity of your truth claims, and to you, as a speaker of truth.

When you explain the validity of your knowledge (truth) claims, you are showing that your work can be believed, in relation to different aspects. You can claim the following forms of validity: these are in addition to those mentioned in Chapter 10; many more exist, and you can create others.

- Personal validity: you ground your insights in your values, and draw on writers such as Polanyi (1958).
- Ontological validity: you ground your work in insights about your relationship with yourself and draw on writers such as Tillich (1973).
- Social validity: you ground your work in insights about communication and the evolution of society and draw on writers such as Habermas (1976).
- Epistemic (epistemological) validity: you ground your work in insights about the nature of knowledge creation processes and draw on writers such as Code (1987).
- Political validity: you ground your work in insights about legitimising knowledge claims and draw on writers such as Chomsky (2002).
- Empathetic validity: you ground your work in insights about personal and social relationships and draw on writers such as Dadds (2008).

You should be creative in the kinds of validity claims you make – but make sure that you are confident about what demonstrating validity involves, because these ideas are at the heart of scholarly work, and readers and reviewers will quickly pick up on them. Explain to your reader what forms of validity you are claiming, and why.

This is where you can have the greatest influence in the learning of others. You demonstrate the validity of your knowledge and truth claims throughout your text: this is part of establishing the methodological rigour of the research. You demonstrate legitimacy through showing that your text is endorsed by critical readers and examiners, that you are trustworthy. If they trust you, people may be willing to try things out for themselves.

Dot Jackson, a senior lecturer in design and technology, writes about learning from her research (2008):

Although this action enquiry was with a small group of students, the quantity and quality of learning has been immense. I will take my new learning into my future practice with all my cohorts and continue with new cycles of reflection-on-action. Since embarking on this research I am able to articulate that my pedagogy has transformed towards collaborative praxis across all my teaching courses, from challenging an expectation of craft and moving towards innovative designerly practice. I have made changes informed by my dynamic reflections towards my own living theory of creative practice. My learning has taken place at a range of levels and in various places from individual conversations to pedagogical reflections. I recognise new ways in which I can support the development of necessary skills and knowledge in design and technology whilst also providing a critical 'creative ecosystem' (Harrington, 1990), where co-creation of knowledge can take place. I continue to work towards empowering students to challenge normative pedagogical practices, recognising their ability to create their own knowledge and to move confidently towards living their values in their practice. My new living theory of practice will be disseminated to the wider academy in papers and at educational conferences as I contribute to a new epistemology for a scholarship of educational knowledge.

My learning may gradually flow into schools through the pedagogy of my students as they take their new learning into schools. I use a river delta as a visual metaphor for my transformational learning as my enquiries develop and branch out in various directions while flowing in the general direction of new understanding and knowledge creation.

(Jackson, 2008: 23–4)

The way to exercise greatest influence is through writing, making public in different forms and for different audiences. This brings us to how to contribute to the education of social formations.

The significance of the fact that you speak for the education of social formations

Now that you have turned yourself into a writer, with academic legitimacy, you are in a position of potentially considerable influence. A key aspect is that you can influence new forms of thinking in your workplace and in the academy; and, given that the academy can influence social and cultural transformation, you are positioned as someone who can influence the future.

You therefore need to be clear about what you wish to say and how to say it. This depends on your values, what you stand for. It is said that unless we stand for something we will fall for anything. Be ready to say what you stand for, and what you are prepared to live (and possibly die) for.

Consider what this means, and how you are advancing the existing range of mainstream literatures, which still speak in a propositional form, about ideas such as self-critique and reflective practices, without always showing what they mean in action.

Here is the greatest source of your influence. You are showing, through the content and form of your text, how you are fulfilling your obligations to the truth, and speaking with your own voice. You are also saying that other people can do this, and should do it. You are pointing out to people in your workplace what needs to be done in order to improve working conditions; and to the academy that their primary responsibility should be finding ways of promoting wisdom for human well-being. You are saying to your academic colleagues that they also should create themselves as public intellectuals and stand up for those who are not able to stand up for themselves.

Sally Aston (2008), a senior lecturer of design and technology, writes about the significance of her research for her ongoing practice.

By undertaking this research I have identified ways I can continue to transform and improve my practice in future, as a practitioner reflecting in and on action. I believe that some [research] participants [now] have the capacity to develop a deeper level of critical consciousness. I feel that if I encourage students to make closer connections with the natural environment and the wider global community, their level of critical engagement will be raised and they will feel that they, as participating and informed citizens, can change things for the better. As this time of transition we have reached what Freire described as an 'historical epoch' which is 'characterised by a series of aspirations, concerns and values in search of fulfilment' (2005: 4). As citizens, we can participate in these epochs by creating, recreating and making decisions which will influence our future. I think it is my responsibility in my position [as a senior lecturer] to influence both future teachers and, indirectly, their pupils, to encourage participation as citizens who have the power to instigate positive change in society. ... With this in mind, I want to continue to develop my learning of ways to improve and understand my practice, as a form of praxis ... where I feel I comfortably inhabit my values.

(Aston, 2008: 22–3)

Through exercising your potentials for educational influence you can contribute to this process of cultural transformation. In Chapter 14 we speak about how you can do this through the development of a knowledge base, how you can make your contribution to the body of public knowledge, and so contribute to discourses about social and cultural evolution.

SUMMARY

This chapter has considered the significance of your research for yourself, the wider community, and for the future. In each of these contexts, you can show its significance for the education of yourself, of others, and of social formations. You can claim significance for what you say, how you say it, and the fact that you say it. Through doing so, you show how you can give meaning to your life, and can contribute to the meaning that others give to theirs.

REFLECTIVE QUESTIONS

Here are some reminders for how you can explain the significance of your knowledge and your text.

- Do you communicate the significance of what you say? Do you explain how you are contributing to your own education, to the education of others, and to the education of social formations? Have you produced a strong evidence base to show the nature of your educational influences in learning, and the range of those influences?

- Do you communicate the significance of how you say what you say? Do you explain how you are contributing to processes of the legitimation of knowledge through your form of communication? Have you produced a strong evidence base to show the procedures involved in exercising your educational influences in learning, and the complexities of those procedures?

- Do you communicate the significance of the fact that you are able to speak for yourself? Do you explain how you are contributing to debates about the legitimacy of all to speak for themselves through showing the potentials involved? Have you produced a strong evidence base to show the legitimacy of the struggles involved to get your knowledge validated and legitimated?

If you have done all these things, you can be fairly confident that your voice will be taken seriously in research and wider communities, and that people will consider your influence in their own processes of learning.

RESEARCH EXERCISE

Write a critical assessment of the significance of your capacity to write for publication; comment on the possibilities of influencing other people's learning through your writing.

We now move to the final chapter, which sets out ideas about creating a new public sphere through creating and sharing the kind of knowledge that is dedicated to improving practice for the benefit of self and others.

FOURTEEN

Some Implications – Where Next?

In *The Old Ways* (2012) Robert Macfarlane produces his third travel work that links travel and the individual's mind. Through real-world travel, he says, we expand our experience of physical landscapes while through metaphorical travel we expand the landscapes of our mind. The book you are reading has been written from my own experience of travelling to work with people across the world, and encouraging them to travel to meet with one another. Together and separately we have travelled far and free, learning collectively as we find ways of expanding our academic and spiritual horizons through the experience of action research and the writing of it.

Each one of us works in institutions that also need to travel in order to find ways of thinking and working that embrace the new while preserving the best of the past. This is not easy, because institutions are not so mobile as individuals, nor do they engage quite so freely. It can be difficult also for individuals whose identity is wrapped up in institutions. Change means changing attitudes and identities, which involves an initial willingness to engage in dialogue; this willingness to engage, says Richard Bernstein (1991), is a prior condition for bringing together different traditions, to leave behind the old and move forward into the new, and can be wonderfully powerful. The outcomes of dialogue are evident in places such as Northern Ireland and South Africa: sworn enemies have come together through their faith in the works of words (Doxtader, 2009). Faith in the works of words means faith in the people who speak them.

Bernstein argues for a more considered approach to debates between research traditions and the consequent demands on researchers working within those traditions to adapt their thinking and practices appropriately. If we are to critique, says Bernstein, we need to question why we do so: 'Critique in the name of what?' Questions about critique are always rooted in deeper questions about how we should live. These are also the kind of questions that real-time researchers ask: they ask, 'How do we manage this moment so that we can live together with dignity and grace?'

I used to think these were the kinds of questions that people interested in researching their practices in action asked, yet these days messages in the literatures are becoming confused and things appear to be different. I was asked some years ago, 'What will you do if and when action research becomes mainstreamed?' My response was, 'It won't get mainstreamed if we keep asking questions.' These days it seems that action research has become mainstreamed in places, and many people have forgotten to ask questions, or are asking the kind of questions to which they expect specific, formulaic answers. While writing this book I received a lot of emails that spoke about a form of action research I did not recognise. One said:

I am a doctoral candidate at [place]. I am using action research to increase understanding about [my topic]. My supervisor has asked me to explain how my objectives can be achieved or demonstrate if the objectives cannot be achieved. What are the variables?

A second said:

I want to change my organisation. Please tell me how action research can help me prove my hypothesis.

I do not engage with these kinds of questions. My view is still that I do not think it is possible to provide pre-packaged answers; I do not think action research is about providing definitive solutions or formulae. However, evidently this is now required in many institutions. Perhaps a new name should enter the field to embrace everything else: Institutionalised Action Research (IAR, perhaps?).

While writing the book I also travelled to several countries where national and institutional power struggles formed an impenetrable backdrop to the work. In these places, colleagues and I spoke about the practices and principles of action research, and they saw the potentials for influencing their workplaces, but when it came to questions such as, 'What shall we do about it?' or 'How shall we implement our action plans?' the conversation tended to stop. One workshop evaluation sheet asked the question, 'What do you think you will do now?' to which the response was 'Nothing'. The trouble with action research is that it is about freedom, but most people are not free, for whatever reason. It seems that people are happy to contribute to the *Big Book of Action Research* that tells you what it is and how to do it; not so many are willing, and many are not able, or allowed, to write their own books to show how they live lives of enquiry together.

Bernstein argues for dialogical perspectives, on the assumption that 'the other has something to say to us and can contribute to our understanding' (1991: 339). He also says there are grounds for optimism:

But there are also counter-tendencies – not towards convergence, consensus and harmony – but towards breaking down of boundaries, a 'loosening of old landmarks' and dialogical encounters where we reasonably explore our differences and conflicts. In this situation, the pragmatic legacy is especially relevant, in particular the call to nurture the type of community and solidarity where there is an engaged fallibilistic pluralism – one that is based on mutual respect, where we are willing to risk our own prejudgments, are open to listening and learning from others, and we respond to others with responsiveness and responsibility. (Bernstein, 1991: 339)

Action research is currently one of the most potent candidates for developing such a pragmatic legacy, and one of the most powerful strategies is through academic writing. In Chapter 10 I spoke about ways to influence the field through introducing small changes in assessment systems; these take the form of introducing democratic and person-centred criteria and standards of judgement. They are achieved through negotiation between candidates, supervisors and examiners. Such a strategy means turning small acts of resistance (Crawshaw and Jackson, 2010) into small acts of transformation. This kind of quiet change strategy, steadily conducted below the radar, tends to be successful: once a small change enters the social and institutional system, it is there and cannot easily be moved. Cumulative small changes solidify into systems, as Habermas (1975) noted: the system takes on a life of its own, and people forget they can change it back.

Such change towards pragmatic perspectives is pressing too in contemporary debates about the nature and role of the university (and in terms of this book, the forms of writing it permits). Further, hope for a breaking down of the boundaries comes from an unexpected quarter – business. Money is persuading the university to refashion itself according to the needs of its new student customers who vote with their credit cards, within a new culture of massive expansionism to accommodate an increasingly diverse student body (Hyland, 2007), and the increased popularity and demand for Mode 2 forms of knowledge. This demand presents an opportunity for action research as a form of theorising practices to come in from the cold and be accepted as an important and necessary part of higher education work. This in turn has implications for how higher degrees will be judged, because real-world working practices cannot be judged only in terms of the objectivity, generalisability and replicability demanded by scientific and social scientific researchers (see Furlong and Oancea, 2005); they also need to be judged in relation to whether the internal goods of the practices that MacIntyre (1985) speaks about are realised, and how this can be achieved. Consequently, universities need to recreate themselves in the image of their students, the people they serve, while helping those students also to appreciate that money is not necessarily the only or most desirable internal good. Love and kindness are more important and money cannot buy them. All kinds of knowledges and their internal goods are potentially legitimate, as are their forms of communication when written according to the criteria generated by the goods themselves. It is for people themselves to decide, but from a position of knowledge, not ignorance.

However, this kind of shape-shifting can be difficult for those universities who remain wedded to the currently dominant epistemology that prioritises abstract theory and a culture of telling. Commitment to these dominant forms has led to the ironic situation outlined by Graf (2003), where, instead of the traditional complaint that students are often not prepared for university, the situation is now reversed in that universities are often not prepared for students. Students live in the real world; they are self- and peer-educated through the Internet and social networking; they appreciate that they are, in the new academic business-speak, higher education's 'customers'. Given that most students now pay for their higher education, they check out what higher education provision is available, and are often as well informed as the sales-people (academic staff) who want to sell it to them. They are technology-savvy, and sophisticated about knowledge of life opportunities and therefore what kind of continuing education will equip them appropriately. They are also aware of the current restrictions on their own employment opportunities, so are looking for ways in which universities can help them maximise their chances.

Universities who wish to attract these potential customers therefore often find they have to change their own self-perceptions about their nature and purposes. This perhaps comes more naturally to those universities who are positioned as 'teaching-led' or 'learning-led', because they already engage with issues of knowledge in the real world, and real-world practice-based methodologies such as action research. Many traditionalist 'research-led' universities, however, still often prioritise more abstract forms of knowledge and are therefore often not well equipped to deal with many of today's students. A colleague in a business school commented to me recently, 'We do not go outside the university very much'. The inclination is still to remain within the safety of the institutional walls and teach the theory of business and management without teaching their real-world practices. Delves-Broughton (2009) says that everyday practice-based subjects such as direct selling are not taught at Harvard Business School (see McDonnell and McNiff, 2014).

I have to emphasise that I am not arguing for the elimination of blue skies research and the pursuit of knowledge for its own sake. I love the idea that we should spend time working with hypothetical issues and imagining possible new directions. Yet research always needs to be linked with the real world. Feynman made this point (2007) when he showed how a reliance on purely abstract thinking led to the *Challenger* disaster. We also need to rely on experience, intuition, and commonsense. We need to recognise all our knowledges, just as we rely on all our senses when walking in the dark.

From this perspective the challenge for universities becomes how to find a middle ground between the demands of students who want to have their practice-based knowledge valued and academically legitimated, which renders them more employable, while maintaining the traditional cultures of knowledge creation, argument, and critically-engaged theory generation. The challenge also lies in encouraging students and staff to see that professional education suffers without such a solidly grounded theoretical base, or without developing a broad understanding and use of a research language to communicate theoretical insights.

This provides an opportunity for action research to realise its full potential, representing, as it does, this middle ground. Action research is grounded in practice, and engages fully with the idea of theory generation from within the practice, with capacity for feeding back into practice in order to enhance it. The challenge for action research is how to achieve its own internal goods of enhanced practice, scholarship and research while also demonstrating the achievement of the established higher education goods of knowledge creation, balanced argument and critical engagement. It is also where newer forms of higher degree education, especially new forms of professional doctorates are achieving greater profile, given that they cater both for the practice-oriented forms of knowledge that many students and staff wish to develop, and also offer new routes to accreditation, assisted through new technologies that support the production of digital dissertations and theses.

I hope this book has gone some way towards reinforcing the need for this brave new world and offered some ideas about how it may be achieved. We all need to learn with and from one another, but this will happen only if we support the development of new dialogical cultures where all voices may be heard and all dialects respected.

Look at the garden. How do you position yourself there? Some people see themselves as the Head Gardener, as it says on their tea mug. It is their job to organise the plants and wildlife, to keep the slugs at bay and clean the ground with insecticide. Others see themselves as part of the garden, visitors like slugs and snails and the occasional ground snake. They delight in the butterflies and the brief glory lives they lead with wings fully spanned. It is said that many species of butterfly live only a few days in their mature form; no butterfly lives for more than a year. Some people capture those short days of free flying and pin butterflies to a board, better to study them and become knowledgeable about them. There is a difference between the practice of butterflies flying and the study of butterflies' flying. There is a difference between doing action research as a practice and studying action research as a topic, between writing action research for personal learning and writing action research for publication.

It is up to you and how your personal acts of transformation can contribute to culture change. You can show how you have transformed your life through studying it, through determination and spiritual resilience, and how you have influenced the learning of other people, so that they learn how to transform their own lives; you have exercised your agency for cultural and social transformation. You have given new meaning to what it means to be a university: not a building so much as people. An institution lives and breathes because of the people within it.

So we continue to work with words, and words make us free. Faust was on dangerous ground when he said, 'In the beginning was the deed' (Goethe, 1957). Deeds, even the most noble, must first and always be grounded in silent and spoken words. You also do this when you do and write action research; you ground your actions in the work of words and show how they transform into deeds through your commitment to offering explanations for what you think and consequently do. We are defined by our words, so it is our responsibility to choose them well.

References

Adams, G. (2008) 'From transmitter of knowledge to mediator of learning', Paper presented at the American Educational Research Association annual meeting, New York. Available at www.jeanmcniff.com/items.asp?id = 81 (accessed March 2014).

al-Takriti, N. (2010) 'Negligent Mnemocide and the Shattering of Iraqi Collective Memory', in R. Baker, S. Ismael and T. Ismael (eds) *Cultural Cleansing in Iraq.* London: Pluto Press. pp. 93–115.

Alford, C.F. (2001) *Whistleblowers: Broken Lives and Organizational Power.* Ithaca: Cornell University Press.

Allport, G. (1955) *Becoming.* New Haven: Yale University Press.

Andrews, R., Borg, E., Davis, S., Domingo, M. and England, J. (eds) (2012) *Digital Dissertations and Theses.* Los Angeles: Sage.

Appadurai, A. (2006) 'The right to research', *Globalizations, Societies and Education,* 4 (2): 167–77.

Arendt, H. (1958) *The Human Condition.* Chicago: University of Chicago.

Arendt, H. (1971) *The Life of the Mind, Vol. 1, Thinking.* New York and London: Harcourt, Brace Jonavich.

Argyris, C. and Schön, D. (1978) *Organisational Learning: A Theory of Action Perspective.* Reading, MA: Addison Wesley.

Argyris, C., Putnam, R. and Smith, D.M. (1985) *Action Science: Concepts, Methods, and Skills for Research and Intervention.* San Francisco: Jossey-Bass.

Argyris, C. and Schön, D. (1974) *Theory in Pracice: Increasing Professional Effectiveness.* San Francisco: Jossey-Bass.

Asiimwe, F.A. and Crankshaw, O. (2011) 'The impact of customary laws on inheritance: A case study of widows in urban Uganda', *Journal of Law and Conflict Resolution,* 3 (1): 7–13.

Aston, S. (2008) Academic Paper: Module 7, MA PVP programme, St Mary's University College, Twickenham.

Barry, P. (2002) *Beginning Theory: An Introduction to Literary and Cultural Theory* (2nd edition). Manchester: Manchester University Press.

Barthes, R. (1970) *S/Z.* New York: Hill & Wang.

Barthes, R. (2000) *Mythologies.* London: Vintage.

Bassey, M. (1999) *Case Study Research in Educational Settings.* Buckingham: Open University Press.

Bateson, G. (1979) *Mind and Nature: A Necessary Unity.* New York: Dutton.

Beardshaw Andrews, Z. (2012) 'Reframing the Performing Arts', in R. Andrews et al. (eds) *The Sage Handbook of Digital Dissertations and Theses.* London: Sage. pp. 101–19.

Benner, P. (1984) *From Novice to Expert: Excellence and Power in Clinical Nursing Practice.* Menlo Park, CA: Addison-Wesley.

Benner, P., Sutphen, M., Leonard, V. and Day, L. (2010) *Educating Nurses: A Call for Radical Transformation.* San Francisco: Jossey-Bass.

Bennett, A. and Hytner, N. (2006) *The History Boys: The Film.* London: Faber and Faber.

Bereiter, C. and Scardamalia, M. (1987) *The Pyschology of Written Composition.* Hillsdale, NJ: Lawrence Earlbaum Associates.

Bergson, H. (1998) *Creative Evolution.* Mineola, NY: Dover Publications (originally published in 1911).

Berlin, I. (1969) *Four Essays on Liberty.* London: Oxford University Press.

Bernstein, R. (1971) *Praxis and Action.* London: Duckworth. (Drawing on some of Marx's unpublished notes written in 1844.)

Bernstein, R. (1991) *The New Constellation.* Oxford: Polity Press.

Bertoft, H. (1996) *The Wholeness of Nature: Goethe's Way of Science.* New York: Floris.

Bhaba, H. (2003), Interview in G. Olson and L. Worsham (2003) *Critical Intellectuals on Writing.* Albany: State University of New York Press.

Biko, S. (1987) *I Write What I Like.* Oxford: Heinemann.

Binnie, A. and Titchen, A. (1998) *Patient-Centred Nursing: An Action Research Study of Practice Development in an Acute Medical Unit.* Report No. 18, Oxford: RCN Institute.

Binnie, A. and Titchen, A. (1999) (ed. J. Lathlean) *Freedom to Practise: The Development of Patient-centred Nursing.* Oxford: Butterworth-Heinemann.

Bleach, J. (2013) 'Community Action Research: Providing Evidence of Value and Virtue', in J. McNiff (ed.) *Value and Virtue in Practice-Based Research.* Poole: September Books. pp. 17–32.

Bohm, D. (1983) *Wholeness and the Implicate Order.* London: Ark Paperbacks.

Bohm, D. (1987) *Unfolding Meaning.* London: Ark Paperbacks.

Bohm, D. (1996) (ed. L. Nichol) *On Dialogue.* London: Routledge.

Bolton, G. (2014) *Inspirational Writing for Academic Publication.* London: Sage.

Bourdieu, P. (1984) *Distinction: A Social Critique of the Judgement of Taste.* London: Routledge.

Bourdieu, P. (1990) *The Logic of Practice.* Cambridge: Polity.

Boyer, E. (1990) *Scholarship Reconsidered: Priorities of the Professoriate.* New Jersey: Carnegie Foundation for the Advancement of Teaching.

Branson, R. (2006) *Screw It, Let's Do It.* London: Virgin.

Brown, L. (2004) *African Philosophy: New and Traditional Perspectives.* Oxford: Oxford University Press.

Bruce Ferguson, P. (2013) 'To Act or Not to Act? That is the Question!', in J. McNiff (ed.) *Value and Virtue in Practice-Based Research.* Poole, September Books. pp. 33–42.

Buber, M. (1937) *I and Thou.* Edinburgh: Clark.

Buber, M. (2002) *Between Man and Man.* London: Routledge.

Bullough, R. and Pinnegar, S. (2001) 'Guidelines for quality in autobiographical forms of self-study research', *Educational Researcher*, 30 (3): 13–22.

Bullough, R. and Pinnegar, S. (2004) 'Thinking About Thinking About Self-Study: An Analysis of Eight Chapters', in J.J. Loughran, M.L. Hamilton, V.K. Labosky and T. Russell (eds) *International Handbook of Teaching and Teacher-Education Practices.* Dordrecht: Kluwer.

Burns, D. (2007) *Systemic Action Research: A Strategy for Whole System Change.* Bristol: The Policy Press.

Bushe, G.R. (2011) 'Appreciative Inquiry: Theory and Critique', in D. Boje, B. Burnes and J. Hassard (eds) *The Routledge Companion to Organizational Change.* Abingdon, Routledge. pp. 87–103.

Butler, J. (1999) *Gender Trouble.* London: Routledge.

Butler-Kisber, L. (2010) *Qualitative Inquiry.* Los Angeles: Sage.

Cahill, M. (2007) *My Living Educational Theory of Inclusional Practice*. PhD thesis, University of Limerick. Available at www.jeanmcniff.com/margaretcahill/index.html (accessed 20 June 2008).

Callahan, R. (1962) *Education and the Cult of Efficiency*. Chicago: University of Chicago.

Calvino, G. (1974) *Invisible Cities*. Florida: Harcourt Brace & Company.

Capra, F. (1996) *The Web of Life*. London: HarperCollins.

Carpenter, J. (2009) *Building Reflective Relationships For and Through the Creation of Educational Knowledge*. Presented at the British Educational Research Association annual meeting, York: York St John University. (Available at: www.jeanmcniff.com/york-st-john-university.asp, accessed March 2014).

Carr, W. and Kemmis, S. (1986) *Becoming Critical: Education, Knowledge and Action Research*. London: Falmer.

Carr, W. and Kemmis, S. (2005) 'Staying critical', *Educational Action Research*, 13 (3): 347–59.

Chandler, D. and Torbert, W. (2003) 'Transforming inquiry and action: Interweaving flavors of action research', *Journal of Action Research*, 1 (2): 133–52.

Chevalier, J. and Buckles, D. (2013) *Participatory Action Research*. Abingdon: Routledge.

Chomsky, N. (1957) *Syntactic Structures*. The Hague: Mouton.

Chomsky, N. (1965) *Aspects of the Theory of Syntax*. Cambridge, MA: MIT Press.

Chomsky, N. (1986) *Knowledge of Language: Its Nature, Origin and Use*. New York: Praeger.

Chomsky, N. (1991) *Media Control: The Spectacular Achievements of Propaganda*. New York: Seven Stories Press.

Chomsky, N. (1996–98) interviewed by D. Barsamian, *The Common Good*. Tucson AZ: Odonian Press.

Chomsky, N. (2000) (ed. D. Macedo) *Chomsky on MisEducation*. Lanham: Rowman & Littlefield.

Chomsky, N. (2002) (edited by P.R. Mitchell and J. Schoeffel) *Understanding Power: The Indispensable Chomsky*. New York: The New Press.

Chomsky, N. (2003) Interview, in G. Olson, and L. Worsham (2003) *Critical Intellectuals on Writing*. Albany: State University of New York Press.

Chomsky, N. (2005) *Imperial Ambitions*. London: Penguin.

Clandinin, J. and Connelly, M. (2000) *Narrative Inquiry*. San Francisco: Jossey-Bass.

Clark, R. and Ivanič, R. (1997) *The Politics of Writing*. London: Routledge.

Code, L. (1987) *Epistemic Responsibility*. Hanover: Brown University Press.

Coetzee, J.M. (1988) *White Writing: On the Culture of Letters in South Africa*. New Haven: Yale University Press.

Coghlan, D. and Brannick, T. (2001) *Doing Action Research in Your Own Organization*. London: Sage.

Collier, J. (1945) 'United States Indian administration as a laboratory of ethnic relations', *Social Research*, 12: 265–303.

Collins, J. (2010) *Bring on the Books for Everybody*. Durham: Duke University Press.

Corcoran, M. and Lalor, K. (2012) *Reflections on Crisis: The Role of the Public Intellectual*. Dublin: Royal Irish Academy.

Cordery, M. (2008) Academic Paper: Module 7, MA PVP programme, St Mary's University College, Twickenham.

Corey, S. (1953) *Action Research to Improve School Practices*. New York: Teachers Press.

Costley, C. and Stephenson, J. (2009) 'Building Doctorates Around Individual Candidates' Professional Experience', in D. Boud and A. Lee (eds) *Changing Practices in Doctoral Education*. Abingdon: Routledge. pp. 171–86.

Crane, J.L. (2014) *Half A Piece of Cloth: The Courage of Africa's Countless Widows*. Rancho Santa Fe: Hearkening Press.

Crawshaw, S. and Jackson, J. (2010) *Small Acts of Resistance*. New York: Sterling Publishing.

Crème, P. and Lea, M. (2008) *Writing at University*. Maidenhead: Open University Press.

Cresswell, J. (2007) *Qualitative Inquiry and Research Design* (2nd edn). Thousand Oaks, CA: Sage.

Csikszentmihalyi, M. (1990) *Flow*. New York: HarperPerennial.

Dadds, M. (2008) 'Empathetic validity', *Educational Action Research*, 16 (2): 279–90.

Dadds, M. and Hart, S. (2001) *Doing Practitioner Research Differently*. London: RoutledgeFalmer.

Daley, P.O. (2007) *Gender and Genocide in Burundi: The Search for Spaces of Peace in the Great Lakes Region*. Oxford: Fountain Publishers.

Davies, M.B. (2007) *Doing a Successful Research Project*. Basingstoke: Palgrave Macmillan.

Deloria, V. (1989) *Custer Died for Your Sins*. Norman: University of Oklahoma Press.

Delves-Broughton, P. (2009) *What They Teach You at Harvard Business School*. London: Penguin.

Derrida, J. (1986) 'But, beyond ... (Open Letter to Anne McClintock and Rob Nixon)' (trans. Peggy Kamul), *Critical Inquiry*, 13 (Autumn): 155–70.

Derrida, J. (1997) *Of Grammatology*. Baltimore: Johns Hopkins Press.

Deutscher, P. (2005) *Derrida*. London: Granta.

Dewey, J. (1938) *Experience and Education*. New York: Macmillan.

Doxtader, E. (2009) *With Faith in the Works of Words*. Claremont: David Philip.

Dutt, V. (2010) 'Invisible Forgotten Sufferers: The Plight of Widows around the World. Why the UN Should Recognize International Widows' Day.' A research study commissioned by the Loomba Foundation and presented to the United Nations on International Widows' Day, 23 June 2010. Research by Risto F. Harma. New Delhi: Konark Publishers Pvt Ltd.

Edvardsen, O. (2010) *Et nettverk av førstehjelpere i det minelagte Nord-Irak*. University of Tromsø, Masters dissertation: September.

Eisner, E. (1997) 'The promise and perils of alternative forms of representation', *Educational Researcher*, 26 (6): 4–10.

Elliott, J. (1991) *Action Research for Educational Change*. Milton Keynes: Open University Press.

Elliott, J. (2007) *Reflecting Where the Action Is*. London: Routledge.

Elliott, J. (2013) 'Introduction: The Spiritual Dimension of Action Research', in J. McNiff (ed.) *Value and Virtue in Practice-Based Research*. Poole, September Books. pp. 6–16.

Esposito, J, and Evans-Winters, V. (2007) 'Contextualizing critical action research: Lessons from urban educators', *Educational Action Research*, 15 (2): 221–37.

Evans, T. (2010) 'Understanding doctoral research for professional practitioners', in M. Walker and P. Thomson (eds) *The Routledge Doctoral Supervisor's Companion*. Abingdon: Routledge.

Feldman, A. (2003) 'Validity and Quality in Self-Study', *Educational Researcher*, 32 (3): 26–8.

Fershleiser, R. and Smith, L. (2008) *Not Quite What I Was Planning*. New York: HarperPerennial.

Festinger, L. (1957) *A Theory of Cognitive Dissonance*. Stanford, CA: Stanford University Press.

Feynman, R. (2001) *The Pleasure of Finding Things Out*. London: Penguin.

Feynman, R. (2007) *What Do You Care What Other People Think?* London: Penguin.

Flood, R.L. (2001) 'The Relationship of "Systems Thinking" to Action Research', in P. Reason and H. Bradbury (eds) *Handbook of Action Research: Participative Inquiry & Practice*. London, Sage. pp. 133–44.

Foucault, M. (1977) 'What is an Author?', in D. Bouchard (ed.) *Language, Counter-Memory, Practice*. Ithaca, NY: Cornell University Press.

Foucault, M. (1979) *Discipline and Punish: The Birth of the Prison*. New York: Vintage Books.

Foucault, M. (1980) (ed. G. Gordon) *Power/Knowledge: Selected interviews and other writings by Michel Foucault, 1972–1977*. New York: Pantheon Books.

Foucault, M. (1994) *Critique and Power: Recasting the Foucault/Habermas debate* (ed. M. Kelly). Cambridge, MA: MIT Press.

Foucault, M. (2001) *Fearless Speech*. Los Angeles: Semiotext(e).

Frankl, V. (1959) *Man's Search for Meaning*. Boston: Beacon.

Freire, P. (1970) *Pedagogy of the Oppressed*. New York: Herder and Herder.

Fromm, E. (1978) *To Have or To Be?* London: Jonathan Cape.

Furlong, J. and Oancea, A. (2005) *Assessing Quality in Applied and Practice-Based Educational Research: A Framework for Discussion*. Oxford: Oxford University Department of Educational Studies.

Galbraith, D. (2009) 'Writing about What We Know: Generating Ideas in Writing', in R. Beard, D. Myhill, J. Riley and M. Nystrand (eds) *The SAGE Handbook of Writing Development*. London: Sage. Chapter 3, pp. 48–64.

Gaventa, J. and Horton, B.D. (1981) 'A citizen's research project in Appalachia, USA', *Convergence: An International Journal of Adult Education*, 14 (3): 30–42.

Ghaye, T. (2010) *Teaching and Learning through Reflective Practice* (2nd edition). Abingdon: Routledge.

Gibbons, M., Limoges, C., Nowotny, H., Schwartzman, S., Scott, P. and Trow, M. (1994) *The New Production of Knowledge: The Dynamics of Science and Research in Contemporary Societies*. London: Sage.

Gibson, J. (1993) *Performance Versus Results*. New York: State University of New York Press.

Gísladóttir, K.R. (2011) *'I am Deaf, Not Illiterate'*. PhD dissertation, Reykjavik, University of Iceland.

Gísladóttir, K.R. (2014) '"Tjaa, I Do Have Ears, But I Do Not Hear": New Literacy Studies and the Awakening of a Hearing Teacher', *Studying Teacher Education: A Journal of self-study of teacher education*, Vol. 10 (2) Online at http://www.tandfonline.com/eprint/m8HNXp4R8K82jRADqqAc/full

Glavey, C. (2008) *Helping Eagles Fly: A Living Theory Approach to Student and Young Adult Leadership Development*. PhD thesis, University of Glamorgan. Available at: www.jeanmcniff.com/items.asp?id=44 (accessed 30 March 2014).

Goethe, J.W. (1957) *Faust: Eine Tragödie*, in *Goethes Werke in Zwei Bänden: Erster Band*. Munich: Droemische Verlagsanstalt Th. Knaur Nachf.

Gordon, S. and Ross-Gordon, J. (2014) 'Multiple approaches to practitioner action research': Paper presented at the Value and Virtue in Practice-Based Research annual conference, York: York St John University, July.

Gould, S.J. (1997) *The Mismeasure of Man*. London: Penguin.

Graf, G. (2003) *Clueless in Academe*. New Haven: Yale University Press.

Gray, J. (1995) *Enlightenment's Wake: Politics and Culture and the Close of the Modern Age*. London: Routledge.

Gray, J. (2002) *Straw Dogs*. London: Granta.

Greenwood, D. and Levin, M. (2007) *Introduction to Action Research* (2nd edition). Thousand Oaks: Sage.

Habermas, J. (1975) *Legitimation Crisis*. Boston: Beacon Press.

Habermas, J. (1976) *Communication and the Evolution of Society*. Boston: Beacon Press.

Habermas, J. (1984) *The Theory of Communicative Action, Volume One*. Boston: Beacon Press.

Habermas, J. (1987) *The Theory of Communicative Action, Volume Two: The Critique of Functionalist Reason*. Oxford: Polity.

Habermas, J. (2001) *The Inclusion of the Other*. Cambridge, MA: MIT Press.

Hall, C., Smith, P. and Wicaksono, R. (2011) *Mapping Applied Linguistics*. Abingdon: Routledge.

Hannerz, U. (1990) 'Cosmopolitans and locals in world culture', *Theory, Culture & Society*, 7: 237–51.

Hansen, S. (2004) 'A constructivist approach to project assessment', *European Journal of Engineering Education*, 29 (2): 211–20.

Harding, S. (ed.) (2004) *The Feminist Theory Standpoint Reader: Intellectual and Political Controversies*. New York: Routledge.

Harland, T. and Pickering, N. (2011) *Values in Higher Education Teaching*. Abingdon: Routledge.

Havel, V. (1990) *Disturbing the Peace*. London: Faber and Faber.

Hawken, P. (2010) *The Ecology of Commerce*. New York: Harper Business.

Heilbroner, R. and Thurow, L. (1998) *Economics Explained*. New York: Simon & Schuster.

Hendrickx, S. and Martin, N. (2011) 'Insights into intimacy from people with Asperger syndrome and their partners', *Good Autism Practice*, 12 (1): 26–34.

Heron, J. (1996) *Cooperative Inquiry: Research into the Human Condition*. London: Sage.

Herr, K. and Anderson, G. (2005) *The Action Research Dissertation*. New York: Sage.

Hofstadter, D. (1979) *Gödel, Escher, Bach: An Eternal Golden Braid*. London: Penguin.

Hogan, P. (2010) *The New Significance of Learning: Imagination's Heartwork*. Abingdon: Routledge.

Holly, P. (1989) 'Reflective writing and the spirit of enquiry', *Cambridge Journal of Education*, 19 (1).

Holy Bible, King James Version. Cambridge: Syndics of Cambridge University Press.

hooks, b. (2003) Interview, in G. Olson, and L. Worsham (2003) *Critical Intellectuals on Writing*. Albany: State University of New York Press.

Horberry, R. (2009) *Brilliant Copywriting*. Harlow: Pearson.

Husserl, E. (1931) *Ideas. A General Introduction to Pure Phenomenology*. London: Allen and Unwin.

Hyland, K. (2007) *Writing in the Academy: Reputation, Education and Knowledge*. University of London: Institute of London Press.

Hymes, D.H. (1966) 'Two types of linguistic relativity', in W. Bright (ed.) *Sociolinguistics*. The Hague: Mouton. pp. 114–58.

Ilyenkov, E. (1977) *Dialectical Logic*. Moscow: Progress.

Jackson, D. (2008) Academic Paper: Module 7, MA PVP programme, St Mary's University College, Twickenham.

James, M. (2013) *Developing a Theopraxis: How Can I Legitimately be a Christian Teacher-Educator?* PhD thesis, University of Leeds. Available at www.jeanmcniff.com

Johnson, S. (2002) *Emergence*. London: Penguin.

Kafka, F. (2003) *The Metamorphosis, In the Penal Colony, and Other Stories*. New York: Simon & Schuster.

Karlsen, A.-G. (2014) 'Public health nursing education as a Master's Programme in Norway: for better or worse?' Paper presented at the Fourth International Conference on Value and Virtue in Practice-Based Research, York, York St John University. 22nd–23rd July.

Kemmis, S. (2009) 'Action research as a practice-based practice', *Educational Action Research*, 17 (3): 463–74.

Kemmis, S. and Smith, T. (2007) *Enabling Praxis: Challenges for Education*. Rotterdam: Sense.

Kemmis, S., McTaggart, R. and Nixon, R. (2014) *The Action Research Planner: Doing Critical Participatory Research*. Singapore: Springer.

King, S. (2000) *On Writing*. London: Hodder Paperbacks.

Kleon, A. (2012) *Steal Like an Artist*. New York: Workman Publishing.

Klos, A. (2014) Papers for annual review meeting. York, York St John University.

Kohn, M. (2000) *As We Know It: Coming to Terms with an Evolved Mind*. London: Granta.

Kress, G. (1982) *Learning to Write*. London: Routledge.

Kress, G. (2010) 'Multimodality', in B. Cope and M. Kalantzis (eds) *Multiliteracies: Literacy Learning and the Design of Social Futures*. London: Routledge. pp. 121–48.

Kress, G. and Bezemer, J. (2009) 'Writing in a Multimodal World of Representation', in R. Beard, D. Myhill, J. Riley and M. Nystrand (eds) *The SAGE Handbook of Writing Development*. London: Sage. pp. 167–81, Chapter 11.

Kuhn, T. (1964) *The Structure of Scientific Revolutions*. Chicago: University of Chicago Press.

Kushner, S. (2000) *Personalizing Evaluation*. London: Sage.

Lather, P. (1991) *Getting Smart: Feminism Research and Pedagogy with/in the Postmodern*. London: Routledge.

Latsone, L. and Pavitola, L. (2013) 'The Value of Researching Civic Responsibility in the Context of Latvia', in J. McNiff (ed.) *Value and Virtue in Practice-Based Research*. Poole, September Books. pp. 93–106.

Lave, J. and Wenger, E. (1991) *Situated Learning: Legitimate Peripheral Participation*. Cambridge: Cambridge University Press.

Law, J. (2004) *After Method: Mess in Social Science Research*. London: Routledge.

Lee, A. and Boud, D. (2009) 'Framing Doctoral Education as Practice', in D. Boud and A. Lee (eds) *Changing Practices in Doctoral Education*. Abingdon: Routledge. pp. 10–25.

Levinas, E. (1998) *Otherwise than Being or Beyond Essence*. Pittsburg: Duquesne University Press.

Levy, N. and Salvadori, M. (2002) *Why Buildings Fall Down*. New York: W.W. Norton & Company.

Lewin, K. (1946) 'Action research and minority problems', *Journal of Social Issues*, 2 (4): 34–46.

Lilla, M. (2001) *The Reckless Mind: Intellectuals in Politics*. New York: The New York Review of Books.

Lodge, D. (2003) *Consciousness and the Novel*. London: Penguin.

Loy, D. (2010) *The World is Made of Stories*. Somerville, MA: Wisdom Publications.

Louw, W. (2011) *Turning Resources into Assets: Improving the Service Delivery and Relevance of a Psychology Training Clinic through Action Research*. The University of Pretoria: PhD in Psychology.

Lyotard, J.-F. (1984) *The Postmodern Condition: A Report on Knowledge*. Manchester: Manchester University Press.

MacDonald, B. (1987) 'The State of Education Today', paper in *The Ides of March Conference Record*: Record of the First C.A.R.E. Conference: Cromer, Centre for Applied Research in Education, University of East Anglia.

Macdonald, J.B. (1995) (ed.) *Theory as a Prayerful Act: The Collected Essays of James B. Macdonald*. New York: Peter Lang.

Macfarlane, R. (2012) *The Old Ways: A Journey on Foot*. London: Penguin.

MacIntyre, A. (1985) *After Virtue* (2nd edition). London: Duckworth.

Macmurray, J. (1957) *The Self as Agent*. London: Faber and Faber.

Macmurray, J. (1961) *Persons in Relation*. London: Faber and Faber.

MacShane, F. (1976) *The Life of Raymond Chandler*. London: Jonathan Cape.

Malgas, Z. (2008) Practitioner Research and Knowledge Transfer, Module 6, MA, PVP Programme, St Mary's University College, Twickenham.

Mansfield, K. (1922) 'Daughters of the Late Colonel', in *The Garden Party, and Other Stories*. New York: Alfred A. Knopf. pp. 83–115.

Marcuse, H. (1964) *One-Dimensional Man*. Boston: Beacon Press.

Marlin, R. (2002) *Propaganda and the Ethics of Persuasion*. Ontario: Broadview Press.

Mason, J. (2002) *Qualitative Researching* (2nd edition). London: Sage.

Mathien, T. and Wright, D.G. (eds) (2006) *Autobiography as Philosophy*. Abingdon: Routledge.

Mavromatis, A. (1991) *Hypnagogia*. London: Routledge.

McCartan, C., Schubotz, D. and Murphy, J. (2012) 'The self-conscious researcher – post-modern perspectives of participatory research with young people', Forum: Qualitative Social Research, 13(1). Retrieved from www.qualitative-research.net/

McDonnell, P. and McNiff, J. (2014) *Action Research for Professional Selling*. Farnham: Gower.

McDonnell, P. and McNiff, J. (in preparation) *Action Research for Nurses*. London: Sage.

McMillan, K. and Weyers, J. (2010) *How to Write Dissertations and Project Reports*. Harlow: Pearson.

McNiff, J. (1984) 'Action research: A generative model for in-service education', *British Journal of Education*, 10 (3): 40–6.

McNiff, J. (1989) *An Explanation for an Individual's Educational Development through the Dialectic of Action Research*. PhD thesis, University of Bath.

McNiff, J. (1990) 'Writing and the Creation of Educational Knowledge', in P. Lomax (ed.) *Managing Staff Development in Schools: An Action Research Approach*. Clevedon: Multilingual Matters. pp. 52–60.

McNiff, J. (2000) *Action Research in Organisations*. London: Routledge.

McNiff, J. (2002) *Action Research: Principles and Practice* (2nd edition). London: Routledge.

McNiff, J. (2012) 'Travels around identity: Transforming cultures of learned colonisation', *Educational Action Research*, 20 (1): 129–46.

McNiff, J. (2013a) *Action Research: Principles and Practice* (3rd edition). Abingdon: Routledge.

McNiff, J. (2013b) 'Becoming cosmopolitan and other dilemmas of internationalisation: Reflections from the Gulf States', *Cambridge Journal of Education*, 43(4): 501–15.

McNiff, J. (2013c) (ed.) *Value and Virtue in Practice-Based Research*. Poole: September Books.

McNiff, J. and Whitehead, J. (2010) *You and Your Action Research Project* (3rd edition). Abingdon: Routledge.

McNiff, J. and Whitehead, J. (2011) *All You Need to Know about Action Research* (2nd edition). London: Sage.

McNiff, J., Norbye, B., Karlsen, A.-G., Olsen, M., Thoresen, A.-L., Törnqvist, M. (2013) Tape recorded conversation in Health Education Research Group, Tromsø: UiT, the Arctic University.

Mee, S. (2014) 'The voice of the expert by experience versus the professional editor: transparency or constitution?' Paper submitted to the Value and Virtue in Practice-Based Research Conference, York St John University, July.

Mellor, N. (1998) 'Notes from a method', *Educational Action Research*, 6 (3): 453–70.

Milgram, S. (1973) *Obedience to Authority*. London: Tavistock.

Miller, J. (1993) *The Passion of Michel Foucault*. London: HarperCollins.

Moustakim, R. (2008) Academic Paper: Module 7, MA PVP programme, St Mary's University College, Twickenham.

Mpondwama, M. (2008) Academic Paper: Module 7, MA PVP programme, St Mary's University College, Twickenham.

Murray, R. (2002) *How to Write a Thesis*. Buckingham: Open University Press.

Murray, R. (2005) *Writing for Academic Journals*. Buckingham: Open University Press.

Ngũgĩ wa Thiong'o (1993) *Moving the Centre: The Struggle for Cultural Freedoms.* Oxford: James Currey.

Noffke, S. (1997a) 'Professional, personal, and political dimensions of action research', *Review of Research in Education,* 22: 305–43.

Noffke, S. (1997b) 'Themes and Tensions in US Action Research', in S. Hollingsworth (ed.) *International Action Research: A Casebook for Educational Reform.* London: Falmer. pp. 2–16.

Noffke, S. (2009) 'Revisiting the Professional, Personal, and Political Dimensions of Action Research', in S. Noffke and B. Somekh (eds) *The SAGE Handbook of Educational Action Research.* London, Sage. pp. 6–23. Chapter 1.

Noffke, S. and Somekh, B. (2009) *The SAGE Handbook of Educational Action Research.* London: Sage.

Norris, C. (1989) *The Deconstructive Turn: Essays in the Rhetoric of Philosophy.* London: Routledge.

Nugent, M. (2000) 'How can I raise the level of self-esteem of second year Junior Certificate School Programme students and create a better learning environment?' MA Thesis, Dublin, University of the West of England. Available at www.jeanmcniff.com/items.asp?id = 53 (accessed March 2014).

Odimmegwa, A.O. (2010) 'Widowhood and the Dignity of Womanhood in Igboland: A Pastoral Challenge to the Discipleship of the Roman Catholic Church in Igboland.' Ph.D. Dissertation, Fordham University, New York.

O'Neill, R. (2008) *ICT as Political Action.* PhD thesis, University of Glamorgan. Available at www.ictaspoliticalaction.com. See also http://www.jeanmcniff.com/theses.asp.

O'Reilly, P. (1994) *Writing for the Market.* Dublin: Mercier Press.

Olsen, M. (2014) 'Learning in a low income country setting', Paper presented at the Collaborative Action Research Network international conference, Tromsø, UiT, the Arctic University, November.

Olson, D. (2009) 'The History of Writing', in R. Beard, D. Myhill, J. Riley and M. Nystrand (eds) *The SAGE Handbook of Writing Development.* London: Sage. pp. 6–16.

Olson, G. and Worsham, L. (2003) *Critical Intellectuals on Writing.* Albany: State University of New York Press.

Oriard, M. (1980) 'Professional football as cultural myth', *Journal of American Culture,* 5.

Orwell, G. (2004) *Why I Write.* London: Penguin Books.

Page, S. (1998) *How to Get Published and Make a Lot of Money!* London: Judy Piatkus Publishers.

Pearson, J. (2008) Academic Paper: Module 7, MA PVP programme, St Mary's University College, Twickenham.

Pearson, J. (2014) Working papers, PhD studies annual review meeting. York: York St John University.

Perlmutter, D.D. (2000) *Policing the Media: Street Cops and Public Perceptions of Law Enforcement.* London: Sage.

Phillips, E.M. and Pugh, D.S. (2005) *How to Get a PhD: A Handbook for Students and their Supervisors* (4th edition). Buckingham: Open University Press.

Pinar, W. (1995) 'Introduction', in B.J. Macdonald (ed.) *Theory as a Prayerful Act: The Collected Essays of James B. Macdonald.* New York: Peter Lang. pp. 1–14.

Pink, D. (2012) *To Sell Is Human.* New York: Riverhead Books.

Polanyi, M. (1958) *Personal Knowledge.* London: Routledge & Kegan Paul.

Polanyi, M. (1967) *The Tacit Dimension.* New York: Anchor Books.

Pollard, A. and Tann, S. (2013) *Reflective Teaching in the Primary School* (2nd edition). London: Continuum.

Popper, K. (1945) *The Open Society and Its Enemies. Vol. 1. Plato*. London, Routledge & Kegan Paul.

Popper, K. (2002) *The Poverty of Historicism*. London: Routledge.

Popplewell, R. and Hayman, R. (2012) *Where, how, and why are Action Research approaches used by international development non-governmental organisations?* Briefing Paper 32. INTRAC [online] (Available at: www.intrac.org/data/files/resources/752/Briefing-Paper-32-Where-how-and-why-are-Action-Research-approaches-used-by-international-development-non-governmentalorganisations.pdf, accessed March 2014).

Pratt-Fartro, T. (2014) 'Do you see what I see? Using a critical lens to build a coaching conceptual framework'. Paper presented at the Fourth International Conference on Value and Virtue in Practice-Based Research, York, York St John University. 22nd–23rd July.

Pressfield, S. (2011) *Do the Work!* The Domino Project, Do You Zoom.

Pring, R. (2000) *Philosophy of Educational Research*. London: Continuum.

QAA (Quality Assurance Agency) (2008) *The Framework for Higher Education Qualifications in England, Wales and Northern Ireland (FHEQ)* [Online]. Available at http://www.qaa.ac.uk/Publications/InformationAndGuidance/Pages/The-framework-for-higher-education-qualifications-in-England-Wales-and-Northern-Ireland.aspx (accessed 28 March 2014).

Rawls, J. (1971) *A Theory of Justice*. Oxford: Oxford University Press.

Raymond, P. (2014) Draft writing for PhD thesis, York, York St John University.

Raz, J. (2003) *The Practice of Value*. Oxford: Oxford University Press.

Reagan, T. (2005) *Non-Western Educational Traditions* (3rd edition). Mahway: New Jersey, Lawrence Erlbaum Associates.

Reason. P. and Bradbury, H. (2001) 'Introduction', in P. Reason and H. Bradbury (eds) *Handbook of Action Research: Participative Inquiry & Practice*. London: Sage. pp. 1–14.

Reason, P. and Bradbury, H. (eds) (2008) *Handbook of Action Research: Participative Inquiry and Practice* (2nd edition). London: Sage.

Reason, P. and Rowan, J. (1981) *Human Inquiry: A Sourcebook of New Paradigm Research*. Chichester: Wiley.

Ricoeur, P. (1992) *Oneself as Another*. Chicago: University of Chicago Press.

Robson, C. (2002) *Real World Research: A Resource for Social Scientists and Practitioner-Researchers* (2nd edition). Oxford: Blackwell.

Rolfe, G. (1996) *Closing the Theory-Practice Gap: A New Paradigm for Nursing*. Oxford: Butterworth-Heinemann.

Rolfe, G. (1998) *Expanding Nursing Knowledge: Understanding and Researching Your Own Practice*. Oxford: Butterworth-Heinemann.

Rorty, R. (2003) Interview in G. Olson and L. Worsham (2003) *Critical Intellectuals on Writing*. Albany: State University of New York Press.

Rose, I., (2005) 'Autistic Autobiography – Introducing the Field.' [Online] Available at: www.cwru.edu/affil/sce/Representing%20Autism.html (accessed 26 April 2013).

Rowell, L., Bruce, C.L., Shosh, J.M. and Riel, M.M. (eds) (in preparation, scheduled for 2016), *Palgrave International Handbook of Action Research*. New York: Palgrave Macmillan.

Rowlands, M. (2005) *Everything I Know I learned from TV*. London: Ebury Press.

Russell, T. and Korthagen, F. (1995) (eds) *Teachers Who Teach Teachers: Reflections on Teacher Education*. London, Falmer.

Ryle, G. (1949) *The Concept of Mind*. Harmondsworth: Penguin.

Sacks, J. (2003) *The Dignity of Difference*. London: Continuum.

Said, E. (1991) *The World, the Text and the Critic*. London: Vintage.

Said, E. (1994) *Representations of the Individual: The 1993 Reith Lectures*. London: Vintage.

Said, E. (1995) *Orientalism*. London: Routledge & Kegan Paul (new Afterword edition).

Said, E. (1997) *Beginnings: Intent and Method*. London: Granta.

Schatzki, T. (2001) 'Introduction: Practice Theory', in T. Schatzki, K. Knorr Gettina and E. von Savigny (eds) *The Practice Turn in Contemporary Theory*. London: Routledge. pp. 1–14.

Schön, D. (1983) *The Reflective Practitioner: How Professionals Think in Action*. New York: Basic.

Schön, D. (1995) 'Knowing-in-Action: The New Scholarship Requires a New Epistemology', *Change*, November–December: 27–32.

Schön, D. and Rein, M. (1994) *Frame Reflection*. New York: Basic Books.

Schutz, A. (1972) *The Phenomenology of the Social World*. London: Heinemann.

Sen, A. (1999) *Development as Freedom*. Oxford: Oxford University Press.

Sen, A. (2007) *Identity & Violence*. London: Penguin.

Sennett, R. (2009) *The Craftsman*. London: Penguin.

Sharples, M. (1999) *How We Write*. London: Routledge.

Sinclair, A. (2008) Academic Paper: Module 7, MA PVP programme, St Mary's University College, Twickenham.

Smith, N. (2000) 'Foreword' in N. Chomsky, *New Horizons in the Study of Language and Mind*. Cambridge: Cambridge University Press.

Somekh, B. (2006) *Action Research: A Methodology for Change and Development*. Maidenhead: Open University Press.

Sowell, T. (1987) *A Conflict of Visions: Ideological Origins of Political Struggles*. New York: William Morrow.

Spinoza, B. (1996) *Ethics*. London: Penguin Books.

Spiro, J. (2008) *How I have Arrived at a Notion of Knowledge Transformation, Through Understanding the Story of Myself as Creative Writer, Creative Educator, Creative Manager, and Educational Researcher*. PhD thesis, University of Bath.

Stenhouse, L. (1975) *An Introduction to Curriculum Research and Development*. London: Heinemann.

Stenhouse, L. (1983) 'Research is systematic enquiry made public', *British Educational Research Journal*, 9 (1): 11–20.

Stern, J. (2014a) *Loneliness and Solitude in Education*. Oxford: Peter Lang.

Stern, J. (2014b) 'Dialogues of Space, Time and Practice: Supporting Research in Higher Education', *Other Education: The Journal of Educational Alternatives*, 3 (2): 3–21.

Stringer, E. (2007) *Action Research* (3rd edition). Los Angeles: Sage.

Tharp, T. (2006) *The Creative Habit: Learn it and Use it For Life*. New York: Simon & Schuster.

Theroux, P. (2012) *The Tao of Travel*. London: Penguin.

Tillich, P. (1973) *The Courage To Be*. London: Fontana.

Titchen, A. (1993) (ed.) *Changing Nursing Practice through Action Research*. Oxford: National Institute for Nursing.

Todd, S. (2003) *Learning from the Other*. New York: State University of New York Press.

Todorov, T. (1990) *Genres in Discourse*. Cambridge, MA: Cambridge University Press.

Todorov, T. (1999) *Facing the Extreme: Moral life in the concentration camps*. London: Weidenfeld and Nicolson.

Torbert, W. (2001) 'The Practice of Action Inquiry', in P. Reason and H. Bradbury (eds) *Handbook of Action Research: Participative Inquiry & Practice*. London: Sage. pp. 250-60.

Torre, M.E. (2009) 'Participatory action research and critical race theory: Fueling spaces for "Nos-otras" to research', *Urban Review*, 41 (1): 106–20.

Vincent, J. (2014) 'Talking about us: using autoethnography to rearticulate autistic spectrum conditions and practice within higher education through a participatory action research approach'. Paper presented at the Value and Virtue in Practice-Based Conference, York St John University, York.

Warren, K. (2001) 'General Introduction' in M. Zimmerman, J. Baird Callicott, G. Sessions, K. Warren and J. Clark (eds) *Environmental Philosophy: From Animal Rights to Radical Ecology.* Upper Saddle River, NJ: Prentice Hall. pp. 1–6.

Wenger, E. (1998) *Communities of Practice: Learning, Meaning, and Identity.* Cambridge: Cambridge University Press.

Whitty, G. (2006) 'Education(al) research and education policy making: is conflict inevitable?', *British Educational Research Journal*, 32 (2): 159–76. April.

Williams, R. (1965) *The Long Revolution.* Harmondsworth: Pelican.

Wing, L. (1996) *The Autistic Spectrum: A Guide for Parents and Professionals.* London: Constable.

Winter, R. (1989) *Learning from Experience.* London: Falmer.

Wittgenstein, L. (1953) *Philosophical Investigations.* Oxford: Blackwell.

Woods, M. (2000) *Knowledge in the Blood.* Dublin: Dedalus.

Yamada-Rice, D. (2012) 'Traditional Theses and Multimodal Communication', in R. Andrews, E. Borg, S. Davis, M. Domingo, and J. England (eds) *Digital Dissertations and Theses.* Los Angeles, Sage. pp. 157–76.

Yee, J. (2012) 'Implications for Research Training and Examining for Design PhDs', in R. Andrews, E. Borg, S. Davis, M. Domingo, and J. England (eds) *Digital Dissertations and Theses.* Los Angeles: Sage. pp. 461–92.

Young, I.M. (2000) *Inclusion and Democracy.* Oxford: Oxford University Press.

Index

critical engagement 38, 55-6, 65, 177-8; with own thinking 191
critical
   friends 81, 83, 115, 118, 136, 151-3; readers 220, 235
criticality, need for 23-4, 116
critique
   need for 6, 33, 118, 180;
   dialectical 84, 122, 179;
   reflexive 84, 122, 176, 179;
   self 104 (see also self-critique)
Czikszentmihalyi, M. 91, 211
Cultural
   imperialism 140;
   relativism 61;
   transformation 258

Dadds, M. 256; and Hart, S. 72
Daley, P.O. 66
data
   coding 82, 115
   disconfirming 82, 113, 182, 191
   forms of 81, 162
   gathering techniques 82, 152, 181-2
   interpreting and analysing 82
   quantitative and qualitative forms 81, 152
   storage 82
Davies, M.B. 173
deadlines 131-3
'death of the author' 71
deconstruction 74-5, 83, 116-7
Deloria, V. 138
Delves-Broughton, P. 264
Derrida, J. 4, 5, 110, 120-1
designing: a text 32, 218; a research project 148-9
Deutscher, P. 4, 110
Dewey, J. 22, 38, 41, 45
Dialogical: cultures 265; forms 28-9, 161, 261; in selling 127
dialogue, need for 25
dairies 132, 134-5, 191
   writing diaries 231
Dick, B. 22
digital texts 3, 73, 128, 265
discourses 1, 29
discoverers and planners 95
dissemination of work 153
do not give up 229
Doxtader, E. 91, 261
draft work 96, 117-8
Dutt, V. 66

e-books 239-40
ecologies of practice 40, 60
editing, discipline in 110
editors, working with them 230-31

educational relationships 159
Edvardsen, O. 98-9, 192
Eisner, E. 154, 252
Elliott, J. 22, 97
emergent form 19, 71
empathetic forms 37 (see also relational forms)
epistemology 28, 33, 43 (see also new epistemology); of traditional higher education 67
epistemological shifts 27, 74
error-free texts 112, 119, 148, 186
Esposito, J. and Evans-Winters, V. 18
essentialism 138-40
ethical conduct 53, 137, 153, 158, 159; how to ensure it 53, 181
ethics
   committees 81, 153
   in action 16
   of natural processes 60
Evans, T. 196
Evidence: base 113; forms of 175; generating it 81, 149; need for 53, 114-5
evolutionary processes 15-16, 60
examiners, finding the right one 199

faith
   in oneself as knower 43, 96, 174
   in one's personal knowledge 77, 87, 90-1, 104
   in the moment 174
   in the work of words 91, 102, 261, 266
Feldman, A. 22, 159, 187
Ferschleiser, R. and Smith, L. 94
Festinger, L. 116
Feynman, R. 183, 252, 264
Flood, J. 188
Flood, R.L. 18-19, 23
flow 91
football, misappropriation of 26-7
Foucault, M. 3, 4, 25, 45, 71, 100, 113, 115, 120, 182, 189-90, 246-7, 252, 255-6
framing and reframing 60-2
Frankl, V. 248, 254
freedom of thinking 2
Freire, P. 21, 121
Fromm, E. 35
funding, allocation of 5
Furlong, J. and Oancea, A. 158, 263

Galbraith, D. 64
Gaventa, J. and Horton, B.D. 21
generative transformational forms of grammar 59
genres of writing through action research 72, 118